Web-Based Learning

What Do We Know?
Where Do We Go?

Web-Based Learning

What Do We Know?

Where Do We Go?

Edited by

**Roger Bruning, Christy A. Horn,
and Lisa M. PytlikZillig**
University of Nebraska–Lincoln

**INFORMATION AGE
PUBLISHING**

80 Mason Street • Greenwich, Connecticut 06830 • www.infoagepub.com

Library of Congress Cataloging-in-Publication Data

Web-based learning : what do we know? where do we go? / edited by Roger
Bruning, Christy A. Horn, and Lisa M. PytlikZillig.
    p. cm.
Includes bibliographical references and index.
  ISBN 1-59311-002-2 (pbk.) – ISBN 1-59311-003-0 (hardcover)
  1. Distance education–Computer-assisted instruction–Congresses. 2.
World Wide Web–Congresses. I. Bruning, Roger H. II. Horn, Christy A.
III. PytlikZillig, Lisa M.
  LC5803.C65W44 2003
  371.3'58–dc21

                                                2003000624

Printed in the United States of America

This volume is dedicated to
Barbara Humes of the U.S. Department of Education
in great appreciation for her outstanding and inspirational work
as the CLASS Project Officer.

CONTENTS

Foreword
Arthur I. Zygielbaum   *ix*

Introduction
Roger Bruning, Christy A. Horn, and Lisa M. PytlikZillig   *xiii*

1. Research on Web-Based Learning: A Half-Full Glass
Richard E. Clark   *1*

2. Nine Ways to Reduce Cognitive Load in Multimedia Learning
Richard E. Mayer and Roxana Moreno   *23*

3. Technology: The Great Equalizer?
Eric J. Jolly and Christy A. Horn   *45*

4. InfoGather: A Tool for Gathering and Organizing Information
from the Web
L. Brent Igo, Roger Bruning, Matthew McCrudden,   *57*
and Douglas F. Kauffman

5. ThinkAboutIt!: A Web-Based Tool for Improving Critical Thinking
Steve Lehman, Roger Bruning, and Christy A. Horn   *79*

6. Teachers, Technology, and Students At Risk
Lisa M. PytlikZillig, Christy A. Horn, and Mary Jane White   *105*

7. At Risk in Cyberspace: Responding to At-Risk Students
in Online Courses
Christy A. Horn, Lisa M. PytlikZillig, Roger Bruning,   *129*
and Douglas F. Kauffman

8. Engineering Issues and Perspectives in Developing Online Courses
Arthur I. Zygielbaum   *153*

9. The Pedagogical Impact of Course Management Systems
   on Faculty, Students, and Institution
   Charles J. Ansorge and Oksana Bendus   169

10. Technological Indicators of Impact of Course Management Systems
    Ashok Samal and Bhuvaneswari Gopal   191

11. Intellectual Property Considerations for Online Educational
    Multimedia Projects: What You Don't Know Could Byte You
    Turan P. Odabasi   209

12. Recommendations and "Voices from the Field":
    Thoughts from the CLASS Summative Evaluation
    Patricia B. Campbell, Lesley K. Perlman, and Earl N. Hadley   231

About the Contributors   253

Author Index   261

Subject Index   267

FOREWORD

Since 1988, the U.S. Department of Education's Star Schools Program has supported the use of distance learning strategies to serve multistate regions primarily by means of satellite and broadcast television. More recently, with the increased capability of schools to make use of resources on the Internet for educational purposes, greater access to high-quality instruction in the full range of core academic subjects has become possible.

In 1996, the University of Nebraska was awarded a multiyear grant under the Department's Star Schools Program to provide high school students and adults with access to online courses that would meet the requirements for a high school diploma issued by the University's existing Independent Study High School and accredited by the North Central Association of Colleges and Schools. The project, known as Communications, Learning, and Assessment in a Student-Centered System (CLASS), proposed to develop forty Web-based–required high school courses and ten elective courses and make them fully accessible online to a national student body. Other goals for the project were to develop the courses so they could be used stand-alone as well as part of a high school curriculum, and to develop a viable framework for Web-based course development, including instructional design and programming.

The CLASS project broke new ground in exploring the development of Web-based, asynchronous, interactive, instructional programming using audio, video, Web links, online assessment, and other features within a seamless navigational system designed to encourage individualized learning, discovery, and exploration. Web-based teaching and learning holds

Web-Based Learning: What Do We Know? Where Do We Go?, pages ix–xi
Copyright © 2003 by Information Age Publishing
All rights of reproduction in any form reserved.

much promise for enabling students to meet challenging, internationally competitive educational standards. However, there are many issues that must still be addressed by telecommunications engineers and experts before the promises of electronic education can become a reality for all students. The experiences of the CLASS project have been highly instructive to the evolving field of information technology in education. The lessons learned from this project were examined during a national symposium held in spring 2002 as a culminating activity of this project.

The symposium hosted speakers who were down-to-earth, avoided the language of academe, and thus were able to reach most everyone in the varied audience of researchers, practitioners, developers, technologists, and teachers. People are obviously hungering for confirmation that there is still a long way to go in knowing what's what in this field and that they are not alone in struggling to make the best of Web-based teaching and learning. The symposium broke down some of the isolation that researchers, practitioners, developers, technologists, and teachers feel about the work they are doing in their own individual arenas and linked them to what is happening in those other arenas. Somehow the "relatedness" came through.

We are pleased to share these lessons with educators, instructional developers, technologists, and others who have an interest in expanding the ways that education can be acquired through electronic technologies.

As the project's current principal investigator, it is appropriate that I acknowledge the dedicated people who made the CLASS project successful. Space and time limitations do not allow naming everyone. Nonetheless, I do say a heartfelt "thank you" to those who shared their intellect, energy, and vision during the project's 6 years.

I do take privilege in recognizing a few individuals involved in the leadership of the project, however. With the concurrence of all involved in the management of CLASS, I wish to acknowledge the steadfast and continuing support we have received from Barbara Humes, the CLASS project officer in the U.S. Department of Education. Beyond the expected role of fiscal and programmatic oversight, Barbara provided guidance based on her considerable educational knowledge and experience. Her direction facilitated innovation and maintained the overall vision of our efforts. We gratefully recognize that the project owes much of its success to her. Sandy Scofield, my predecessor as principal investigator, led the project through a particularly challenging period and helped foster the concept of the symposium. We are grateful for her leadership. Char Hazzard was project director from the inception of CLASS. She showed great perseverance through the difficult times and deserves well to relish the successes. Char also was responsible for leading the mechanics of the symposium and taking care of the myriad of details involved in such an enterprise. Finally, I would like to recognize the contributions of Roger Bruning and Christy Horn. As co-directors of the Center for Instructional Innovation, they provided the research foundation for the CLASS project and the intellectual leadership for the symposium. I am grateful for their skill, patience, and dedication.

—Arthur I. Zygielbaum
Principal Investigator, CLASS Project
Co-Director, National Center for Information Technology in Education

This book was produced in part with funds from the U.S. Department of Education under Grant No. R203D960003. The content does not necessarily reflect the position or policy of the Department of Education or any other agency of the federal government.

The U.S. Department of Education's Star Schools Program currently funds 23 projects that encourage improved instruction in mathematics, science, and foreign languages as well as other skills, such as literacy, workplace, and life skills through distance education. These projects serve K–12 and adult learners and various underserved populations including limited English proficient students and students with disabilities. The Star Schools Program is one of the largest networks of public and private sector partners (schools, school districts, state departments of education, telecommunications entities, universities, regional service centers) helping to build the capacity of the education community to make effective use of the information superhighway.

Further information about the Star Schools Program can be found at *www.WestEd.org/tie/dlrn/starschools.html*, or by contacting Joe Wilkes at (202) 219-2186.

INTRODUCTION

This volume contains the proceedings from the first Nebraska Symposium on Information Technology in Education, held in Lincoln, Nebraska, on May 15–17, 2002. This symposium, titled "Web-Based Learning: What Do We Know? Where Do We Go?," brought to an informal close the research and development activities of the CLASS (Communications, Learning, and Assessment in a Student-Centered System) project, which, beginning in 1996, had been continuously supported by major funding from the Star Schools Program of the U.S. Department of Education. The Nebraska Symposium enabled us to report on many of the experiences in CLASS and CLASS-supported research, and to reflect on them in light of what is known about multimedia learning.

We conceived of this symposium as drawing on two critical resources for designing excellent Web-based education: solid instructional theory and broad experience in teaching using Web-based technologies. For the former, we went to outstanding researchers and theorists in multimedia and technology-based learning. For the latter, we drew primarily on the experience of participants in CLASS, who had been intimately associated with the challenges of creating and delivering a complex system of Web-based instruction.

From its inception, CLASS was a remarkable endeavor. CLASS was the largest project ever funded by the Star Schools Program. It was also the first Web-based project in Star Schools, which in the past had focused primarily on television- and satellite-based instruction. CLASS was a collaboration of several different partners: the University of Nebraska's Independent Study

Web-Based Learning: What Do We Know? Where Do We Go?, pages xiii–xxii
Copyright © 2003 by Information Age Publishing

High School (ISHS) and its parent unit, the Division of Continuing Studies (DCS) at the University of Nebraska–Lincoln (UNL); Nebraska Educational Telecommunications (NET); the David Sarnoff Research Institute of Princeton, New Jersey; the Nebraska Department of Education (NDE); and UNL's Center for Instructional Innovation (CII). The central goal for CLASS was tremendously ambitious: developing more than 50 full-semester, fully accredited, multimedia, online high school courses constituting the core curriculum needed for high school graduation.

As described in its proposal to Star Schools, CLASS would create "...a dynamically interactive, student-centered course environment within an electronically available communication, learning, and assessment system [where] students access moving imagery, graphics, sound, and text via a transparent interactive navigational system that encourages individualized learning, discovery, and exploration." In the proposed partnership, ISHS would provide instructors and the course enrollment/student support framework; DCS, the course content and instructional design; NET, the Web-based multimedia design and course production; Sarnoff, the tracking software needed for teachers to monitor student activities in a virtual environment; NDE, the learning standards and accreditation review for all courses; and CII, research, development, and evaluation.

While this structure evolved over the life of the project, by 2001 CLASS had reached its major goals, which included producing more than 50 courses constituting the core curriculum needed to complete an accredited high school diploma. Many of these courses now are available through the commercial unit spawned by CLASS—CLASS.COM™. In producing these courses, CLASS developed an instructional design framework integrating voice, data, and video elements and created inventive ways for linking students with other students and instructors in an online environment. CLASS also produced a uniform navigation system for moving through course content and worked out the complex system of advisory, instructional, and support services needed by online students.

In many ways, the story of CLASS is a classic story of struggle—against daunting odds, significant obstacles were faced and overcome by dedicated people showing great determination and perseverance. What was proposed in 1995 and funded by Star Schools in 1996 would be considered remarkable even today. In those early days of 1996, however, the Internet was not today's Internet—access was limited and downloads were very slow. Browsers were balky and incompatible and authoring tools were not today's accessible and forgiving systems. From day one of the project, it seemed that participants were led inexorably into *terra incognita*. Deep expertise was a precious commodity; in virtually every area of CLASS activity, there were few established methods and processes on which to draw. CLASS needed to grow its expertise as it went along.

In retrospect, it is probably fair to say that there was a certain amount of naiveté in the initial vision for CLASS and in the early ideas about how CLASS might accomplish its goals. What some saw as a relatively straightforward transfer of existing content to the Web turned out to be immensely challenging on multiple dimensions. Some of the most prominent of these challenges were as follows:

- *Course content.* The decision to place the bulk of the content online and to move away from textbooks placed great pressure on curriculum development. Without the usual resource of textbooks, which traditionally had supplied curriculum frameworks for the independent study offerings of ISHS, the need for primary curriculum development expanded enormously. Moreover, intellectual property issues connected to obtaining permissions to use content and tools in courses were quickly apparent. Whereas copyright owners often were generous in their granting permissions for use by the nonprofit entities connected to the project itself, use of materials in for-profit ventures developing out of CLASS was another matter.

- *Course design.* At the beginning of the CLASS project, designers were encouraged to try out a variety of course designs. Some early courses were essentially explorations, while others focused on student-to-student interaction based on a social-cognitive, constructivist view of learning. While all involved sophisticated multimedia, some had high levels of student activities and others remained primarily text based. Although divergence of approaches in the early courses was instructive for the remainder of CLASS course development, project designers realized as the courses unfolded that they needed to have a standard framework for course development.

- *Course assessments.* The assessment challenges for CLASS were also considerable. The assessments needed to function simultaneously on multiple and varied dimensions. For example, in addition to providing effective, timely feedback for students and useful management information for teachers, the assessments needed to map onto state and national standards. The assessments needed to be efficient as well as effective. The ISHS teachers, for example, were able to effectively manage quite large numbers of students in the traditional print environment. CLASS's Internet-based courses, however, brought greatly increased expectations for rapid turnaround of assessments. The expectation of rapid turnaround by the students and the nature of available technology tools also tended to limit assessments to forms that could be self-scored within the technology, or easily scored by instructors.

- *Course toolbars and navigation.* The early courses were essentially hand crafted by CLASS instructional designers working together with NET Web development and media development specialists. It was soon obvious, however, that the courses needed to have a common look and feel, including standardized page format, course and resource access, navigation tools, and online utilities. Additionally, similar courses needed a way to share modularized functions. Thus, significant efforts were devoted to creating a "standardized" look and functionality for the CLASS courses.

- *Student tracking.* Under a prior military contract, Sarnoff Research Institute had already developed technology for tracking Web-based activity. Thus, CLASS initially had contracted with Sarnoff to adapt those systems to CLASS courses. The vision for this tracking system was that instructors would be able to directly observe student progress in courses by consulting course "maps" showing key course elements and displaying student progress relative to these elements. This visionary approach turned out to be impractical from both the design and technical perspectives. Today's CLASS courses do have considerable internal tracking capability, but of a more conventional sort based on logs of student activity keyed to course elements. Typically, however, this information was not used by instructors but by CLASS designers and researchers.

- *Divergent expectations.* Arguably the greatest challenge facing all of the participants involved with CLASS was the wide variety and often divergent expectations placed on the project. The proposal to Star Schools indicated that CLASS would create an instructional design structure for online, distance-delivered courses, developing courses that would reach diverse populations and accommodate a variety of learning styles and educational needs. However, CLASS simultaneously had promised to quickly produce an exceptional number of courses, a goal not easily reconciled with careful research and evaluation leading to validated design frameworks. CLASS courses and their delivery also were expected to be marketable and commercially viable. All of these certainly are valid expectations for online courses, but when expectations came into conflict, which they often did, they placed considerable stress on the project and its staff.

- *Research and evaluation.* When CLASS began in 1996, the amount of well-designed research on Web-based learning was still very small, with few established methods for gathering and aggregating data from Web-based applications, and virtually no data available on the performance of students in online, multimedia-based courses. Producing the complex course designs in CLASS involved expending large amounts of project resources, and as CLASS designers began to move course after course from design to development to tryout stages, needs were great for significant amounts of formative evaluation. Meeting these needs required an approach in which results of studies could be very rapidly produced, fed back to designers, and immediately incorporated into course designs. For the most part, this was not possible, especially early on, as demands for careful research design, data aggregation, and responsible reporting conflicted with project production needs. More often than not, evaluation information fed into the development of the next courses rather than into the course that was being evaluated. It also became clear during this period of time that there was a need for summative evaluation conducted by evaluators outside the UNL environment. Campbell-Kibler Associates became the outside evaluator and fulfilled a critical role in the project. Their reports on the CLASS projects can be found at http://www.campbell-kibler.com.

In meeting challenges like these, a tremendous amount has been learned. This volume, in many ways, is the story of the "lessons learned" from the CLASS project. These lessons include some pertaining to the design and management of online instruction, others about developing and maintaining Web-based instructional technologies, and still others about issues of intellectual property and about conducting valid research and evaluation in the online environment. The need to meet multiple challenges led to advances on virtually every front, including technological innovation, course design, and approaches to research. The chapters in this book highlight many of these advances.

To better understand some of the issues encountered in CLASS, we began our planning for the conference and subsequently for these proceedings by stepping back and taking a larger, theory-based perspective. The first three chapters introduce overarching issues of general import when considering the potential benefits and limitations of Web-based learning. These issues include misconceptions about Web-based learning, cognitive load as a primary concern in the design of Web-based materials, and the appropriate characterization of the so-called "digital divide."

In Chapter 1, Richard Clark discusses the state of research on learning in Web-based distance-education environments. In his discussion, Clark debunks and clarifies six popular misconceptions about Web-based learning, including misconceptions about the use of different media, highly active program elements, and problem-based discovery instruction. He also recommends research-based strategies for effectively designing and delivering Web-based courses and for preventing the further propagation of misconceptions. In his conclusion, Clark notes that designers, rather than being driven by an enthusiasm for novel technologies, need to pay attention to current research and be aware of design elements that may unduly increase cognitive load.

The topic of cognitive load is expanded in Chapter 2, in which Richard Mayer and Roxana Moreno describe a cognitive theory of multimedia learning. Their theory is based on assumptions that conceptualize multimedia learners as active learners who are separately processing and then integrating limited amounts of visual and auditory information. Their theory explicates three types of demands (essential processing, incidental processing, and representational holding) that may overload a learner's cognitive system and interfere with transferable learning. In light of these assumptions and demands, Mayer and Moreno offer several recommendations for reducing a variety of different types of cognitive overload. They also review research supporting the utility of these recommendations.

While Mayer and Moreno consider the cognitive aspects of Web-based learning, Eric Jolly and Christy Horn discuss potential limitations existing at the social and cultural levels. In Chapter 3, they discuss current controversies over the extent of the "digital divide," that is, the divide separating those who do and do not have access to the technology needed to deliver Web-based courses. As Jolly and Horn aptly point out, while past controversies have debated the "breadth" of the divide, a more important issue today may be the "depth" of the divide. For while there are fewer and fewer groups who totally lack access to Web-based technologies, the extent, quality, and effectiveness of access varies greatly.

Following these three primarily conceptual chapters are four chapters concerning specific lessons learned from CLASS-related project activities. In Chapter 4, Brent Igo, Roger Bruning, Matthew McCrudden, and Douglas Kauffman describe a series of studies systematically exploring the translation of a pen-and-paper note-taking tool into a Web tool. Rather than assuming that the beneficial effects of pen-and-paper matrix note-taking activities would transfer to Web-based activities, these researchers studied the effects of the translation, varying one environmental variable at a time. To their surprise, though students were found to benefit from pen-and-paper matrix note taking applied to Web material, the effects disappeared when students used *InfoGather* (a Web-based matrix note-taking tool) to record their notes. These researchers used observational data and two additional studies to solve the mystery of the missing effects. As a result, they also uncovered important factors affecting the design of seemingly equivalent tools in traditional versus Web-based environments.

In Chapter 5, Steve Lehman and Roger Bruning describe the development of a second Web-based tool, called *ThinkAboutIt!*, designed to promote deeper processing and learning of information in the online environment. The *ThinkAboutIt!* tool was developed in line with current theories in cognitive science and designed to promote (1) learner organization of content, (2) integration with background knowledge, (3) connections to relevant contexts, and (4) metacognition through social interaction. Like Igo and colleagues, Lehman and Bruning present research to support the utility of *ThinkAboutIt!*, while exemplifying the systematic application of theory to the design of new tools unique to the online environment.

Chapters 6 and 7 discuss project findings that specifically pertain to students at risk for academic failure, revisiting issues introduced by Jolly and Horn in Chapter 3. In Chapter 6, Lisa PytlikZillig, Christy Horn, and Mary Jane White discuss the results of a statewide survey of Nebraska teachers' use of technology with at-risk students. Results from that survey found that teachers both observe and recommend simple rather than complex technology use by at-risk students; however, teacher observations and recommendations were themselves unrelated and difficult to predict. The authors note that their findings are consistent with prior research, but contrast with current research-based recommendations for motivating students at risk. Finally, they underscore the need for additional research to determine the causes and effects of these persistent patterns of results.

In Chapter 7, Christy Horn, Lisa PytlikZillig, Roger Bruning, and Douglas Kauffman describe the experiences of at-risk students in Web-based high school courses as viewed in two rich and detailed data sets. In the first data set, intensive qualitative observations and quantitative assessments of the experiences of at-risk students and those not at risk suggested a number of preliminary principles for the implementation of Web-based courses with students from at-risk populations. These principles stress the effectiveness of online technology for promoting student engagement and the importance of factors such as student expectations, teacher workload, and the intensive pilot testing of new technology. Teacher relationships were found to be especially important for motivating at-risk student course engagement; and the second data set, which involved experimental methodology, revealed qualities of teacher–student interaction that could be manipulated to enhance student motivation.

The next four chapters turn toward the more technical aspects of Web-based course design and implementation. In Chapter 8, Art Zygielbaum, who served as the final principal investigator for the CLASS Project, discusses the development of online courses from an engineering perspective. Throughout the 5-year period during which CLASS personnel attempted to meet the project's research and development and production goals, a number of technical and management problems were encountered and lessons were learned. After reviewing these challenges and reflecting upon major project successes and mistakes, Zygielbaum offers practical advice to educators who wish to mitigate the risks inherent in the development of online courses and course content.

Chapters 9 and 10 specifically focus on campus-wide studies of the use of online course management systems (CMSs). In Chapter 9, Charles Ansorge and Oksana Bendus provide a historical overview of CMS use at UNL and then describe current attitudes and practices related to CMS use. Through Web-based and telephone surveys of students, faculty, and administrators, Ansorge and Bendus identify several important and universal issues. Among their findings were generally positive reactions to Blackboard, UNL's integrated course management system. However, faculty also reported that use of the system required additional course preparation time, and faculty and administrators alike recognized the need to somehow compensate faculty members for this additional effort. In addition, they found that faculty members felt the ability to post documents was one of the most useful features of Blackboard. Similarly, students reported using the system primarily to print or review course documents.

Chapter 10 builds on the Ansorge and Bendus chapter by providing complementary information on the use of the Blackboard system, as revealed by technical indicators. Ashok Samal and Bhuvaneswari Gopal report results based on data collected directly from various system log files. Their findings, like those reported by Ansorge and Bendus, suggest that instructors use the Web primarily for dissemination of information, rather than to promote student discussion or to conduct student assessment. In addition, they provide evidence for the wide use of Blackboard by students, but somewhat less use by faculty. Finally, comparison of use by faculty and students from different colleges and at different times provides important technical information for administrators needing to determine how to allocate technical resources.

In Chapter 11, Turan Odabasi provides an overview of issues concerning Web-based content as legally owned intellectual property. By providing simple, applicable explanations of "intellectual property," "copyright," works in the "public domain," "fair use," "patents," "trademarks," and other legal concepts, Odabasi's chapter provides important background information for anyone using or developing Web-based content. As he notes, in the midst of one's attempts to enhance student learning by developing the best content possible, "it is easy to place intellectual property concerns behind many other considerations. But unlike most other considerations, failure to properly understand and address intellectual property issues can lead to tremendous financial liability and can render entire projects useless."

The final chapter of the volume contains a selection of recommendations and short reports that were done as part of the summative evaluation by Campbell-Kibler Associates. In Chapter 12, Patricia Campbell, Lesley Perlman, and Earl Hadley present a brief report and three brochures. These documents contain recommendations to students, parents, designers, and administrators compiled by some of the many individuals who have had the opportunity to engage with the CLASS courses during the last 6 years.

We conclude our introduction by attempting to recognize the host of people whose creativity, hard work, and dedication to CLASS are reflected in this volume. The CLASS project and the online high school curriculum that it produced were the product of so many people's efforts that it is almost impossible to know where to begin. As we have indicated, its courses were produced and refined over a multiyear period by people in many different units working together: instructional designers and content experts whose knowledge and creativity generated the content and design for the courses; programmers, engineers, and Web designers from NET, whose creative talents transformed the courses into exciting Web-based multimedia forms; the teachers and administrators in UNL's Independent Study High School, whose dedication and caring were felt by every CLASS student; and the evaluators and researchers of Campbell-Kibler Associates and the Center for Instructional Innovation, whose work helped focus attention on the design, processes, and outcomes of the courses.

Many individuals also worked very hard to make the Nebraska Symposium on Information Technology in Education a success. Special recognition is due to Char Hazzard, who coordinated the project over its entire span, and to her administrative team. Special thanks are due to Sandy Scofield, principal investigator for CLASS during its final year of production, and Barbara Humes, U.S. Department of Education program officer for CLASS, who helped to conceptualize the idea of the symposium and arranged for the no-cost extension that helped fund it. We also wish to acknowledge the members of the Symposium planning team, led by Sandy Scofield and Art Zygielbaum. Members of the team included Char Hazzard, Kathy Northrop, Jim Schiefelbein, Jean Jones, Marie Dvorak, Sandra Gahn, Christy Horn, Roger Bruning, Art Zygielbaum, and Mary Bodvarsson. In addition to its Star Schools funding, the conference also had several additional sponsors. These include the National Center for Information Technology in Education (NCITE), which hosted the Web site for the conference and provided the electronic framework for conference submissions, and the Center for Instructional Innovation, which provided logistic support and coordinated the poster sessions for the conference. Special credit is also due to the Scholarship, Technology, and Educational Practice (STEP) project, a Preparing Tomorrow's Teachers to Use Technology federal grant, which enriched the conference greatly through its cosponsorship by involving its affiliated Nebraska school personnel and administrators in conference activities.

Finally, thanks are due to those individuals who have made significant contributions to this volume through their editorial skills and attention to its details. Three people deserve particular recognition. Mary Bodvarsson of the Center for Instructional Innovation and NCITE acted as a reader and editorial assistant on each of the chapters and volume sections; Xiongyi Liu of the Center for Instructional Innovation provided editing, referencing, and cross-referencing assistance, as well as general administrative assistance; and Art Zygielbaum, co-director of NCITE and CLASS principal investigator, provided helpful feedback on the volume's introduction and to the structure of the volume as a whole.

—Roger Bruning
Christy Horn
Lisa PytlikZillig

CHAPTER 1

RESEARCH ON WEB-BASED LEARNING

A Half-Full Glass

Richard E. Clark
Rossier School of Education,
University of Southern California

ABSTRACT

This chapter discusses six common but mistaken ("half-empty") assumptions about learning in Web-based "distance" instruction environments in light of current cognitive learning and motivation research, including (1) some media enhance learning more than others, (2) newer media are more motivating, (3) highly active visual and auditory screen design techniques enhance motivation and learning, (4) providing problem-based discovery instruction and high levels of learner control will increase learning and motivation, (5) available instructional design models are adequate for the complex knowledge presented in many online courses, and (6) formatting instruction so that it is compatible with various "learning styles" will increase learning. After each half-empty discussion, the half-full part of the research "glass" is examined by briefly describing a number of effective, research-

Web-Based Learning: What Do We Know? Where Do We Go?, pages 1–22
Copyright © 2003 by Information Age Publishing
All rights of reproduction in any form reserved.

1

based strategies for (1) selecting media to enhance learning, (2) motivating learning during instruction to prevent dropout, (3) designing screen displays, (4) scaffolding instructional support in online courses, (5) using instructional design models for complex learning, and (6) considering individual differences in learning. The final section of the chapter describes research and design strategies that may help eliminate misconceptions about learning from media.

For at least a century various types of technology-based distance education programs have attracted enthusiastic supporters. All communication technologies have been used at some point as vehicles to transmit instruction and support education at a distance, including letters, newspapers, film, radio, television, and most recently, computers with Web-based connections. Over the years, researchers have uncovered very positive benefits of using media in distance education. Among those benefits are decreased cost per student by those who provide education and those who purchase it (Levin, Glass, & Meister, 1987; Levin & McEwan, 2001), increases in convenience for students and educators, and increased access to instruction by people whose educational alternatives are severely limited by geography or other handicapping conditions such as economic, social, or physical barriers (Office of Technology Assessment, 1988).

What is very interesting about media-based distance education is that its advocates have tended to avoid stressing the positive results in past research in favor of arguing that new media have benefits that, according to the research evidence, are at best very uncertain and at worst wrong. The goal of this chapter is to describe at least six misconceptions that appear to have special relevance to the design and assessment of Web-based instruction. Following a description of each problem area are brief suggestions about research that may help correct the misconception or that may help to remedy the current situation so that the misconception is turned into a positive reality.

ARE THERE LEARNING BENEFITS FROM WEB-BASED INSTRUCTION?

The best example of our tendency to emphasize uncertain benefits is that most discussions of new media emphasize their impact on learning, rather than their economic or access benefits. Compelling evidence for greater amounts of learning from newer media or mixes of media when compared with more traditional media has not surfaced even when thousands of studies over many years have examined media use with wide variations in subject matter, learning contexts, and types of learners (Clark, 2001).

Media advocates have always experienced problems providing credible, research-based evidence of learning benefits when new media are compared with more traditional media (Clark, 2001; Clark & Salomon, 1986; Mielke, 1968; Salomon, 1984; Schramm, 1977). Until recently, the time lag between each new communication technology tended to be approximately the span of a generation. This led many media advocates to ignore the lack of learning benefits in past research and to assume that their new technology was unique. One damaging result of a failure to learn from the past is that mistakes tend to be repeated.

There is no evidence of learning benefits from any medium that cannot be explained by other factors besides the medium, which have not been ruled out by inadequacies in the research or evaluation design (Clark, 2001). This conclusion extends to "media attributes" and multimedia or hypermedia formats (Clark, 1994). A number of researchers have claimed that the most promising approach to learning is to assume that it is influenced by instructional methods (Cronbach & Snow, 1977), not by media. This approach implies, for example, that the increased interactivity between learner and instructional presentations afforded by computers is an instructional method issue rather than a media issue. Instructional methods are defined as "...any way to shape information that compensates for or supplants the cognitive processes necessary for achievement or motivation. For example, students often need an example to connect new information in a learning task with information in their prior experience. If students cannot (or will not) give themselves an adequate example, an instructional (method) must provide it for them" (Clark, 2001, p. 208). Variations in interactivity can be provided to learners by a number of media, including computers. Even Kozma (1994), a critic of this conclusion, has acknowledged that no evidence exists to support the argument that media has influenced learning in past research and there is no indication that media or media attributes alone (including the "Web-based" media attributes) will influence learning in the future.

Suggestions for Overcoming the "Learning Benefit" Misconception

Because research has so consistently shown that media per se does not impact learning, those concerned with online instructional assessment should exercise caution when making inferences about the origin of measured differences between online instruction and other mediated forms of the same or similar programs (see Clark, 2000, for specific suggestions for evaluation strategies and questions). One approach to overcoming misconceptions concerning media-associated learning benefits from Web-based instruction is to shift the emphases in research and writings about Web-based instruction. Instead of looking for and proclaiming learning benefits, education scholars should seek to demonstrate that Web-based learning is at least as effective as similar instruction presented in the classroom or by other media. The "no significant difference" finding in research can be interpreted as "equally effective" or "equally ineffective." This approach focuses our attention away from the media and toward the importance of using powerful instructional design models for Web instruction. David Merrill (2000) has recently described a number of powerful design models that could be used in the development of Web-based courses. The important fact to remember is that when highly successful classroom instruction is translated into Web-based instruction, the learning results are likely to continue to be solid provided that effective instructional methods continue to operate in the Web environment. Of course, the reverse is also true. Poor classroom instruction may also become poor Web-based instruction.

Media selection studies

A parallel approach to this problem is to draw on past research in media selection in order to make decisions about which delivery platform is best for a particular course offering. Sugrue and Clark (2000) provide a very comprehensive review of nearly all published media selection schemes, including those based on research. They suggest ways to select media based on the goals of the course being offered, the learners, and the organizational setting in which the course is presented. Additional empirical research to test the validity of their claims would be useful.

Access benefits

In addition to shifting the focus from issues concerning learning benefits to issues concerning instructional methods, researchers could focus attention on the established strengths of Web-based instruction. There are at least two strong areas that advocates should explore. First, new media offer the opportunity to extend access to instruction much more widely than classroom-based programs. Many examples of access benefits and research in this area are described, for example, in a report by the now-defunct federal Office of Technology Assessment (1988). Updates of access research reports can be found in the many new journals that have sprung up to handle Web and distance education research and practice.[1]

Cost–benefit analysis

Second, media offer the potential for considerable economic benefits in the form of increased speed of learning and a reduction in per-student cost. On the one hand, researchers are investigating the possibility that "cognitive efficiencies" might be achieved with the right mix of media attributes, sensory mode, learning task, and learners. For example, Cobb (1997) has suggested that some media and symbolic modes, such as pictures and narrated descriptions of the same information, lead to quicker and/or less cognitively demanding learning and performance outcomes for some people. A related approach is to assess the cost-effectiveness of different instructional delivery platforms. A variety of strategies provide advance estimates of cost of various alternative ways to deliver instruction. Under some conditions, the financial and social benefits of Web-based instruction are considerable. Examples are described by Levin and colleagues (1987). However, benefits are not guaranteed; a number of studies have questioned the cost–benefit of new media as they are presently being used (Levin & McEwan, 2001).

ARE THERE MOTIVATIONAL BENEFITS FROM WEB-BASED INSTRUCTION?

Part of the justification for Web-based instruction is based on assumptions that it is more motivating than other forms. Abrahamson (1998) most likely speaks for the majority of media advocates when stating "a primary function of the use of television, computers, and telecommunications in distance learning is to motivate students rather than just to provide information to them" (p. 2). However, evidence for the motivational qualities of Web-based instruction has been mixed at best. As reviewed next, one finds the most positive evidence in qualitative studies but very negative indicators in empirical and quantitative studies. Even in the qualitative studies, there are indications that the motivational benefits observed are not due to the Web-based nature of instruction, but are due to changes in instructional method that are sometimes correlated with the use of newer media. Dropout studies further support the potentially negative impact of Web-based media on student motivation (persistence).

Qualitative Research

Qualitative studies of students' motivation for Web-based instruction yield mostly positive motivational results. In many of these studies, students who report motivational benefits from Web-based courses may be attracted to the online collaboration with other students. For example, in a study of online learners at the New Jersey Institute of Technology, 55% of the respondents indicated that they were "more motivated to work hard on their assignments because other students would be reading them" (Hiltz, 1997, p. 12). Kitchen and McDougall (1998) report that in an online graduate course, 60% of participants reported that collaborative work reduced their tendency to procrastinate. However, collaborative learning effects on motivation are not exclusive to the Web. Student collaborative work is possible to arrange in nondistance settings and without Web-based media. It is also important to note the possibility that collaborative distance settings may attract learners who have stronger social and collaborative needs. Thus, supposedly positive effects of collaborative Web-based media could be due to selection effects rather than to the media. A study of Web-based students who seemed to lack strong collaborative needs was reported by Valenta, Therriault, Dieter, and Mrtek (2001). They surveyed a large group of prospective Web students at the University of Illinois at Chicago Circle in order to categorize their acceptance or resistance to different features of Web-based instruction. Using Q-methodology, they characterized students' views into three categories: time and structure in learning, convenience in learning, and social interaction in learning. Of primary importance to the time and structure group was the flexibility of online courses (this is an access issue); however, they were ambivalent about concerns of social interaction in the classroom. The convenience group liked working from home and saving travel time (access and efficiency). This group was neutral on social interaction. The social interaction group was most attracted to Web offerings where there was "potential for *less* participant discussion, ...fewer subtleties in teaching...[and less] immediate feedback" (Valenta et al., p. 7, emphasis added). When these students were given the Canfield Learning Styles Inventory, a large proportion (74%) were classified as independent learners. These data suggest that individual and group differences in students will produce different patterns of motivation in all instructional settings, including Web-based instruction. A very intelligent discussion of motivation in Web-based instruction can be found in a Web-based article authored by Thierry Karsenti (1999). He finds evidence for shifting patterns of motivation across time in Web courses and different motivational patterns being experienced by students with different levels of autonomy and self-efficacy. His hypotheses about shifting motivational patterns in Web courses should be explored further in quantitatively oriented research.

Quantitative Studies

The evidence found in more quantitatively oriented empirical research is quite different than the picture presented in a number of qualitative studies. Many empirical quasi-experimental studies have been conducted in this area, often with very disappointing results (e.g., Clark, 1999). For example, Yang (1991–1992) examined the effects of computer-based versus print-based instruction on motivation, continuing motivation, and content recall. In his study, a total of 52 eleventh graders were randomly assigned to either a computer-based or a print-based instruction group. Both groups received the same history lesson on the decisions President Abraham Lincoln made during his presidency. Immediate and delayed recall was tested with 16 multiple-choice items. The results indicated that the computer-based instruction group showed higher motivation and higher immediate recall scores over the print-based group but the results of the delayed recall were not significant, suggesting only short-term gains that may not justify the relative greater cost of the computer-based materials.

In another typical empirical study, Eveland and Dunwoody (2000) examined a variety of Web-based approaches versus print-based instruction on the flu virus. University undergraduates who were experienced computer users completed questionnaires concerning their motivation, Web expertise, and cognitive load following the reading of an article about the flu virus in (1) a linear Web version, (2) a nonlinear Web version, (3) an advertisement Web version, and (4) a print version. Results indicate that learning from print was better than learning from linear and nonlinear Web designs, but no different than learning from the advertisement. No significant differences across media conditions were found using cued recall as the measure of learning. In this study, students who were more motivated by Web-based instruction tended to get significantly lower learning scores on the post-test.

Studies of Course Dropout

An important indicator of motivation in all learning environments is the level of persistence at learning tasks over time (Pintrich & Schunk, 2001). More motivated students tend to focus on learning tasks over time and not become distracted by other goals or activities. Because persistence is a key motivational index, student "dropout" from Web courses might be a good indication of motivational problems. Web-based instruction is likely to be more accessible to more students, yet once they enroll, motivation in the form of persistence is one of the key processes that keeps them enrolled and working over time.

The National Center for Education Statistics reported that from 1995 to 1997–98 the total number of community college and four-year college students enrolled in distance education courses across all degree-granting institutions increased from 754,000 to 1.6 million (Lewis, Snow, Farris, Levin, & Greene, 1999). The percentage of public institutions offering Web-based learning options increased from 62% in fall 1995 to 79% in 1997–98 in the public 4-year institutions, and from 58 to 72% in public 2-year institutions. The survey also indicated that in 1997–98, an additional

12% of public 4-year and 19% of public 2-year institutions planned to offer them in the next 3 years (Lewis et al., 1999). However, studies constantly demonstrate high levels of dropout in distance education programs. According to Potashnik and Capper (1998), the dropout rates for distance education students range from 19 to 90%. They estimate an average 40% dropout rate for most distance courses. An article in the *Chronicle of Higher Education* reports that the dropout rates in online courses range from 20 to 50%, so student retention becomes a real challenge (Carr, 2000). In addition, anecdotal evidence constantly indicates that Web-based courses have a much higher dropout rate than traditional courses (Hiltz, 1994, 1997). Thus, while most advocates of Web-based instruction have argued for motivational benefits, existing evidence suggests that important components of motivation may actually be decreased by common features of Web-based instruction. Salomon (1984) presented compelling evidence that students who express a preference for instruction presented via new media tend to expect that it will be a less demanding way to learn. This expectation results in the investment of lower levels of mental effort and lower achievement levels when compared to instructional conditions, which are perceived as more demanding. This finding has been replicated a number of times with different media (see, e.g., the discussion of related studies in Clark, 2001). Salomon's theory may be the reason why the Eveland and Dunwoody (2000) study of different ways to teach about the flu virus (described above) found that the most motivated students learned the least.

Suggestions for Overcoming Misconceptions about Motivational Benefits

Rather than assuming that certain media have monolithically positive (or negative) effects on motivation, online assessment strategies that attempt to capture motivational benefits should adopt a more fine-grained approach (or pay attention to more types of motivation—not just to rather surface-level and immediate indices such as choice and interest). For example, Pintrich and Schunk (2001) suggest three "indexes" of motivation: (1) active choice (actively starting to do something that one formerly "intended" to do but had not started), (2) persistence (continuing to work toward a goal, despite distractions), and (3) mental effort, defined by Salomon (1984) as "the number of non-automatic elaborations invested in learning" (p. 647). Each of these indices may play a different role in, or relate differently to, the learning process. For example, it is possible that active choice (e.g., enrollment in Web-based instruction) may be facilitated by optimistic expectations about ease of access and flexibility of scheduling; however, this is an "access" issue, not a learning issue. Meanwhile, as discussed in more detail next, mental effort is required for all learning, and delays in finishing online courses and rumors about high dropout rates suggest the need for more research on persistence.

Persistence in Web-based courses

The very high level of enrollment followed by unusually high levels of dropout in Web-based courses is an indication that students may be exercising what motivation theorists call "active choice" but not persistence. They are obviously choosing to enroll in these courses and projections indicate that enrollments may continue to increase in the future. Yet it also seems that too many students are not persisting after they have enrolled. Why not? Persistence has been found to be associated with the value students place on the interest and utility they associate with the learning objectives or instructional strategies provided in the course or the benefits of finishing it (Eccles & Wigfield, 2002). There are suggestive indicators in existing Web-based case studies about what features students value in courses and which of those features are often missing in Web-based instruction. For example, many prospective distance-learning students may be trying to overcome their perceived lack of contact with instructors in large enrollment, classroom-based courses. Hiltz (1997) found that 71% of the students surveyed at the New Jersey Institute of Technology felt that asynchronous learning networks provided better access to their professors than they received in traditional, face-to-face courses. She does provide the caveat that this access is dependent upon the instructor making himself or herself available online daily. Similarly, Shaw and Pieter (2000) found that 66% of their respondents said that the asynchronous learning environment made their lecturer more accessible than those in traditional classrooms. The students in an online program at Drexel echoed these sentiments: in one cohort 55% of students believed they interacted with the professor more than they would have in a face-to-face class (Hislop, 2000).

Online courses may be chosen over other forms of distance education, for similar reasons (i.e., heightened instructor contact). In Kennedy's (2000) survey of a group of online students, 68% of the 40 respondents said they enrolled online rather than self-study because they wanted instructor feedback and guidance through the course. Most students also believe that the heightened instructor contact enhanced their learning in the course. The State University of New York students who reported the highest levels of instructor interaction also reported the highest levels of value for the course (Fredericksen, Pickett, Shea, Pelz, & Swan, 2000). UCLA has also reduced dropout with a system, in which course managers contact "missing" students to prod them into persisting (Frankola, 2001).

Thus, though it seems clear that Web-based instruction *can* include (or be perceived to include) more instructor–student contact, and that this increased interaction may enhance the value of the course and student persistence to the extent that such increased interaction is missing, motivation to persist may be lacking as well. Additional studies concerning the factors and strategies that would further enhance student persistence in Web-based courses would be useful.

Mental effort

Not much is known about the direct impact of online instructional formats on mental effort (aside from Salomon's cautions), but the early research is not promising. Recent studies by John Sweller and others (e.g., Mousavi, Low, & Sweller, 1995; Sweller & Chandler, 1994) indicate that many instructional strategies and complex screen displays risk overloading working memory and causing "automated" cognitive defaults where mental effort is both reduced and directed to nonlearning goals. Complicating this finding is strong evidence that learners are not aware when they become overloaded and enter a default state (Gimino, 2000). Because all methods used to measure mental effort involve self-report (e.g., Bandura, 1997), this finding is very distressing. Pintrich and Schunk (2001) suggest the use of various measures for ongoing assessment of motivation including self-efficacy (Bandura, 1997), value for learning goals (Eccles & Wigfield, 2000), mood or emotionality, and dual task measures for mental effort (Gimino, 2000). In general, it seems that mental effort may be influenced in large part by the amount of perceived difficulty in a Web-based course. It is possible that when moderately challenging learning goals and tasks are presented, mental effort increases. When learning tasks are too easy or impossibly difficult, mental effort decreases radically. Students seem to be able to accurately report the amount of mental effort they are investing in easy to moderately difficult tasks. Yet there is disturbing evidence that they seem unaware when they stop investing mental effort as learning tasks become extremely difficult or impossible. Designers must exercise caution not to overwhelm Web students with extremely complex tasks or screen design features that overload working memory. Meanwhile, researchers should continue to study how specific tasks and design features impact mental effort.

DOES ACTIVE SCREEN DESIGN HELP
OR DAMAGE LEARNING?

Another common but misplaced assumption concerning Web-based instruction is that highly active visual and auditory screen design techniques enhance the motivation and learning of most students. In fact, there is increasing evidence that the "busy" screen designs often found in online learning environments may either be irrelevant or actually cause learning problems. Many Web-based instructional designers are tempted toward instructional presentations that include very active animated figures, music and other background sounds, motion video depictions of course concepts, "voiceover" narration, and other visually and aurally exciting displays. While many learners seem to welcome the visual and aural entertainment, the best evidence suggests that learners are often overloaded by seductive but irrelevant distractions or the effort of processing redundant information so their learning is reduced (Moreno & Mayer, 2000; see also Mayer & Moreno, Chapter 2, this volume). Screen designs that separate visual and text-based explanations or demonstrations, and/or are heavily text laden seem to overload the working memory of many students and decrease their learning. This is not to say, however, that all screen activity or complexity is damaging. Mayer and his colleagues advise the spatial and temporal integration of verbal and visual information. They also recommend the use of narration rather than large bodies of text. Furthermore, there is some evidence that animation may not hurt (or may even slightly improve) learning if used appropriately. We turn to that evidence next.

Two experiments on animated agents and other screen design strategies. Two recently published studies of the effects of animated pedagogical agents extend Mayer's work and illustrate the complex nature of issues that surround screen design for the presentation of Web courses. Animated agents are defined by Craig, Gholson, and Driscoll (2002) as "a computerized character (either humanlike or otherwise) designed to facilitate learning" (p. 428). Atkinson (2002) suggests that these animated agents "reside in the learning environment by appearing as animated 'humanlike' characters, which allows them to exploit nonverbal communication typically reserved for human–human interaction...[and] can focus a learner's attention by moving around the screen, using gaze and gesture, providing nonverbal feedback and conveying emotions" (pp. 416–417). Atkinson describes a complex study where a variety of aural (spoken narration) and visual instructional aids were either used with an animated agent or employed alone in a lesson that used worked examples to teach mathematical proportion problems to university undergraduates. In two experiments, Atkinson achieved some interesting but mixed results. In general, giving a voiceover description of the elements of the worked example in his study was as effective as voice plus the pedagogical agent in most outcome measures. There was some indication that the agent helped and voiceover helped performance on transfer tasks but the effect was "not as dramatic or pervasive as might be expected" (p. 423). Atkinson also found that when his animated agent gestured toward key elements of the worked example, more learning occurred than a narration-only condition. Of course, methods of highlighting the key elements in an instructional display that do not require animated pedagogical agents are available.

A powerful and less expensive alternative to pedagogical agents was examined in a study by Craig and colleagues (2002), who partially replicated some of Atkinson's (2002) treatments and studies conducted by Mayer and his colleagues (Mayer, 2001). Craig and colleagues provided instruction about lightening formation developed by Mayer to university undergraduates. They employed a spoken narration that was presented with three different agent conditions crossed with three visual conditions for a 3 × 3 factorial study. A "no agent" condition provided narration coordinated with pictures, an agent only condition where the agent "speaks" narration coordinated with pictures, and finally an agent with gestures condition where the agent looked and pointed toward relevant parts of the display while the narration described it. In one of the three visual conditions, the narration and agent were accompanied by static pictures. In a visual condition called "sudden onset," different areas of the static pictures were highlighted with color when the narration discussed them. In the final condition, the static picture was replaced by animation that covered the same information. The results of this experiment indicated that the "sudden onset" highlighting of the areas being discussed in the static pictures was as effective as the agent and the animation conditions. In a second experiment, Craig and colleagues examined the harmful redundancy effect found by Mayer (2001) when both a text and narrated version of the same information is presented together on the screen. As expected, they found that when they added printed text to a narration of the text, students were overloaded by the redundancy involved in trying to process two forms of the same information. They also replicated Mayer's finding that when the computer screen presents narrated information (without pictures or text), information is learned better than a printed version of the narration.

So What Do We Know about Screen Design?

These lines of research are providing valuable guidance for screen designers. These studies seem to indicate that we must focus learners constantly on information that is directly related to learning goals. Designers must also resist the temptation to offer visually and aurally enticing and aesthetically pleasing but irrelevant screen design formats and features that overload the attention and cognitive processing resources of learners. Evidence mounts that simpler screen design features may be most successful when they present important information to be learned in cognitively manageable chunks and focus learners' attention on key elements of instructional displays. Both studies reviewed above provide strong evidence that less expensive and less technologically challenging pedagogical features may be more effective at promoting learning. More information about related research and suggested ways to overcome screen design learning problems can be found in Mayer (2001).

ARE PROBLEM-BASED DISCOVERY LEARNING AND LEARNER NAVIGATION CONTROL EFFECTIVE?

It is often assumed that providing problem-based discovery instruction and high levels of learner control over navigation will increase learning and motivation. However, major disagreements surround the question of how much structure and instructional control should be imposed on learners in Web-based programs. The reasoning that brings most people to advocate providing students with as much control as possible during learning seems sensible. How will students "learn to learn" if they are not encouraged to exercise self-control over their own learning? Yet here also one finds a split between Web designers and instructional researchers. On the one hand, it is possible to find many passionate arguments for maximum learner control by designing Web-based courses that encourage learners to navigate freely within and between lessons and instructional presentations to discover knowledge (Friend & Cole, 1990; Jonassen, 1994). On the other hand, most of the research that has examined the effects of discovery learning and high levels of learner navigation control during learning has found only very limited benefits (Dillon & Gabbard, 1998; Hannafin & Sullivan, 1996). The most typical finding in research on both discovery learning and high levels of learner control (versus more structure and program control of instructional events) indicate that only students with very high ability and more prior knowledge are helped by exercising more control. Thus students benefiting from very high control levels constitute a very small percentage of students who enroll in any Web-based course.

Why is learner control and discovery the wrong method for many students? Working memory overload may account for much of the research evidence that discovery-based instruction and high levels of learner navigation control are not effective for most students. There is a long history of cautions about these approaches in educational research. For example, Cronbach (1966) reviewed research from the 1930s to the 1960s and found discovery benefits for only the highest aptitude students. In Cronbach and Snow's (1977) monumental review of instructional research, they presented convincing evidence that discovery and learner control may be beneficial only for students with very advanced prior knowledge and/or exceptionally high general ability. They also found considerable evidence that these methods depress learning for those with average to lower ability or prior knowledge. Cronbach and Snow argued that the very high cognitive load imposed by these two methods easily overloads low ability students but may permit exceptionally high ability students to use their own automated learning strategies. Designers should therefore be aware that only about one in five students will benefit from high levels of navigation and discovery while others may be harmed by them.

How Do We Provide Maximum Learner Control without Damaging Learning?

Designs that effectively scaffold instructional support seem to be most effective. An ideal strategy would be to gradually withdraw system control of learning strategies and the presentation of conceptual knowledge only when student practice data and/or reliable assessments of relevant prior knowledge indicate that they can work more independently. This seems to be the approach being taken by researchers such as Dillon and Gabbard (1998), Hanafin and Sullivan (1996), Sweller (1994), Sweller and Chandler (1994), Paas and van Merrienboer (1994) and van Merrienboer (1997). What we can hope for in the future are clearer guidelines about how to anticipate and identify those learners who will benefit from different levels of learner control and discovery in specific kinds of learning tasks. This question is only one of those being investigated by instructional theorists who are concerned with designs for very complex learning.

IS ISD ADEQUATE FOR COMPLEX ONLINE LEARNING ENVIRONMENTS?

In the past it has been assumed that available instructional design models could adequately provide successful blueprint designs for the complex knowledge presented in many online courses. However, recent criticisms of the Instructional Systems Design (ISD) model for developing training blueprints have argued that it does not adequately represent "complex" knowledge (van Merrienboer, 1997). One result of the use of inadequate design models is a huge variation in the learning and transfer by students in Web-based programs. Evidence for the need to address the issue of complex learning is clearer in specific areas such as the learning of very complex concepts (Corneille & Judd, 1999) and verbal information (Pointe & Engle, 1990). Complex knowledge requires that students learn to coordinate and integrate both recurrent (procedural) and nonrecurrent (declarative) knowledge. Jeroen van Merrienboer (1997) makes a strong case for a heuristic insight about complex learning when he suggests that when practicing new and complex knowledge "the whole is not the sum of the parts" (p. 95). Learners must coordinate the integration of two types of knowledge that require a great deal of problem-solving practice geared to specific application contexts. In the past, practice exercises were most often offered in sequence across a course with very little opportunity for larger and more inclusive exercises. Adequate learning of complex knowledge requires the full integration of all knowledge being learned in increasingly large and inclusive practice exercises. Instructional methods of choice for complex knowledge seem to be focused on the development of adequate mental models for declarative knowledge and deductive expository methods for procedural, nonrecurrent knowledge. Scaffolding can be accomplished by the gradual replacement of deductive with inductive expository methods as students gain expertise.

What Instructional Design Models Support Complex Learning on the Web?

There are a variety of research-based approaches to developing new instructional designs that are capable of supporting the learning of complex knowledge. Examples include new constructivist design theories for problem solving (Jonassen, 1994, 1999; Reigeluth, 1999a, 1999b; Schwartz, Brophy, Lin, & Bransford, 1999), arguments for new context and technology-based design (Driscoll & Dick, 1999; Kozma, 2000; Richey, 1998), two decades of systematic design research and development on complex learning issues by John Anderson (1983, 1993, 1996; Anderson & Lebiere, 1998), innovative work on "first principles of instruction" by designer-researcher David Merrill (2000), and a new comprehensive design model proposed by van Merrienboer (1997). These welcome discussions have at least one important goal in common: the gradual evolution of design theory to accommodate complex learning.

At this point, there appears to be only one fully explicated design model that specializes in supporting the development of complex learning, whether it is Web or classroom based. Jeroen van Merrienboer and his colleagues (van Merrienboer, 1997; van Merrienboer, Clark, & de Croock, 2002) have described a full design model, solidly based on research in cognitive learning and advanced expertise. David Merrill (2000) has provided a very useful summary of the key features of a number of popular and successful design models (including van Merrienboer's model) and has translated them into a set of "first principles of design." The principles he finds in the successful approaches assume that complex learning is facilitated when (1) learners are engaged in solving real-world problems, (2) existing knowledge is activated as a foundation for new knowledge (and skills), (3) new knowledge is demonstrated to the learner, and (4) new knowledge is integrated into the learner's world. We can expect more design models for complex learning to be available in the next few years. What is less certain is whether the models will be adequately tested before they are widely used.

SHOULD ONLINE INSTRUCTION BE ADJUSTED TO ACCOMMODATE DIFFERENT LEARNING STYLES?

Most educators hope that many of the obvious individual, cultural, and group differences between learners can be accommodated by adjusting Web-based instructional presentations to "fit" different styles. Thus, they assume that formatting instruction so that it is compatible with various "learning styles" will increase learning. Learning styles are generally defined as a reliable and distinct mode of acquiring knowledge. Styles are often confused with learning preferences or values (favoring one method of instruction or type of learning task over another), learning strategies (plans for learning knowledge and/or skills), cognitive strategies (plans for processing specific kinds of information), or cognitive styles (habitual and distinct modes of processing specific kinds of information). Examples of learning styles can be found in references to "visual" or "verbal" learners, "convergers/divergers/assimilators/accommodators," or "Meyers Briggs Types." Learning styles are expected to remain more or less constant across a wide variety of learning tasks. Web-based instruction is thought to offer an ideal platform for tailoring instruction to fit different styles.

Yet the research evidence for learning styles is not very solid. In some cases, clear evidence exists in research that popular style measures are not reliable and that their validity is questionable. One example is the very popular Myers Briggs Types, which has been criticized often by measurement and learning researchers (e.g., Pittenger, 1993). Yet these criticisms have seemingly done nothing to discourage its use in instruction. Unreliable style measures cannot reliably support learning. In most cases, research examining the utility of different style measures is either not available, inadequately designed, or strongly indicates that the style measure does not work. Yet the number of Web sites that give advice on how to use style measures to design Web instruction seems to be increasing.

Cronbach and Snow's (1977) landmark review of the interaction of aptitudes and individual differences clearly suggested that there are no reliable learning style differences that can be adopted for instruction. They also criticized a number of cognitive style measures such as field dependence/independence. Their conclusion has been checked and reinforced by more recent reviews (see, e.g., Chall, 2000). These reviews indicate that adjusting instructional formats to accommodate "visual" or "verbal" learners, "field dependent," or Meyer's Briggs Types does not result in measured learning gains. Clark (1988) has argued that under some conditions, attempts to adjust instructional formats to accommodate learning styles may actually decrease learning.

So How Do We Accommodate Individual and Cultural Differences in Learning?

The recommendation given by Cronbach and Snow (1977) and adopted by most researchers (see Everson & Tobias, 1998), is that only general ability and relevant prior knowledge will reliably predict different capacities to benefit from different types of instruction. In general, they recommended that learners with higher levels of general ability and prior knowledge require less instructional support and benefit from more freedom to apply their own learning plans, methods, and strategies. For students with moderate to lower levels of prior knowledge and ability, more learning support is necessary. A promising developmental approach was described by Corno and Snow (1986). They point to a variety of motivational and domain-specific approaches that attempt to tap learners' ability to assemble learning strategies that help them adapt their prior knowledge and existing learning strategies to new learning challenges. They are very enthusiastic about motivational differences of the type recently described by Pintrich and Schunk (2001). It is likely that in the future we will find that most of the important learning differences between students not accounted for by ability or prior knowledge will be due to motivational differences in values, self-efficacy, or emotionality.

CONCLUSION AND SUGGESTIONS

At the root of most of the online instructional misconceptions discussed in this chapter is a lack of attention to past research on various instructional design and learning support strategies. Too many design strategies are selected out of enthusiasm and the personal preferences of the designers without checking their support in well-designed laboratory and field studies. As a result, designers seem not to be aware of the need for constant concern with the amount of cognitive load imposed on learners by a variety of techniques, including popular screen design strategies, the information "chunk size" presented, the navigation rules provided to learners, the use of discovery methods, and the lack of design models that accommodate complex learning. To avoid these problems, it is useful to check the research evidence that supports (or fails to support) design approaches. It is also useful to separate instructional design (often defined as the assembly of instructional "blueprints" or plans) and development (the construction of instructional materials and media presentations used to implement an instructional design blueprint). When design and development are conducted at the same time, the separate concerns of the two stages of instructional program development tend to become confused and the resulting Web-based instruction may often cause learning and assessment problems (Clark, 2000). It also appears that different types of instructional methods are helpful to support learning goals, on the one hand, and motivational goals, on the other hand (Clark, 2000). Separating the design of instructional methods to support learning and motivation is necessary to fully appreciate how these two complex cognitive processes can be yoked to work together (and how they sometimes can be placed in conflict). In addition, online designers must integrate the teaching and learning of both declarative and procedural knowledge (van Merrienboer, 1997).

AUTHOR NOTE

Correspondence concerning this chapter should be addressed to Richard E. Clark, Rossier School of Education, University of Southern California, 3664 Hightide Drive, Rancho Palos Verdes, CA 90275-6135. Email: clark@usc.edu

NOTE

1. The following Web site lists more than a dozen new journals dealing with distance education and a large number of Web-based newsletters: http://webster.commnet.edu/HP/pages/darling/journals.htm

REFERENCES

Abrahamson, C. E. (1998). Issues in interactive communication in distance education. *College Student Journal, 32*(1), 33–42.

Anderson, J. R. (1983). *The architecture of cognition.* Cambridge, MA: Harvard University Press.

Anderson, J. R. (1993). *Rules of the mind.* Hillsdale, NJ: Erlbaum.

Anderson, J. R. (1996). ACT: A simple theory of complex cognition. *American Psychologist, 51*(4), 355–365.

Anderson, J. R., & Lebiere, C. (1998). *The atomic components of thought.* Mahwah, NJ: Erlbaum.

Atkinson, R. K. (2002). Optimizing learning from examples using animated pedagogical agents. *Journal of Educational Psychology, 94*(2), 416–427.

Bandura, A. (1997). *Self-efficacy: The exercise of control.* New York: Freeman.

Carr, S. (2000, February). As distance education comes of age, the challenge is keeping the students [Online]. Retrieved June 30, 2002, from http://chronicle.com/free/v46/i23/ 23a00101.htm

Chall, J. (2000). *The academic achievement challenge: What really works in the classroom.* New York: Guilford Press.

Clark, R. E. (1994). Media will never influence learning. *Educational Technology Research and Development, 42*(2), 21–29.

Clark, R. E. (1988). When teaching kills learning: Research on mathemathantics. In H. Mandl, E. DeCorte, N. Bennett, & H. F. Friedrich (Eds.), *Learning and instruction: European research in an international context* (Vol. 22, pp. 1–22). Oxford, UK: Pergamon Press.

Clark, R. E. (1999). Yin and Yang cognitive motivational processes operating in multimedia learning environments. In J. van Merrienboer (Ed.), *Cognition and multimedia design.* Herleen, Netherlands: Open University Press.

Clark, R. E. (2000). Evaluating distance education: Strategies and cautions. *Quarterly Journal of Distance Education, 1*(1), 5–18.

Clark, R. E. (2001). *Learning from media: Arguments, analysis and evidence.* Greenwich, CT: Information Age.

Clark, R. E., & Salomon, G. (1986). Media in teaching. In M. Wittrock (Ed.), *Handbook of research on teaching* (3rd ed.). New York: Macmillan.

Cobb, T. (1997). Cognitive efficiency: Toward a revised theory of media. *Educational Technology Research and Development, 45*(4), 21–35.

Corneille, O., & Judd, C. M. (1999). Accentuation and sensitization effects in the categorization of multifaceted stimuli. *Journal of Personality and Social Psychology, 77*(5), 927–941.

Corno, L., & Snow, R. E. (1986). Adopting teaching to individual differences among learners. In M. C. Wittrock (Ed.), *Handbook of research on teaching* (3rd ed., pp. 605–629). New York: Macmillan.

Craig, S. D., Gholson, B., & Driscoll, D. M. (2002). Animated pedagogical agents in multimedia educational environments: Effects of agent properties, picture features and redundancy. *Journal of Educational Psychology, 94*(2), 428–434.

Cronbach, L. J. (1966). The logic of experiments on discovery. In L. S. Shulman & E. R. Keislar (Eds.), *Learning by discovery: A critical appraisal* (pp. 76–92). Chicago: Rand McNally.

Cronbach, L., & Snow, R. E. (1977). *Aptitudes and instructional methods.* New York: Irvington.

Dillon, A., & Gabbard, R. (1998). Hypermedia as an educational technology: A review of the quantitative research literature on learning comprehension, control and style. *Review of Educational Research, 68*(3), 322–349.

Driscoll, M., & Dick, W. (1999). New research paradigms in instructional technology: An inquiry. *Educational Technology, Research and Development, 47*, 1042–1062.

Eccles, J.S., & Wigfield, A. (2002). Motivational beliefs, values and goals. *Annual Review of Psychology, 53,* 109–132.

Eveland, W. P., & Dunwoody, S. (2000, June). *A test of competing hypotheses about the impact of the World Wide Web versus traditional print media on learning.* Paper presented at the annual meeting of the International Communications Association, Acapulco, Mexico.

Everson, H. T., & Tobias, S. (1998). The ability to estimate knowledge and performance in college: A metacognitive analysis. *Instructional Science, 26,* 65–79.

Frankola, K. (2001). Why online learners drop out. *Workforce, 80*(10), 52–60.

Fredericksen, E., Pickett, A., Shea, P., Pelz, W., & Swan, K. (2000). *Student satisfaction and perceived learning with on-line courses: Principles and examples from the SUNY learning network* [Online]. Retrieved June 30, 2002, from http://www.aln.org/alnweb/journal/Vol4_issue2/le/Fredericksen/LE-fredericksen.htm

Friend, C. L., & Cole, C. L. (1990). Learner control in computer-based instruction: A current literature review. *Educational Technology, 30*(11), 47–49.

Gimino, A. (2000). *Factors that influence students' investment of mental effort in academic tasks: A validation and exploratory study.* Unpublished doctoral dissertation, University of Southern California, Los Angeles.

Hannafin, R. D., & Sullivan, H. J. (1996). Preferences and learner control over amount of instruction. *Journal of Educational Psychology, 88*(1), 162–173.

Hiltz, S. R. (1994). *The virtual classroom: Learning without limits via computer networks.* Norwood, NJ: Ablex.

Hiltz, S. R. (1997). Impacts of college-level courses via asynchronous learning networks: Some preliminary results. *Journal of Asynchronous Learning Networks, 1*(2) [Online]. Retrieved June 30, 2002, from http://www.aln.org/alnweb/journal/issue2/hiltz.htm

Hislop, G. (2000). *Working professionals as part-time on-line learners* [Online]. Retrieved June 30, 2002, from http://www.aln.org/alnweb/journal/Vol4_issue2/le/hislop/LE-hislop.htm

Jonassen, D. (1994). Thinking technology: Toward a constructivist design model. *Educational Technology, 34*(4), 34–37.

Jonassen, D. (1999). Designing constructivist learning environments. In C. M. Reigeluth (Ed.), *Instructional design theories and models: A new paradigm of instructional theory* (Vol. 2, pp. 371–396). Mahwah, NJ: Earlbaum.

Karsenti, T. (1999, October). *Student motivation and distance education on the Web: Love at first sight?* [Online]. Paper presented at the Web-Based Learning Conference, University of New Brunswick. Retrieved June 30, 2002, from http://naweb.unb.ca/proceedings/1999/karsenti/karsenti.html

Kennedy, C. (2000). *Quick online survey summary* [Online]. Retrieved June 30, 2002, from http://www.smccd.net/kennedyc/rsch/qcksrv.htm

Kitchen, D., & McDougall, D. (1998). Collaborative learning on the Internet. *Journal of Educational Technology Systems, 27*(3), 245–258.

Kozma, R. B. (1994). Will media influence learning? Reframing the debate. *Educational Technology Research and Development, 42*(2), 7–19.

Kozma, R. (2000). Reflections on the state of educational technology. *Educational Technology, Research and Development, 48,* 5–15.

Levin, H.M., Glass, G., & Meister, G. R. (1987). Cost-effectiveness of computer assisted instruction. *Evaluation Review, 11*(1), 50–72.

Levin, H.M., & McEwan, P. J. (2001). *Cost-effectiveness analysis: Methods and applications* (2nd ed.). Thousand Oaks, CA: Sage.

Lewis, L., Snow, K., Farris, E., Levin, D., & Greene, B. (1999, December). *Distance education at postsecondary education institutions: 1997–98* [Online]. Retrieved June 30, 2000, from http://nces.ed.gov/pubs2000/2000013.pdf

Mayer, R. (2001). *Multi-media learning.* Cambridge, UK: Cambridge University Press.

Merrill, D. M. (2000). *First principles of instruction* [Online]. Paper presented at the annual convention of the Association for Educational Communications and Technology, Denver, CO. Retrieved June 30, 2002, from http://www.id2.usu.edu/Papers/5FirstPrinciples.PDF

Mielke, K. W. (1968). Questioning the questions of ETV research. *Educational Broadcasting, 2,* 6–15.

Moreno, R., & Mayer, R. (2000). *A learner centered approach to multi media explanations: Deriving instructional design principles from cognitive theory* [Online]. Retrieved from http://imej.wfu.edu/articles/2000/2/05/printver.asp

Mousavi, S. Y., Low, R., & Sweller, J. (1995). Reducing cognitive load by mixing auditory and visual presentation modes. *Journal of Educational Psychology, 87,* 319–334.

Office of Technology Assessment. (1988, September). *Power on: New tools for teaching and learning* [Online]. Retrieved June 30, 2002, from http://www.wws.princeton.edu/~ota/ disk2/1988/8831_n.html

Paas, F. G. W. C., & van Merrienboer, J. J. G. (1994). Variability of worked examples and transfer of geometrical problem-solving skills: A cognitive-load approach. *Journal of Educational Psychology, 86*(1), 122–133.

Pintrich, P. R., & Schunk, D. H. (2001). *Motivation in education: Theory, research and practice* (2nd ed.). Englewood Cliffs, NJ: Prentice Hall.

Pittinger, D. J. (1993). The utility of the Myers-Briggs Type Indicator. *Review of Educational Research, 63*(4), 467–488.

Pointe, L. B., & Engle, R. W. (1990). Simple and complex word spans as measures of working memory capacity. *Journal of Experimental Psychology: Learning, Memory and Cognition, 16*(6), 1118–1133.

Potashnik, M., & Capper, J. (1998). *Distance education: Growth and diversity* [Online]. Retrieved June 30, 2002, from http://www.worldbank.org/fandd/english/0398/articles/0110398.htm

Reigeluth, C. M. (1999a). The elaboration theory: Guidance for scope and sequence decisions. In C. M. Reigeluth (Ed.), *Instructional design theories and models: A new paradigm of instructional theory* (Vol. 2). Mahwah, NJ: Erlbaum.

Reigeluth, C. M. (Ed.). (1999b). *Instructional design theories and models: A new paradigm of instructional theory* (Vol. 2). Mahwah, NJ: Erlbaum.

Richey, R. (1998). The pursuit of useable knowledge in instructional technology. *Educational Technology, Research and Development, 46,* 7–22.

Salomon, G. (1984). Television is "easy" and print is "tough": The differential investment of mental effort in learning as a function of perceptions and attributions. *Journal of Educational Psychology, 76,* 774–786.

Schramm, W. (1977). *Big media, little media.* Beverly Hills, CA: Sage.

Schwartz, D., Brophy, S., Lin, X., & Bransford, J. (1999). Flexibly adaptive instructional design: A case study from an educational psychology course. *Educational Technology, Research and Development, 47,* 39–60.

Shaw, G. P., & Pieter, W. (2000). *The use of asynchronous learning networks in nutrition education: Student attitude, experiences, and performance* [Online]. Retrieved June 30, 2002, from http://www.aln.org/journal/Vol4_issue1/shawpieter.htm

Sugrue, B., & Clark, R. E. (2000). Media selection for training. In S. Tobias & D. Fletcher (Eds.), *Training handbook.* New York: Macmillan.

Sweller, J. (1994). Cognitive load theory, learning difficulty, and instructional design. *Learning and Instruction, 4,* 295–312.

Sweller, J., & Chandler, P. (1994). Why some material is difficult to learn. *Cognition and Instruction, 12,* 185–233.

Valenta, A., Therriault, D., Dieter, M., & Mrtek, R. (2001, September). *Identifying student attitudes and learning styles in distance education* [Online]. Retrieved from http://www.aln.org.alnweb/journal/Vol5_issue2/Valenta/Valenta.htm

van Merrienboer, J. J. G. (1997). *Training complex cognitive skills: A four-component instructional design model for technical training.* Englewood Cliffs, NJ: Educational Technology Publications.

van Merrienboer, J. J. G., Clark, R. E., & de Croock, M. B. M. (2002). Blueprints for complex learning: The 4C/ID model. *Educational Technology Research and Development, 50*(2), 39–64.

Yang, Y. C. (1991–1992). The effects of media on motivation and content recall: Comparison of computer and print-based instruction. *Journal of Educational Technology Systems, 20,* 95–105.

CHAPTER 2

NINE WAYS TO REDUCE COGNITIVE LOAD IN MULTIMEDIA LEARNING[1]

Richard E. Mayer
University of California, Santa Barbara

Roxana Moreno
University of New Mexico

ABSTRACT

First, we propose a theory of multimedia learning based on the assumption that humans possess separate systems for processing pictorial and verbal material (dual channel assumption), that each channel is limited in the amount of material that can be processed at one time (limited capacity assumption), and that meaningful learning involves cognitive processing including building connections between pictorial and verbal representations (active processing assumption). Second, based on the cognitive theory of multimedia learning, we examine the concept of cognitive overload in which the learner's intended cognitive processing exceeds the learner's available cognitive capacity. Third, we examine five overload scenarios. For each overload scenario, we offer one or two theory-based suggestions for how to

Web-Based Learning: What Do We Know? Where Do We Go?, pages 23–44
Copyright © 2003 by Information Age Publishing

reduce cognitive load and we summarize our research results aimed at testing the effectiveness of each suggestion. Overall, our analysis shows that cognitive load is a central consideration in the design of multimedia instruction.

WHAT IS MULTIMEDIA LEARNING AND INSTRUCTION?

The goal of our research is to figure out how to use words and pictures to foster meaningful learning. We define *multimedia learning* as learning from words and pictures, and we define *multimedia instruction* as presenting words and pictures that are intended to foster learning. The words can be printed (such as onscreen text) or spoken (such as narration). The pictures can be static (such as illustrations, graphs, charts, photos, or maps) or dynamic (such as animation, video, or interactive illustrations). An important example of multimedia instruction is a computer-based narrated animation that explains how a causal system works (such as how pumps work, how a car's braking system works, how the human respiratory system works, how lightning storms develop, how airplanes achieve lift, or how plants grow).

We define meaningful learning as a deep understanding of the material, which includes attending to important aspects of the presented material, mentally organizing it into a coherent cognitive structure, and integrating it with relevant existing knowledge. Meaningful learning is reflected in the ability to apply what was taught to new situations, so we measure learning outcomes by using tests of *problem-solving transfer* (Mayer & Wittrock, 1996). In our research, meaningful learning involves the construction of a mental model of how a causal system works. In addition to asking whether learners can recall what was presented in a lesson (i.e., retention test), we also ask them to solve novel problems using the presented material (i.e., transfer test). All the results reported in this chapter are based on problem-solving transfer performance.

In pursuing our research on multimedia learning, we have repeatedly faced the challenge of cognitive load: Meaningful learning requires that the learner engage in substantial cognitive processing during learning, but the learner's capacity for cognitive processing is severely limited. Instructional designers have come to recognize the need for multimedia instruction that is sensitive to cognitive load (Clark, 1999; Sweller, 1999; van Merrienboer, 1997). A central challenge facing designers of multimedia instruction is the potential for cognitive overload, in which the learner's intended cognitive processing exceeds the learner's available cognitive capacity. In this chapter we present a theory of how people learn from multimedia instruction, which highlights the potential for cognitive overload.

Then, we describe how to design multimedia instruction in ways that reduce the chances of cognitive overload in each of five overload scenarios.

INTRODUCTION TO REDUCING COGNITIVE LOAD IN MULTIMEDIA LEARNING

How the Mind Works

We begin with three assumptions about how the human mind works, based on research in cognitive science: the dual channel assumption, the limited capacity assumption, and the active processing assumption. These assumptions are summarized in Table 2.1.

Table 2.1.   Three Assumptions about How the Mind Works in Multimedia Learning

Assumption	Definition
Dual channel	Humans possess separate information-processing channels for verbal and visual material.
Limited capacity	There is only a limited amount of processing capacity available in the verbal and visual channels.
Active processing	Learning requires substantial cognitive processing in the verbal and visual channels.

First, the human information processing system consists of two separate channels: an auditory/verbal channel for processing auditory input and verbal representations and a visual/pictorial channel for processing visual input and pictorial representations.[2] The dual channel assumption is a central feature of Paivio's (1986) dual coding theory and Baddeley's (1998) theory of working memory, although all theorists do not characterize the subsystems exactly the same way (Mayer, 2001).

Second, each channel in the human information-processing system has limited capacity—only a limited amount of cognitive processing can take place in the verbal channel at any one time and only a limited amount of cognitive processing can take place in the visual channel at any one time. This is the central assumption of Chandler and Sweller's (1991; see also Sweller, 1999) cognitive load theory and Baddeley's (1998) theory of working memory.

Third, meaningful learning requires a substantial amount of cognitive processing to take place in the verbal and visual channels. This is the central assumption of Wittrock's (1989) generative learning theory and Mayer's (1999, 2002) Selecting–Organizing–Integrating (SOI) theory of active learning. These processes include paying attention to the presented material, mentally organizing the presented material into a coherent structure, and integrating the presented material with existing knowledge.

Let's explore these three assumptions within the context of a cognitive theory of multimedia learning, which is summarized in Figure 2.1. The theory is represented as a series of boxes arranged into two rows and five columns, along with arrows connecting them. The two rows represent the two information-processing channels, with the auditory/verbal channel on top and the visual/pictorial channel on the bottom (see Footnote 2). This aspect of Figure 2.1 is consistent with the dual channel assumption.

The five columns in Figure 2.1 represent the modes of knowledge representation: physical representations (such as words or pictures that are presented to the learner), sensory representations (in the ears or eyes of the learner), shallow working memory representations (such as sounds or images attended to by the learner), deep working memory representations (such as verbal and pictorial models constructed by the learner), and long-term memory representations (such as the learner's relevant prior knowledge). The capacity for physically presenting words and pictures is virtually unlimited and the capacity for storing knowledge in long-term memory is virtually unlimited, but the capacity for mentally holding and manipulating words and images in working memory is limited. Thus, the working memory columns in Figure 2.1 are subject to the limited capacity assumption.

The arrows represent cognitive processing. The arrow from words to eyes represents printed words impinging on the eyes; the arrow from words to ears represents spoken words impinging on the ears; and the arrow from pictures to eyes represents pictures (such as illustrations, charts, photos, animations, and videos) impinging on the eyes. The arrow labeled *selecting words* represents the learner's paying attention to some of the auditory sensations coming in from the ears, whereas the arrow labeled *selecting images* represents the learner's paying attention to some of the visual sensations coming in through the eyes.[3] The arrow labeled *organizing words* represents the learner's constructing a coherent verbal representation from the incoming words, whereas the arrow labeled *organizing images* represents the learner's constructing a coherent pictorial representation from the incoming images. Finally, the arrows labeled *integrating* represent the merging of the verbal model, the pictorial model, and relevant prior knowledge. In addition, we propose that the selecting and organizing processes may be guided partially by prior knowledge activated by the learner. In multimedia learning, active processing requires five cognitive processes: selecting words, selecting images, organizing words, organizing images, and integrating. Consistent with the active processing assumption, these processes place demands on the cognitive capacity of the information-processing sys-

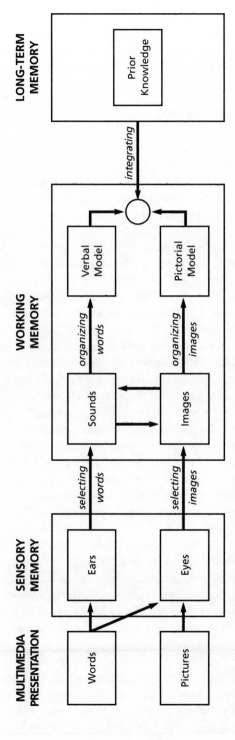

Figure 2.1. Cognitive theory of multimedia learning.

tem. Thus, the labeled arrows in Figure 2.1 represent the active processing required for multimedia learning.

The Case of Cognitive Overload

Let's consider what happens in multimedia learning, that is, a learning situation in which words and pictures are presented. A potential problem is that the processing demands evoked by the learning task may exceed the processing capacity of the cognitive system—a situation we call *cognitive overload*. The ever-present potential for cognitive overload is a central challenge for instructors (including instructional designers) and learners (including multimedia learners); meaningful learning often requires substantial cognitive processing using a cognitive system that has severe limits on cognitive processing.

We distinguish among three kinds of cognitive demands: essential processing, incidental processing, and representational holding.[4] *Essential processing* refers to cognitive processes that are required for making sense of the presented material, such as the five core processes in the cognitive theory of multimedia learning: selecting words, selecting images, organizing words, organizing images, and integrating. For example, in a narrated animation presented at a fast pace and consisting of unfamiliar material, essential processing involves using a great deal of cognitive capacity in selecting, organizing, and integrating the words and the images.

Incidental processing refers to cognitive processes that are not required for making sense of the presented material but are primed by the design of the learning task. For example, adding background music to a narrated animation may increase the amount of incidental processing to the extent that the learner devotes some cognitive capacity to processing of the music.

Representational holding refers to cognitive processes aimed at holding a mental representation in working memory over a period of time. For example, suppose that an illustration is presented in one window and a verbal description of it is presented in another window, but only one window can appear on the screen at one time. In this case, the learner must hold a representation of the illustration in working memory while reading the verbal description or must hold a representation of the verbal information in working memory while viewing the illustration.

Table 2.2 summarizes the three kinds of cognitive processing demands in multimedia learning. The total processing intended for learning consists of essential processing plus incidental processing plus representational holding. Cognitive overload occurs when the total intended processing exceeds the learner's cognitive capacity.[5] Reducing cognitive load can involve redistributing essential processing, reducing incidental processing, or reducing representational holding.

Table 2.2.   Three Kinds of Demands for Cognitive Processing in Multimedia Learning

Type of processing	Definition
Essential processing	Processing aimed at making sense of the presented material, including selecting, organizing, and integrating words and selecting, organizing, and integrating images.
Incidental processing	Processing aimed at nonessential aspects of the presented material.
Representational holding	Processing aimed at holding verbal or visual representations in working memory.

RESEARCH ON REDUCING COGNITIVE LOAD IN MULTIMEDIA LEARNING

In the following sections, we explore nine ways to reduce cognitive load in multimedia learning. We describe five different scenarios involving cognitive overload in multimedia learning. For each overload scenario we offer one or two suggestions for how to reduce cognitive overload based on the cognitive theory of multimedia learning, and we review the effectiveness of our suggestions based on a 12-year program of research carried out at the University of California, Santa Barbara. Our recommendations for reducing cognitive load in multimedia learning are summarized in Table 2.3.

Type 1 Overload: Offloading when One Channel is Overloaded with Essential Processing Demands

Problem: One channel is overloaded with essential processing

Consider the following situation: A student is interested in understanding how lightning works. She goes to a multimedia encyclopedia and clicks on the entry for *lightning*. A 2-minute animation appears on the screen depicting the steps in lightning formation along with concurrent onscreen text describing the steps in lightning formation. The onscreen text is presented at the bottom of the screen so while the student is reading, she cannot view the animation and while she is viewing the animation, she cannot read the text.

This situation creates what Sweller (1999) has called a *split-attention effect* because the learner's visual attention is split between viewing the anima-

Table 2.3. Load-Reduction Methods for Five Overload Scenarios in Multimedia Instruction

Type of overload scenario	Load-reducing method	Description of research effect	Effect size
Type 1: Essential Processing in Visual Channel > Cognitive Capacity of Visual Channel			
Visual channel is overloaded by essential processing	**Offloading:** Move some essential processing from visual channel to auditory channel	**Modality effect:** Better transfer when words are presented as narration rather than as onscreen text	1.17 (6)
Type 2: Essential Processing (in Both Channels) > Cognitive Capacity			
Both channels are overloaded by essential processing	**Segmenting:** Allow time between successive bite-size segments	**Segmentation effect:** Better transfer when lesson is presented in learner-controlled segments rather than as continuous unit	1.36 (1)
	Pretraining: Provide pretraining in names and characteristics of components	**Pretraining effect:** Better transfer when students know names and behaviors of system components	1.00 (3)
Type 3: Essential Processing + Incidental Processing (Caused by Extraneous Material) > Cognitive Capacity			
One or both channels overloaded by essential and incidental processing (attributable to extraneous material)	**Weeding:** Eliminate interesting but extraneous material	**Coherence effect:** Better transfer when extraneous material is excluded	0.90 (5)
	Signaling: Provide cues for how to process the material to reduce processing of extraneous material	**Signaling effect:** Better transfer when signals are included	0.74 (1)

Table 2.3. Load-Reduction Methods for Five Overload Scenarios in Multimedia Instruction (Cont.)

Type of overload scenario	Load-reducing method	Description of research effect	Effect size
Type 4: Essential Processing + Incidental Processing (Caused by Confusing Presentation) > Cognitive Capacity			
One or both channels overloaded by essential and incidental processing (attributable to confusing presentation of essential material)	**Aligning:** Place printed words near corresponding parts of graphics to reduce need for visual scanning	**Spatial contiguity effect:** Better transfer when printed words are placed near corresponding parts of graphics	0.48 (1)
	Eliminating redundancy: Avoid presenting identical streams of printed and spoken words	**Redundancy effect:** Better transfer when words are presented as narration rather than narration and onscreen text	0.69 (3)
Type 5: Essential Processing + Representational Holding > Cognitive Capacity			
One or both channels overloaded by essential processing and representational holding	**Synchronizing:** Present narration at same time as corresponding animation to minimize need to hold representations in memory	**Temporal contiguity effect:** Better transfer when corresponding animation and narration are presented at the same time	1.30 (8)
	Individualizing: Make sure learners possess skill at holding mental representations	**Spatial ability effect:** High spatial learners benefit more from well-designed instruction than do low spatial learners	1.13 (2)

Note. Number in parentheses indicates number of experiments upon which effect size is based.

tion and reading the onscreen text. This problem is represented in Figure 2.1 by the arrow from picture to eyes (for the animation) and the arrow from words to eyes (for the onscreen text). Thus, the eyes receive a lot of concurrent information but only some of that information can be selected for further processing in visual working memory (i.e., the arrow from eyes to images can only carry a limited amount of information).

Solution: Offloading

One solution to this problem is to present words as narration. In this way, the words are processed—at least initially—in the verbal channel (indicated by the arrow from words to ears in Figure 2.1), whereas the animation is processed in the visual channel (indicated by the arrow from picture to eyes in Figure 2.1). The processing demands on the visual channel are thereby reduced, so the learner is better able to select important aspects of animation for further processing (indicated by the arrow from eyes to images). The processing demands on the verbal channel are also moderate, so the learner is better able to select important aspects of the narration for further processing (indicated by the arrow from ears to sounds). In short, the use of narrated animation represents a method for offloading (or reassigning) some of the processing demands from the visual channel to the verbal channel.

In a series of six studies carried out in our lab at Santa Barbara, students performed better on tests of problem-solving transfer when scientific explanations were presented as animation and narration rather than as animation and onscreen text (Mayer & Moreno, 1998, Experiments 1 and 2; Moreno & Mayer, 1999, Experiments 1 and 2; Moreno, Mayer, Spires, & Lester, 2001, Experiments 4 and 5). The median effect size was 1.17. We refer to this result as a *modality effect*. Students understand a multimedia explanation better when the words are presented as narration rather than as onscreen text. A similar effect was reported by Mousavi, Low, and Sweller (1995) in a book-based multimedia environment. The robustness of the modality effect provides strong evidence for the viability of offloading as a method of reducing cognitive load.

Type 2 Overload:
Segmenting and Pretraining When Both Channels Are Overloaded with Essential Processing Demands in Working Memory

Problem: Both channels are overloaded with essential processing

Suppose a student views a narrated animation that explains the process of lightning formation, based on the strategies discussed in the previous section. In this case, some of the narration is selected to be processed as words in the verbal channel and some of the animation is selected to be processed as images in the visual channel (as shown by the arrows in Figure 2.1 labeled *selecting words* and *selecting images*, respectively). However, if the information content is rich and the pace of presentation is fast, learners may not have enough time to engage in the deeper processes of organizing the words into a verbal model, organizing the images into a visual model, and integrating the models (as shown by the *organizing words, organizing images*, and *integrating* arrows in Figure 2.1). By the time that the learner selects relevant words and pictures from one segment of the presentation, the next segment begins, thereby cutting short the time needed for deeper processing.

This situation leads to cognitive overload, in which available cognitive capacity is not sufficient to meet the required processing demands. Sweller (1999) refers to this situation as one in which the presented material has *high intrinsic load*, that is, the material is conceptually complex. Although it might not be possible to simplify the presented material, it is possible to allow learners to intellectually digest one chunk of it before moving on to the next.

Solution: Segmenting

A potential solution to this problem is to allow some time between successive segments of the presentation. In segmenting, the presentation is broken down into bite-size segments. The learner is able to select words and select images from the segment. Then, the learner also has the time and capacity to organize and integrate the selected words and images. Then, the learner is ready for the next segment, and so on. In contrast, when the narrated animation is presented continuously—without time breaks between segments—the learner can select words and select images from the first segment; but, before the learner is able to complete the additional processes of organizing and integration, the next segment is presented, which demands the learner's attention for selecting words and images.

For example, Mayer and Chandler (2001, Experiment 2) broke down a narrated animation explaining lightning formation into 16 segments. Each segment contained one or two sentences of narration and approximately 8 to 10 seconds of animation. After each segment was presented, the learner could start the next segment by clicking on a button labeled "Continue." Although students in both groups received identical material, the segmented group had more study time. Students who received the segmented presentation performed better on subsequent tests of problem-solving transfer than did students who received a continuous presentation. The effect size in the one study we conducted was 1.36. We refer to this as a *segmentation effect*. Students understand a multimedia explanation better when it is presented in learner-controlled segments rather than as a continuous presentation. Further research is needed to determine the separate effects of segmenting and interactivity, such as comparing how students learn from multimedia presentations that contain built-in or user-controlled breaks after each segment.

Solution: Pretraining

Although segmenting appears to be a promising technique for reducing cognitive load, sometimes segmenting might not be feasible. An alternative technique for reducing cognitive load when both channels are overloaded with essential processing is pretraining, in which learners receive prior instruction concerning the components in the to-be-learned system. Constructing a mental model involves two steps: building component models (i.e., representations of how each component works) and building a causal model (i.e., a representation of how a change in one part of the system causes a change in another part, and so on). In processing a narrated animation explaining how a car's braking system works, learners must simultaneously build component models (concerning how a piston can move forward and back, how a brake shoe can move forward and back, and so on) and a causal model (when the piston moves forward, brake fluid is compressed, and so on). By providing pretraining about the components, learners can more effectively process a narrated animation—devoting their cognitive processing to building a causal model. Without pretraining, students must try to understand each component and the causal links between them—a task that can easily overload working memory.

In a series of three studies involving narrated animations about how brakes work and how pumps work, students performed better on problem-solving transfer tests when the narrated animation was preceded by short pretraining about the names and behaviors of the components (Mayer, Mathias, & Wetzell, 2002, Experiments 1, 2, and 3). The median effect size comparing the pretrained and nonpretrained groups was 1.00. Similar results were reported by Pollock, Chandler, and Sweller (2002). We refer to this result as a *pretraining effect*. Students understand a multimedia presentation better when they know the names and behaviors of the components in the system. Pretraining involves a specific sequencing strategy, in which components are presented before a causal system is presented. The results provide support for pretraining as a useful method of reducing cognitive load.

Type 3 Overload:
Weeding and Signaling When the System Is Overloaded by Incidental Processing Demands Due to Extraneous Material

Problem: One or both channels are overloaded by the combination of essential and incidental processing

In the two foregoing scenarios, the cognitive system was required to engage in too much essential processing—such as when complex material is presented at a fast rate. Let's consider a somewhat different overload scenario where a learner seeks to engage in both essential and incidental processing, which together exceed the learner's available cognitive capacity. For example, suppose a learner clicks on the entry for *lightning* in a multimedia encyclopedia and receives a narrated animation describing the steps in lightning formation (i.e., which requires essential processing) along with background music or inserted narrated video clips of damage caused by lightning (i.e., which requires incidental processing).

According to the cognitive theory of multimedia learning, adding interesting but extraneous[6] material to a narrated animation may cause the learner to use limited cognitive resources on incidental processing, leaving less cognitive capacity for the essential processing. As a result, the learner will be less likely to engage in the cognitive processes required for meaningful learning of how lightning works, indicated by the arrows in Figure 2.1. Sweller (1999) refers to the addition of extraneous material in an instructional presentation as an example of *extraneous load.*

Solution: Weeding

In order to solve this problem, we suggest eliminating interesting but extraneous material, a load-reducing technique that can be called *weeding.* Weeding involves making the narrated animation as concise and coherent as possible so the learner will not be primed to engage in incidental processing. In a concise narrated animation, the learner is primed to engage in essential processing. In contrast, in an embellished narrated animation—such as one containing background music or inserted narrated video of lightning damage—the learner is primed to engage in both essential and incidental processing.

In a series of five studies carried out in our lab at Santa Barbara, students performed better on problem-solving transfer tests after receiving a concise narrated animation than an embellished narrated animation (Mayer, Heiser, & Lonn, 2001, Experiments 1, 3, and 4; Moreno & Mayer, 2000, Experiments 1 and 2). The added material in the embellished narrated animation consisted of background music or adding short narrated video clips showing irrelevant material. The median effect size was 0.90. We refer to this result as a *coherence effect.* Students understand a multimedia explanation better when interesting but extraneous material is excluded rather than included. The robustness of the coherence effect provides strong evidence for the viability of weeding as a method for reducing cognitive load. Weeding seems to help facilitate the process of selecting relevant information.

Solution: Signaling

When it is not feasible to remove all the embellishments in a multimedia lesson, cognitive load can be reduced by providing cues to the learner about how to select and organize the material, a technique that has been called *signaling* (Lorch, 1989; Meyer, 1975). For example, Mautone and Mayer (2001) constructed a 4-minute narrated animation explaining how airplanes achieve lift, which contained many extraneous facts and somewhat confusing graphics. Thus, the learner might engage in lots of incidental processing by focusing on nonessential facts or nonessential aspects of the graphics. A signaled version guided the learner's cognitive processes of (a) selecting words by stressing key words in speech, (b) selecting images by adding red and blue arrows to the animation, (c) organizing words by adding an outline and headings, and (d) organizing images by adding a map showing which of the three parts of the lesson was being presented. In the one study we conducted on signaling of a multimedia presentation (Mautone & Mayer, 2001, Experiment 3), students who received the signaled version of the narrated animation performed better on a subsequent test of problem-solving transfer than did students who received the nonsignaled version. The effect size was 0.74. We refer to this result as a *signaling effect*: Students understand a multimedia presentation better when it contains signals concerning how to process the material. Although there is substantial research literature on signaling of text in printed passages (Lorch, 1989), Mautone and Mayer's study offers the first examination of signaling for narrated animations. Signaling seems to help in the process of selecting and organizing relevant information.

Type 4 Overload:
Aligning and Eliminating Redundancy When the System Is Overloaded by Incidental Processing Demands Attributable to How the Essential Material is Presented

Problem: One or both channels are overloaded by the combination of essential and incidental processing

The problem is the same in Type 3 and Type 4 overload—namely, that the learning task requires incidental processing—but the cause of the problem is different. In Type 3 overload the source of the incidental processing is that extraneous material is included in the presentation, but in

Type 4 overload the source of the incidental processing is that the essential material is presented in a confusing way. For example, Type 4 overload occurs when onscreen text is placed at the bottom of the screen, whereas corresponding graphics are placed toward the top of the screen.

Solution: Aligning words and pictures

In Type 3 overload scenarios, incidental cognitive load was created by adding extraneous material. Another way to create incidental cognitive load is to misalign words and pictures on the screen, such as presenting an animation in one window with concurrent onscreen text in another window elsewhere on the screen. In this case, which we call *separated presentation*, the learner must engage in a great deal of scanning to figure out which part of the animation corresponds with the words, creating what we call incidental processing. In eye-movement studies, Hegarty and Just (1989) have shown that learners tend to read a portion of text and then look at the corresponding portion of the graphic. When the words are far from the corresponding portion of the graphic, the learner is required to use limited cognitive resources in visually scanning the graphic in search of the corresponding part of the picture. The amount of incidental processing can be reduced by placing the text within the graphic, next to the elements it is describing. This form of presentation, which we call *integrated presentation*, allows the learner to devote more cognitive capacity to essential processing.

Consistent with this analysis, Moreno and Mayer (1999, Experiment 1) found that students who learned from integrated presentations (consisting of animation with integrated onscreen text) performed better on a problem-solving transfer test than did students who learned from separated presentations (consisting of animation with separated onscreen text). The effect size in this single study was 0.48. Similar effects have been found with text and illustrations in books (Mayer, 2001). We refer to this result as a *spatial contiguity effect*: Students understand a multimedia presentation better when printed words are placed near rather than far from corresponding portions of the animation. Thus, spatial alignment of words and pictures appears to be a valuable technique for reducing cognitive load. As you can see, aligning is similar to signaling in that it guides cognitive processing, eliminating the need for incidental processing. Aligning differs from signaling in that aligning applies to situations in which essential words and pictures are separated and signaling applies to situations in which extraneous material is placed within the multimedia presentation.

Solution: Eliminating redundancy

Another example of Type 4 overload occurs when a multimedia presentation consists of simultaneous animation, narration, and onscreen text. In this situation, which we call *redundant presentation*, the words are presented both as narration and simultaneously as onscreen text. However, the learner may devote cognitive capacity to processing the onscreen text and reconciling it with the narration, thus priming incidental processing that reduces the capacity to engage in essential processing. In contrast, when the multimedia presentation consists of narrated animation, which we call *nonredundant presentation*, the learner is not primed to engage in incidental processing. In a series of three studies (Mayer, Heiser, & Lonn, 2001, Experiments 1 and 2; Moreno & Mayer, 2002, Experiment 2), students who learned from nonredundant presentations performed better on problem-solving transfer tests than did students who learned from redundant presentations. The median effect size was 0.69, indicating that eliminating redundancy is a useful way to reduce cognitive load. We refer to this result as a *redundancy effect.* Students understand a multimedia presentation better when words are presented as narration rather than as narration and onscreen text. We use the term redundancy effect in a more restricted sense than does Sweller (1999). As you can see, eliminating redundancy is similar to weeding in that both involving cutting aspects of the multimedia presentation. They differ in that weeding involves cutting interesting but irrelevant material, whereas eliminating redundancy involves cutting an unneeded duplication of essential material.

When no animation is presented, students learn better from a presentation of concurrent narration and onscreen text (i.e., verbal redundancy) than from a narration-only presentation (Moreno & Mayer, 2002, Experiments 1 and 3). An explanation for this effect is that adding onscreen text does not overload the visual channel because it does not have to compete with the animation.

Type 5 Overload:
Synchronizing and Individualizing When the System is Overloaded by the Need to Hold Information in Working Memory

Problem: One or both channels are overloaded by the combination of essential processing and representational holding

In the foregoing two sections, cognitive overload occurred when the learner attempted to engage in essential and incidental processing, and the solution was to reduce incidental processing through weeding or signaling (when extraneous material was included), or through aligning words and pictures or reducing redundancy (when the same essential material was presented in printed and spoken formats). In the fifth and final overload scenario, cognitive overload occurs when the learner attempts to engage in both essential processing (i.e., selecting, organizing, and integrating material that explains how the system works) and representational holding (i.e., holding visual and/or verbal representations in working memory during the learning episode).

For example, consider a situation in which a learner clicks on the *lightning* entry in a multimedia encyclopedia. First, a short narration is presented describing the steps in lightning formation, and next a short animation is presented depicting the steps in lightning formation. According to a cognitive theory of multimedia learning, this successive presentation can increase cognitive load because the learner must hold the verbal representation in working memory while the corresponding animation is being presented. In this situation, cognitive capacity must be used to hold a representation in working memory, thus depleting the learner's capacity for engaging in the cognitive processes of selecting, organizing, and integrating.

Solution: Synchronizing

A straightforward solution to the problem is to synchronize the presentation of corresponding visual and auditory material. When presentation of corresponding visual and auditory material is simultaneous, there is no need to hold one representation in working memory until the other is presented. This situation minimizes cognitive load. In contrast, when the presentation of corresponding visual and auditory material is successive, there is a need to hold one representation in one channel's working memory until the corresponding material is presented in the other channel. The additional cognitive capacity used to hold the representation in working memory can contribute to cognitive overload.

For example, in a series of eight studies carried out in our lab at Santa Barbara (Mayer & Anderson, 1991, Experiments 1 and 2a; Mayer & Anderson, 1992, Experiments 1 and 2; Mayer, Moreno, Boire, & Vagge, 1999, Experiments 1 and 2; Mayer & Sims, 1994, Experiments 1 and 2), students performed better on tests of problem-solving transfer when they learned from simultaneous presentations (i.e., presenting corresponding animation and narration at the same time) than from successive presentations (i.e., presenting the complete animation before or after the complete narration). The median effect size was 1.30, indicating robust evidence for synchronizing as a technique for reducing cognitive load. We refer to this result as a *temporal contiguity effect*. Students understand a multimedia presentation better when animation and narration are presented simultaneously rather than successively.

Importantly, the temporal contiguity effect is eliminated when the successive presentation is broken down into bite-size segments that alternate between a few seconds of narration and a few seconds of corresponding animation (Mayer et al., 1999, Experiments 1 and 2; Moreno & Mayer,

2002, Experiment 2). In this situation, working memory is not likely to become overloaded because only a small amount of material is subject to representational holding.

Solution: Individualizing

In cases where synchronization may not be possible, an alternative technique for reducing cognitive load is to be sure that the learners possess skill in holding mental representations in memory.[7] For example, high spatial ability involves the ability to hold and manipulate mental images with a minimum of mental effort. Low spatial learners may not be able to take advantage of simultaneous presentation because they must devote so much cognitive processing to hold mental images. In contrast, high spatial learners are more likely to benefit from simultaneous presentation by being able to carry out the essential cognitive processes required for meaningful learning. Consistent with this prediction, Mayer and Sims (1994, Experiments 1 and 2) found that high spatial learners performed much better on problem-solving transfer tests from simultaneous presentation than from successive presentation, whereas low spatial learners performed at the same low level for both. Across two experiments involving a narrated animation on how the human respiratory system works, the median effect size was 1.13. We refer to this interaction as the *spatial ability effect*, and note that individualization—matching high-quality multimedia design with high-spatial learners—may be a useful technique for reducing cognitive load.

CONCLUSION

Meeting the Challenge of Designing Instruction that Reduces Cognitive Load

A major challenge for instructional designers is that meaningful learning can require a heavy amount of essential cognitive processing but the cognitive resources of the learner's information processing system are severely limited. Therefore, multimedia instruction should be designed in ways that minimize any unnecessary cognitive load. In this chapter we summarized nine ways to reduce cognitive load, with each load-reduction method keyed to an overload scenario.

Our research program—conducted at UCSB over the last 12 years— convinces us that effective instructional design depends on sensitivity to cognitive load, which, in turn, depends on an understanding of how the human mind works. In this chapter, we shared the fruits of 12 years of research, aimed at contributing to cognitive theory (i.e., understanding the nature of multimedia learning) and building an empirical database (i.e., research-based principles of multimedia design).

Theory

We began with a cognitive theory of multimedia learning based on three core principles from cognitive science, which we labeled as dual channel, limited capacity, and active processing (in Table 2.1). Based on the cognitive theory of multimedia learning (in Figure 2.1) we derived predictions concerning various methods for reducing cognitive load. In running scores of controlled experiments to test these predictions, we were able to refine the theory and offer substantial empirical support. Thus, the seemingly practical search for load-reducing methods of multimedia instruction has contributed to theoretical advances in cognitive science—namely, a well-supported theory of how people learn from words and pictures. Overall, our approach has been based on the idea that the best way to improve instruction is to begin with a research-based understanding of how people learn.

Database

Our search for theory-based principles of instructional design led us to conduct scores of well-controlled experiments, thereby producing a substantial research base (summarized in Table 2.3). For each of our recommendations for how to reduce cognitive load, we see the need to conduct multiple experiments. In some cases where we report only a single preliminary study (i.e. segmenting, signaling, and aligning), more empirical research is needed. Clear and replicated effects are the building blocks of both theory and practice. Overall, our approach has been based on the idea that the best way to understand how people learn is to test theory-based predictions in the context of student learning scenarios.

Future directions

The measurement of cognitive load is a major area of needed research. In particular, we need ways to directly gauge cognitive load experienced by learners, to gauge the cognitive demands of instructional materials, and to gauge the cognitive resources available to individual learners. Although we hypothesize that our nine recommendations reduce cognitive load, it would be useful to have direct measures of cognitive load.

In our research, concise narrated animation fostered meaningful learning without creating cognitive overload. However, additional research is needed to examine situations in which certain kinds of animation can overload the learner (Schnotz, Boeckheler, & Grzondziel, 1999) and to determine the role of individual differences in visual and verbal learning styles in influencing cognitive overload (Plass, Chun, Mayer, & Leutner, 1998;

Riding, 2001). In addition, it would be worthwhile to examine whether the principles of multimedia learning apply to the design of online courses that require many hours of participation, to problem-based simulation games, and to multimedia instruction that includes onscreen pedagogical agents (Clark & Mayer, 2003).

In short, our program of research convinces us that the search for load-reducing methods of instruction contributes to cognitive theory and educational practice. Research on multimedia learning has promise for continuing to be an exciting venue for educational psychology.

AUTHOR NOTE

Richard E. Mayer's postal address is Department of Psychology, University of California, Santa Barbara, CA 93106-9660, USA. Richard E. Mayer's email address is mayer@psych.ucsb.edu. Roxana Moreno's postal address is Educational Psychology Program, University of New Mexico, Albuquerque, NM 87131. Roxana Moreno's email address is moreno@unm.edu. This research was supported by grant N00014-01-1-1039 from the Office of Naval Research.

NOTES

1. This chapter was reprinted from an article in press in the *Educational Psychologist.* Copyright 2002 by Lawrence Erlbaum Associates. Reprinted with permission.

2. Based on research on discourse processing (Graesser, Millis, & Zwaan, 1997), it is not appropriate to equate a verbal channel with an auditory channel. Mayer (2001) provides an extended discussion of the nature of dual channels.

3. *Selecting words* refers to selecting aspects of the text information rather than only specific words. *Selecting images* refers to selecting parts of pictures rather than only whole pictures.

4. *Essential processing* corresponds to the term *intrinsic load,* as used by Sweller (1999). *Incidental processing* corresponds to the term *extraneous load,* as used Sweller (1999).

5. In order to maintain conceptual clarity, we use the term *processing demands* to refer to properties of the learning materials or situation, and the term *processing* to refer to internal cognitive activity of learners.

6. Extraneous material may be related to the topic but does not directly support the educational goal of the presentation.

7. Individualization is not technically a design method for reducing cognitive load, but rather a way to select individual learners who are capable of benefiting from a particular multimedia presentation.

REFERENCES

Baddeley, A. (1998). *Human memory.* Boston: Allyn & Bacon.

Chandler, P., & Sweller, J. (1991). Cognitive load theory and the format of instruction. *Cognition and Instruction, 8,* 293–332.

Clark, C. C. (1999). *Developing technical training* (2nd ed.). Washington, DC: International Society for Performance Improvement.

Clark, C. C., & Mayer, R. E. (2003). *E-learning and the science of instruction.* San Francisco: Jossey-Bass.

Hegarty, M., & Just, M. A. (1989). Understanding machines from text and diagrams. In H. Mandl & J. R. Levin (Eds.), *Knowledge acquisition from text and pictures* (pp. 171–194). Amsterdam: Elsevier.

Lorch, R. F., Jr. (1989). Text signaling devices and their effects on reading and memory processes. *Educational Psychology Review, 1,* 209–234.

Mautone, P. D., & Mayer, R. E. (2001). Signaling as a cognitive guide in multimedia learning. *Journal of Educational Psychology, 93,* 377–389.

Mayer, R. E. (1999). *The promise of educational psychology: Volume 1. Learning in the content areas.* Upper Saddle River, NJ: Prentice Hall.

Mayer, R. E. (2001). *Multimedia learning.* New York: Cambridge University Press.

Mayer, R. E. (2002). *The promise of educational psychology: Volume 2. Teaching for meaningful learning.* Upper Saddle River, NJ: Prentice Hall.

Mayer, R. E., & Anderson, R. B. (1991). Animations need narrations: An experimental test of a dual-coding hypothesis. *Journal of Educational Psychology, 83,* 484–490.

Mayer, R. E., & Anderson, R. B. (1992). The instructive animation: Helping students build connections between words and pictures in multimedia learning. *Journal of Educational Psychology, 84,* 444–452.

Mayer, R. E., & Chandler, P. (2001). When learning is just a click away: Does simple user interaction foster deeper understanding of multimedia messages? *Journal of Educational Psychology, 93,* 390–397.

Mayer, R. E., Heiser, J., & Lonn, S. (2001). Cognitive constraints on multimedia learning: When presenting more material results in less understanding. *Journal of Educational Psychology, 93,* 187–198.

Mayer, R. E., Mathias, A., & Wetzell, K. (2002). Fostering understanding of multimedia messages through pretraining: Evidence for a two-stage theory of mental model construction. *Journal of Experimental Psychology: Applied, 8,* 147–154.

Mayer, R. E., & Moreno, R. (1998). A split-attention effect in multimedia learning: Evidence for dual processing systems in working memory. *Journal of Educational Psychology, 90,* 312–320.

Mayer, R. E., Moreno, R., Boire, M., & Vagge, S. (1999). Maximizing constructivist learning from multimedia communications by minimizing cognitive load. *Journal of Educational Psychology, 91,* 638–643.

Mayer, R. E., & Sims, V. K. (1994). For whom is a picture worth a thousand words? Extensions of a dual-coding theory of multimedia learning. *Journal of Educational Psychology, 84,* 389–460.

Mayer, R. E., & Wittrock, M. C. (1996). Problem-solving transfer. In D. Berliner & R. Calfee (Eds.), *Handbook of educational psychology* (pp. 45–61). New York: Macmillan.

Meyer, B. J. F. (1975). *The organization of prose and its effects on memory.* New York: Elsevier.

Moreno, R., & Mayer, R. E. (1999). Cognitive principles of multimedia learning: The role of modality and contiguity. *Journal of Educational Psychology, 91,* 358–368.

Moreno, R., & Mayer, R. E. (2000). A coherence effect in multimedia learning: The case for minimizing irrelevant sounds in the design of multimedia instructional messages. *Journal of Educational Psychology, 92,* 117–125.

Moreno, R., & Mayer, R. E. (2002). Verbal redundancy in multimedia learning: When reading helps listening. *Journal of Educational Psychology, 94,* 156–163.

Moreno, R., Mayer, R. E., Spires, H. A., & Lester, J. C. (2001). The case for social agency in computer-based multimedia learning: Do students learn more deeply when they interact with animated pedagogical agents? *Cognition and Instruction, 19,* 177–214.

Mousavi, S., Low, R., & Sweller, J. (1995). Reducing cognitive load by mixing auditory and visual presentation modes. *Journal of Educational Psychology, 87,* 319–334.

Paivio, A. (1986). *Mental representations: A dual coding approach.* Oxford, UK: Oxford University Press.

Plass, J. L., Chun, D. M., Mayer, R. E., & Leutner, D. (1998). Supporting visual and verbal learning preferences in a second language multimedia learning environment. *Journal of Educational Psychology, 90,* 25–36.

Pollock, E., Chandler, P., & Sweller, J. (2002). Assimilating complex information. *Learning and Instruction, 12,* 61–86.

Riding, R. (2001). The nature and effects of cognitive style. In R. J. Sternberg & L. Zhang (Eds.), *Perspectives on thinking, learning, and cognitive styles* (pp. 47–72). Mahwah, NJ: Erlbaum.

Schnotz, W., Boeckheler, J., & Grzondziel, H. (1999). Individual and co-operative learning with interactive animated pictures. *European Journal of Psychology of Education, 14,* 245–265.

Sweller, J. (1999). *Instructional design in technical areas.* Camberwell, Australia: ACER Press.

van Merrienboer, J. J. G. (1997). *Training complex cognitive skills.* Englewood Cliffs, NJ: Educational Technology Press.

Wittrock, M. C. (1989). Generative processes of comprehension. *Educational Psychologist, 24,* 345–376.

CHAPTER 3

TECHNOLOGY: THE GREAT EQUALIZER?

Eric J. Jolly
Education Development Center, Inc.

Christy A. Horn
Center for Instructional Innovation, University of Nebraska–Lincoln

ABSTRACT

The term *digital divide* entered our vocabulary in the mid-1990s as a response to the large gaps in computer access and use among people. Recently there have been mixed reports on the status of this gap, the pace at which it is closing, and the shape of our dreams for technology as an equalizing force. Clearly the measures used to make the original diagnosis for the problem are showing healthy signs of improvement. But as technology has advanced, so have our expectations of quality, access, and utility. Because what we measure will often define what we seek to accomplish, it is important to reexamine our notions of this so-called divide. This chapter seeks to address the data behind the reports that might suggest that our measures of the digital differences we've labeled a *divide* should also be reconsidered.

Web-Based Learning: What Do We Know? Where Do We Go?, pages 45–56
Copyright © 2003 by Information Age Publishing
All rights of reproduction in any form reserved.

For more than a decade now, governmental leaders from across our political spectrum have been holding out the hope that technology would one day be the great equalizer. Especially in education, there have been extensive initiatives to facilitate the spread of technology and connectivity in schools. The goal is to take advantage of the Internet content explosion in the hope of providing high-quality education to all children. In the midst of all this progress, however, there has been the concomitant fear captured by the alarming phrase "the digital divide." The term *digital divide* entered our vocabulary in the mid-1990s as a response to the large gaps in computer access and use among people. In common use, the term implies that there are individuals on the "wrong side" of the digital divide who have limited access to information (and thus education) and that merely providing access will serve to close the divide and provide equal educational access to all individuals in our society. The emphasis of a myriad of government programs has been to close the gap created by the digital divide by providing more computers and Internet connections. Recently there have been mixed reports on the status of this gap, the pace at which it is closing, and the shape of our dreams for technology as an equalizing force.

Technology as an equalizing force is not a new concept. So often, when a new technological breakthrough occurs, it immediately has been embraced as a mechanism for the improvement of the educational and social system. In 1922, Thomas Edison proclaimed that "the motion picture is destined to revolutionize our educational system and that in a few years it will supplant largely, if not entirely, the use of textbooks" (as cited in Cuban, 1986, p. 9). When radio became a reality, Benjamin Darrow (1932), founder and first director of the Ohio School of the Air and a tireless promoter of radio in the classroom, proclaimed, "The central and dominant aim of education by radio is to bring the world to the classroom, to make universally available the services of the finest teachers, the inspiration of the greatest leaders... and unfolding world events which through the radio may come as a vibrant and challenging textbook of the air" (cited in Cuban, 1986, p. 19).

Despite the enthusiasm surrounding revolutionary technologies, they never seem to reach their potential. The Radio Division of the U.S. Department of Commerce began licensing commercial and educational stations beginning in 1920. State departments of education sponsored radio use and by 1932 nine states were providing regular broadcasts of either weekly or monthly programs. In 1943, a 6-year study sponsored by the Federal Communications Commission concluded, "radio has not been accepted as a full-fledged member of the educational family" (Woelfel & Tyler, 1945, cited in Cuban, 1986, p. 24). Problems with federal regulations, commercial development of the airwaves, and the obstacles teachers faced in accessing and utilizing the technology in the classroom prevented widespread use of radio as an educational tool. The radio never became the "textbooks of the air," apparently due to many of the same challenges that create the barriers to technology as the great equalizer today.

THE CHANGING ETHERSCAPE

The so-called digital divide grew out of reports in the early 1990s that proclaimed our nation's poorest children were at risk for exclusion from the Internet revolution as a result of concerns over access to high quality equipment. It was this concern that prompted the 1996 Telecommunications Act to support subsidized access to high-speed telecommunications links in every public school and library across the nation. More than $5 billion has been committed to public school districts, private schools, public libraries, states, and consortia since the first wave of E-rate commitments in November 1998. In 2000, the Urban Institute (Puma, Chaplin, & Pape, 2000) reported that the E-rate is having the intended effect of supporting the development of Internet and telecommunications services, especially in poor areas. In that same report, the Urban Institute indicated that the programs' objectives are being met, as applications rates and overall total funding are higher for higher-poverty districts, schools, and libraries. During this same period of time, the government began to track Internet access and use in schools, in the workplace, and in the home. In the last decade, a dramatic increase in individual and classroom access to computers and the Internet has been documented, resulting in reports of 53.9% of Americans using the Internet. The dramatic increase of access in our nation's schools and libraries is largely attributable to federal programs like the E-rate, the Technology Innovation Challenge Fund, and the Community Technology Centers, coupled with significant state and local investments. According to the most recent reports, the government believes that increased access has provided much of the answer to the "divide" problem (National Telecommunications and Information Administration [NTIA], 2002).

This astonishing progress has led digerati such as noted columnist Sonia Arrison (2002) to point out that the digital divide has all but vanished, echoing the stance of the U.S. Department of Commerce, which is reflected in its latest report concerning Americans' use of computers and the Internet. Commerce Secretary Donald Evans stated, "I am heartened by this report's findings that all groups of individuals are using [computers and Internet] technologies in increasing numbers." While it is true that the data from the most current report clearly show that increasing numbers of Americans are connected to the Internet, the same data show how some segments of our society—particularly underserved communities—continue to lag behind. Andy Carvin of the Benton Foundation takes a different view and concludes that the digital divide not only still exists but also has actually become "more acute" (Carvin, 2002). The new dispute that is forming is over whether we can continue to measure this gap in access in the same ways (for examples, see Table 3.1). Clearly, the measures used to make the original diagnosis of the problem are showing healthy signs of improvement. However, as the technology has advanced, so have our expectations of quality, access, and utility.

Table 3.1.   Comparison of Views of the Department of Commerce (DOC) Report: A Nation Online

Sonia Arrison (2002) Center for Technology Studies	Andy Carvin (2002) Benton Foundation
"The DOC report proves that even lower income people can get wired if they see it as a priority."	Since 1997, the gap between the poorest and richest households online has increased from 35 to 54 points. "The digital divide hasn't vanished by any means—instead, it's become more acute."
"Many of the Internet's so-called 'have nots' are really 'want-nots.'"	"...despite the overwhelming amount of Internet content, almost none of it address the specific needs of underserved, at-risk audiences: the poor, rural communities, the disabled, non-native English speakers and ethnic minorities."
"Unless people can read and understand what they find on the Internet, all the computers and networks in the world won't be of much use."	"Approximately, 44 million adults are functionally illiterate.... The mistake that Arrison and others have made is that they separate the digital divide and education as if they were two mutually exclusive issues that can be tackled separately."

Because what we measure will often define what we seek to accomplish, it is important to reexamine our notions of this so-called divide. As children, we would frequently ask our parents, "How big am I?" We would then walk to the inside of the closet door where we would stand very tall and they would mark off our height and note the date. Over the course of childhood, this measure allowed us to track the rapid progress of normal development. As we age, however, this measure becomes far less useful, and by 18 years of age it seems to track a dimension that is no longer relevant to healthy growth and development. Alas, today, as adults, the tape measure is more aptly used to track our girth rather than our height. Similarly, the developmental pathways of information technology might suggest that our measures of the digital differences we've labeled a "divide" should also be reconsidered. We must now be concerned with more than mere access. While questions of access still exist, they are more specific in nature. The critical questions we must ask include access "To what?" (content and equipment), "For what purpose?", "With what support?", and "For whose goals?"

There are still significant divides between high- and low-income households, among different racial groups, between northern and southern states, disabled and nondisabled users, and rural and urban households. These gaps mean that people within these underserved communities are not able to participate in the social, civic, educational, and economic opportunities offered by information technologies (NTIA, 2002).

Although it has been reported that there are 35 states with more than half their populations online, a look behind these data reveals that we have not yet found our great equalizer. There are still 15 states in which use is either at or below 50%. Twelve of those 15 states are located in the South and the Southwest and are also states that have a high percentage of minority and rural populations (NTIA, 2002). Only one in four of America's poorest households were online in late 2001—compared to 8 in 10 homes earning over $75,000 a year.

According to *Nation Online* (NTIA, 2002) report, 90% of all school-age children (between ages 5–17) use computers and 58.5% use the Internet, primarily to complete school assignments. However, that statistic only tells a piece of the story. Roughly 80% of children (ages 10–17) in the lowest income category were using computers in their schools, a percentage that is little different from the 88.7% of the highest income levels. In 1999, the ratio of students per instructional computer was 15 to 1 for the poorest schools in the United States, and 7 to 1 for the wealthiest schools. The disadvantage of inequitable access in the schools is compounded by the lack of access at home. Although the percentage of homes with computers has increased, household income clearly dictates the likelihood of computer ownership. It is still true in 2002 that in the lowest income category only 33.1% of children are using computers at home, in contrast to 91.7% of the children in the highest income categories.

Hispanic and African American children also have lower computer use rates at home, compared to those of whites and Asian American/Pacific Islanders (see Table 3.2). Hispanic (38.9%) and African American (44.7%) children rely more heavily on schools for their computer access than do whites (15.1%) and Asian American/Pacific Islanders (11.1%). In addition to school, children who do not have computer access at home make use of community resources to use the Internet. For example, 16.6% of Internet users in the 10–17 age bracket use the Internet in a public library. This percentage rises to 29.3% among children who have access at school but not at home. As household income rises, the need for community-based access decreases. Accessing the Internet at the public library is more common among those with lower incomes (20%). Racial and ethnic groups also make use of community resources for access. Among racial and ethnic groups, 12.7% of whites, 19.4% of African Americans, and 16% of Hispanics using the Internet at libraries do not have access to the Internet at home, school, or work (NTIA, 2002).

Table 3.2.   Percent of U.S. Households with Internet Access by Race, 2001

Location	White	African American	Asian American/ Pacific Islander	Hispanic
U.S.	55.4	30.8	68.1	32.0
Rural	51.0	24.4	68.2	29.9
Urban	57.2	31.6	68.1	32.2

Note. Table data found online at: *http://www.ntia.doc.gove/ntiahome/dn/html/anationonline2.htm*

According to *Nation Online* (NTIA, 2002), while computers in schools have played a crucial role in narrowing the technology gap for low-income children, they still remain behind their more affluent classmates (34.3% of low-income children, compared to 62.7% high-income children). Inequitable access to technology in schools and classrooms for low-income students is compounded by the fact that these students are not likely to have access to computers or the Internet at home. For some ethnic minorities, the issue may not be cost as much as culture. Internet use among Hispanic individuals varies considerably depending on the language spoken in the household. In households where Spanish is the only language spoken (1 in 9 Hispanic households), only 14.1% of Hispanics used the Internet in contrast to 37.6% of Hispanics who lived in households where Spanish is not the only language spoken. Although *Nation Online* does not report on computer and Internet adoption by Native Americans, an earlier report by the Department of Commerce (Riley, Nassersharif, & Mullen, 1999) indicates that only 39% of rural households in Native communities have telephones, compared to 94% for non-Native communities. Of the rural Native households, only 22% have cable television, 9% have personal computers, and of those, only 8% have Internet access.

ACCESS TO MORE THAN A SEAT

Too often access is defined as a count of the number of machines, or, in the case of the Internet, connections that are in existence. There have been a multitude of studies that address the inequalities of access to and use of the Internet among various segments of the population: low-income and underserved Americans (The Children's Partnership, 2000), race (Hoffman & Novak, 1999), gender (Bimber, 2000), children (Wilhelm, Carmen, & Reynolds, 2002), teachers, (NCES, 2000) and rural communities (Strover, 1999). Technology hasn't eliminated the real barriers to opportunity—education, language, literacy, poverty, and discrimination (Senyak & Fong, 2000). Teachers in schools with the highest minority enrollments (50% or more minority enrollment) were less likely to have Internet available in the classroom (51% as compared to 69% for teachers in schools with low minority enrollments; NCES, 2000, pp. ii–iii). In addition, high poverty schools were more likely to use computers for academic drill and practice, whereas the schools with very low rates of students eligible for free or reduced-price lunches were more likely to use computers and the Internet for more complex learning and communication. In addition, teachers in schools with high minority enrollments were more likely to indicate that outdated, incompatible, or unreliable computers were a significant problem.

These data indicate that while access is almost universal, the students' use of the technology is not equitable across groups. Classrooms with high-achieving students were more likely to use computers for communication and learning while greater use of game software was reported in low-achieving classrooms. In general, the use of technology in high-achieving classrooms appeared to be related to teacher assessments of student achievement potential (Ravitz, Becker, & Wong, 2000).

The NCES (2000) study also found that teachers in high minority schools were significantly less likely to communicate with parents using the Internet (14%) than their peers in school with less than 50% minority enrollments (25–30%). Teachers in schools with high minority populations were less likely to assign students to use technologies for multimedia presentations (36% in high minority enrollment schools vs. 49% of teachers in low minority enrollment schools), CD-ROM research (38% of high minority enrollment schools vs. 55% of teachers in low minority enrollment schools), and for Internet research (41% of high minority enrollment schools vs. 57% of teachers in low minority enrollment schools).

The digital divide has gotten a great deal attention but it has always been focused on issues of access. Fifty million underserved Americans face one or more content-related barriers that stand between them and benefits offered by the Internet. Despite the overwhelming amount of Internet content, almost none of it addresses the specific needs of underserved, at-risk audiences: the poor, rural communities; disabled, non-native English speakers; or ethnic minorities. According the Children's Partnership (2000) study, for Americans on the wrong side of the content divide, useful content would include the following: (a) employment, education, business development, and other information, (b) information that can be clearly understood by limited-literacy users, (c) information in multiple languages, and (d) opportunities to create content and interact with others online in culturally appropriate ways. The Children's Partnership research included discussion groups with more than 100 low-income Internet users, interviews with nearly 100 community technology leaders and other experts, analysis of 1,000 Web sites, and a review of the literature and promising activities across the country. The audit had three purposes: (a) to describe the groups of Americans who are underserved by Internet content, (b) to analyze the online content currently available for low-income and underserved Americans, and (c) to provide a road map for action— identifying ways in which the public and private sectors working with underserved communities might improve Internet access and content.

The Children's Partnership (2000) research found that although many underserved communities have gained access to the Internet, many are not receiving any appreciable benefit as a result of a number of barriers that still exist. The study found four significant barriers that affect large numbers of Americans: (a) lack of local information, (b) literacy barriers, (c) language barriers, and (d) lack of cultural diversity.

Lack of Local Information

Likely the most wide-ranging barrier is the lack of the kind of information that users want and need the most: local information about their community. While this is a barrier to most Americans, it disproportionately impacts Americans living on limited incomes, particularly the nearly 21 million Americans over age 18 whose annual income is at or below the poverty level. Precisely the information that would be of most use to the individuals interviewed in the study (e.g., local job resources or job listings for entry-level positions) proved to be the most rare and difficult to find (1%). Additionally, information about local low-cost housing was, with very few exceptions, unavailable (1%). The study found that adults want practical information about their own communities such as local job listings requiring entry-level skills, local housing listings, and community information (Children's Partnership, 2000).

Literacy Barriers

Literacy is another significant barrier for more than 32 million Americans who speak a language other than English as their primary language. Most of the online information written at a limited-literacy level is designed for young children and doesn't provide the information needed by adults with limited-literacy skills (only 1% of Web sites were found to meet this need). The study found that adults with basic literacy skills want to be able to prepare for securing high school equivalency degrees and to be able to find online resources that utilize multimedia capabilities to compensate for their limited-literacy skills (Children's Partnership, 2000).

Language Barriers

An estimated 87% of documents on the Internet are in English while as previously cited at least 32 million Americans speak a language other than English as their primary language. The most common multilingual content found on the Internet is in Spanish. Most of this content originates in Latin America or Spain, making it of little use to non-English speakers in this country who express a need for local information, online translation tools, and instructional materials (Children's Partnership, 2000).

Cultural Barriers

Finally, the Internet has the potential to bring people together and provide information organized around their unique cultural interests and practices. Twenty-six million foreign-born Americans can find some cultural resources on the Internet, but only about 1% is local information. (However, general cultural sites are growing for African American, Hispanic, and Asian communities.) Adults interviewed in the Children's Partnership (2000) study wanted to have opportunities for cultural exploration and development, cultural spaces that provide information about ethnic and local cultural interests, and health information.

Actually being able to navigate the Internet is another critical issue, of the 45 Internet users who participated in the Children's Partnership (2000) Web search exercise, 80% said it took too long to find the information they were asked to find, 65% did not find the material understandable when they did find it, and 65% did not find the portals assigned easy to use. These findings draw attention to the need for training and support as well as better searching tools.

CONCLUSION

As one dimension of potential develops, there evolves a need to measure other dimensions. Today, the gap (or chasm) is a different one than was envisioned when the digital divide was initially identified. The context has changed, but the yardstick by which we measure has not. What you measure matters. We should not be concerned with the political debate over choosing "the number" that best describes a gap previously defined. Rather, we need to choose new numbers and new yardsticks that more accurately and better describe the disparity. In developing nations, access alone is an accurate and useful measure. For example, 2 billion people worldwide have never dialed a telephone. But if we are looking at the kind of access to technology in the United States that drives the economic engines, we need to look at a very different set of statistics. Research has demonstrated that the presence of educational resources in the home makes a difference in academic achievement in science and mathematics (NCES, 1997). Thus, the fact that our minority and poor children do not yet have access in their homes does matter. How teachers use technology with their students is also likely to matter. It is important to know if a teacher facing an underachieving child will most likely engage that child in game or drill and practice software rather than using technologies that will promote the development of expertise or critical thinking (see PytlikZillig, Horn, & White, Chapter 6, this volume). Knowing that the lower-achieving students are half as likely to be engaged in higher-order learning tasks on the Web as our higher-achieving students is important information.

We need to move beyond access and opportunity and address the issue of outcomes. It is no longer about connectivity. The social and technological support and training necessary to implement the technology, access to high quality content, materials that meet the broader goals of all communities, and outcomes in student learning are what need to be measured now. If we are ever going to truly bridge the gap, it will require strategic, ongoing, public–private partnerships at local, national, and international levels. Our efforts must address literacy and content as well as access, quality, utility, and support. These efforts must also be ongoing because there will always be new technologies available.

The digital divide may not be the most serious issue facing Americans seeking a better life, but it still exists, and is one critical element to achievement in America. As Senyak and Fong (2000) point out, "Computers and the Internet must be available to all, regardless of ethnicity or geography or income. Not because the technology is somehow special or revolutionary, but exactly because it's so ordinary" (p. 2).

AUTHOR NOTE

Correspondence concerning this chapter should be addressed to Eric J. Jolly, Education Development Center, Inc., 55 Chapel Street, Newton, MA 02458. Email: ejolly@edc.org

REFERENCES

Arrison, S. (2002, March 13). What digital divide? *Tech News First* [Online]. Retrieved May 13, 2002, from http://news.com.com/2010-1078-858537.html

Bimber, B. (2000). *Losing ground bit by bit: Low-income communities in the information age* [Online]. Retrieved March 13, 2002, from http://www.Benton.org/Library/Low-income/

Carvin, A. (2002). Digital divide: Still very real. *Tech News First* [Online]. Retrieved May 13, 2002, from http://news.com.com/2010-1078-872138.html

The Children's Partnership. (2000). *Online content for low-income and underserved Americans: The digital divide's new frontier* [Online]. Retrieved May 15, 2002, from http://www.childrenspartnership.org/pub/low_income/

Cuban, L. (1986). *Teachers and machines.* New York: Teachers College Press.

Hoffman, D. L., & Novak, T. P. (1999). *The evolution of the digital divide: Examining the relationship of race to Internet access and usage over time* [Online]. Retrieved September 18, 2002, from http://ecommence.vanderbilt.edu/research/papers/pdf/manuscripts/Evolution/DigitalDivide-pdf.pdf/

National Center for Education Statistics (NCES). (1997). *Pursuing excellence: A study of U.S. fourth-grade mathematics and science achievement in international context* (Rep. No. NCES 97255) [Online]. Retrieved November 30, 2002, from http://nces.ed.gov/pubsearch/pubsinfo.asp?pubid=97255

National Center for Education Statistics (NCES). (2000). *Teachers tools for the 21st century: A report on teachers' use of technology* (Rep. No. NCES 2000-102) [Online]. Retrieved September 18, 2002, from http://lnces.ed.gov/pubsearch/ pubsinfo.asp?pubid=2000102

National Telecommunications and Information Administration (NTIA). (2002). *A nation online: How Americans are expanding their use of the Internet* [Online]. Retrieved August 15, 2002, from http://www.ntia.doc.gov/ntiahome/dn/

Puma, M. J., Chaplin, D., & Pape, A. D. (2000). *E-Rate and the digital divide: A preliminary analysis from the integrated studies of educational technology* [Online]. Washington, DC: U.S. Department of Education, Urban Institute. Retrieved August 22, 2002, from http://www.urban.org/education/erate.html

Ravitz, J., Becker, H., & Wong, Y. T. (2000). *Constructivist-compatible beliefs and practices among U.S. teachers: 1998 National Survey* (Rep. No. 4). Irvine, CA & Minneapolis, MN: Center for Research on Information Technology and Organizations.

Riley, R. A., Nassersharif, B., & Mullen, J. (1999). *Assessment of technology infrastructure in native communities* (Rep. No. 99-07-13799) [Online]. Washington, DC: U.S. Department of Commerce, Economic Development Administration

(EDA). Retrieved September 12, 2002, from http://www.doc.gov/eda/pdf/ 1G3_13_atinc.pdf

Senyak, J., & Fong, A. (2000). Bridging the digital divide: Thinking about community technology. *TechSoup* [Online]. Retrieved May 13, 2002, from http:// www.techsoup.org/ articlepage.cfm?articleid=164&topicid=12

Strover, S. (1999). *Rural Internet connectivity* [Online]. Retrieved August 22, 2002, from http://www.rupri.org/pubs/archive/reports/1999/P99-13/

Wilhelm, T., Carmen, D., & Reynolds, M. (2002). *Connecting kids to technology: Challenges and opportunities* [Online]. Retrieved September 25, 2002, from http:// www.aecf.org/publications/data/snapshot_june2002.pdf

CHAPTER 4

INFOGATHER: A TOOL FOR GATHERING AND ORGANIZING INFORMATION FROM THE WEB

L. Brent Igo
Roger Bruning
Center for Instructional Innovation,
University of Nebraska–Lincoln

Matthew McCrudden
University of Nevada–Las Vegas

Douglas F. Kauffman
University of Oklahoma

ABSTRACT

Six studies were conducted in a design experiment framework to guide the development of *InfoGather,* an online, note-taking tool. Experiment 1 justi-fied the development of the tool's chart (or matrix) layout. Students recorded more propositions into paper-and-pencil notes using a matrix than with an open-ended format. In Experiment 2, students who recorded their notes in paper-and-pencil matrices learned more from Web-based text than students who used an outline format. Experiments 3 and 4 were first attempts to use *InfoGather* in online note-taking experiments. Observational data gathered in those experiments aided in the design of Experiments 5 and 6. In Experiment 5, students who created notes with an *InfoGather* matrix learned more from Web-based text than students who created notes with a blank *InfoGather* tool. The results were congruent with previous research on paper-and-pencil note taking. Experiment 6 tested the effect of copy and paste restrictions on learning. Students whose note taking was restricted and who were forced to make deeper note-taking decisions (restricted copy and paste) learned more facts, concepts, and relationships than students in an unrestricted copy and paste condition.

The Web, with its nearly limitless access to information on almost any topic, seems to have tremendous educational possibilities. For many students and teachers, having easy access to such a huge network of information may seem like an educational panacea, removing the barriers between the need for information and its availability. Perhaps this is why more and more American students are using the Internet for research purposes (Lenhart, Simon, & Graziano, 2001). Gathering information from the Internet is only the first step in the process of learning that information, however. Simply having an abundance of Internet sources from which to gather information might not improve learning and comprehension.

Students struggle to learn from multiple information sources (Dreher & Guthrie, 1990). For example, while hearing a lecture or reading from a textbook, students tend to use inferior note-taking strategies—jotting down only the most general points and often failing to make connections among information (Kiewra & Dubois, 1998). Furthermore, typical students are unable to synthesize the necessary concepts from a single information source efficiently (e.g., a newspaper article), let alone multiple sources (e.g., a book, a lecture, and an article) (Dreher & Guthrie, 1990). The sheer amount of information available on the Internet may present students with as many problems as solutions.

The process of gathering information from sources, however, can be a powerful learning experience. Although many students are ineffective note-takers, note taking can be a beneficial activity when done properly (King, 1992). For example, students learn more when they are prompted to decide which information is and is not important to a good set of notes (Brown, Bransford, Ferrara, & Campione, 1983; Kiewra, 1991). Such decisions lead to deeper processing of the information and in turn help students learn (Glover, Bruning, & Plake, 1982). Similarly, students who are required to summarize information learn more than students who are not prompted to go beyond their usual note-taking habits (King, 1992; Loranger, 1997). Again, the requirement to summarize leads students to deeper interactions with information. In short, gathering information from sources such as journals or books can be a constructive learning exercise. But as with physical exercise, information gathering must be performed properly to achieve the desired effect.

Given what we already know about approaches to gathering information from text sources, it would seem learners might gather information from the Internet with varying degrees of effectiveness. With this in mind, the Center for Instructional Innovation (CII) at the University of Nebraska–Lincoln (UNL) began the development of an online note-taking tool, *InfoGather*, to help students gather information from the Internet. Our ideas regarding the design features of such a tool were simple. First, we wanted it to function much like a word processing program, one that would follow users as they moved about the Internet. We sought to give students the ability to add, amend, or remove information at any time while using the tool. Note-taking tools with these features, of course, are readily available in a variety of computer-based environments. What are not available, however, are tools with an organizational dimension prompting students to store information in terms of categories and relationships. Thus, we sought to design a tool with features that would allow structural organization before, during, or after note taking. Such a capability would allow the student to sort the chosen information by topic, characteristic, or category.

Our developmental approach to *InfoGather* was guided by three criteria: (1) provision of sound instruction, (2) collaboration with teachers, and (3) execution of theory-driven research on technology-based learning using naturalistic investigative methods. Because our goal was that a fully developed *InfoGather* tool would eventually find its way into classrooms, we sought from the beginning to contextualize our research in the schools and in students' day-to-day classroom activities. It was critical for us to provide our student participants with pertinent content, beneficial activities, and an application they could actually use.

Related to our aim of providing instructional support was our desire to collaborate with teachers in developing *InfoGather*. We knew that, for our student participants to do their best in the experimental activities, the content addressed in the activities should be congruent with both existing course curriculum and the teachers' instructional goals. Use of *InfoGather* needed to flow naturally from what the teachers covered in the classrooms and their approaches to teaching and learning. Although we wanted to gather data on the tool's effectiveness, our overriding purpose was the development of an application that would facilitate learning and that teachers and students would want to use. Consequently, the teachers became integral members of our research team and took part in decisions about content, construction of experimental materials, approaches to conducting experiments, and the features of the tool.

Our final criterion for our work with the *InfoGather* tool was the execution of sound, theory-driven educational research. Good experimental research is grounded in theory and there is a need to explore instructional theory in the context of the Internet; much of what we currently know about teaching and learning processes has not been tested in Web-based settings (Bonk & Cummings, 1998). Because the *InfoGather* tool is essentially a Web-based note-taking device, we chose to explore the generalizability of one particular note-taking research genre, *matrix organizers.*

A matrix (also called a graphic organizer or a chart) is a two-dimensional, cross-classification table with topics across its top row, categories comparing those topics down the first column, and related facts in its corresponding cells (see Figure 4.1). The previous research on matrix organizers has shown quite consistently that students who study with matrices learn more facts and relationships among those facts than students who study with linear (or outline) notes (e.g., Kiewra, Dubois, Christian, & McShane, 1988; Kiewra, Kauffman, Robinson, Dubois, & Staley, 1999; Robinson & Kiewra, 1995). Presumably, matrix organizers help students connect ideas (see Figure 4.1) by more clearly displaying relationships among information within specific topics (such as "Butterfly") and related information across topics (such as "Butterfly" and "Moth") than do outlines. However,

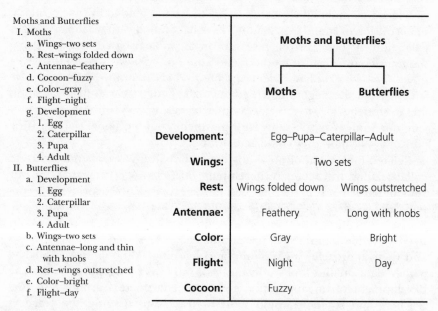

Figure 4.1.   Examples of linear/outline (left) and matrix (right) notes.

matrix organizers had not been tested in an online environment and our research was designed to fill that gap in the research literature.

We developed the *InfoGather* tool using a design-experiment approach (Brown, 1992). This approach includes a series of studies in a naturalistic context aimed at making incremental improvements in design. Design experiments are similar to traditional educational experiments in that the effectiveness of an instructional intervention is tested experimentally. Design experiments, however, are conducted in real world environments where the instructional effects are tested in situations identical to actual practice and improvements in design are made incrementally. Challenges that are eliminated through control in traditional experiments are treated as they arise in design studies. For example, consider how many challenges a high school teacher might encounter with 28 students using the Internet in a media lab setting. Instead of posing confounds, however, such challenges offer information useful for altering instructional approaches, design of the tool, and the focus of the next study. Design changes from one study to the next not only provide evidence of instructional effects, but also do so in the presence of obstacles that teachers face every day. In this chapter we report six studies designed and implemented to guide development of the *InfoGather* tool's features. We briefly describe each study and the impact it had on the tool's development.

These studies began in the fall of 2000, when our research team began interacting with a local high school where the senior author previously had taught. Social studies was selected as the content area; it matched both the needs of the school's social science department and our desire to examine information gathering and summarization of expository information. Our starting point for planning was a focus group session attended by three government and history teachers. During the session, the researchers and the teachers discussed two issues: (1) ways *InfoGather* might be used in helping students learn from Web-based instructional materials, and (2) the use of research as a basis for development of the *InfoGather* tool. After several additional conversations about logistics—curriculum prescriptions, media lab availability, and content delivery—an initial date was set for the first experiment. Included in that deadline were smaller, but important sub-deadlines, such as the need for writing and editing content to ensure the maximum relevance of the experiment to student learning goals.

EARLY EXPERIMENTS:
FROM PAPER AND PENCIL TO THE INTERNET

Our first two experiments were transitional first steps from paper-and-pencil note-taking experiments to studies of online note taking. Before our Web designers and programmers could become fully engaged in the task of creating an alpha version of *InfoGather*, we needed information justifying the spatial layout for the tool; that is, how should the tool actually appear on the screen? What kind of note-taking organization should be provided for users? At face value the existing research on matrix organizers seemed to supply this justification, in that matrices presented in paper-and-pencil form have been shown to facilitate student learning. In previous research, however, students typically have been presented with notes to study and, in those studies where they took notes themselves, they took notes from texts or lectures, not from information displayed on a computer screen. Consequently, our first experimental step was to examine the impact of students taking typical notes (with paper and pencil) from text delivered via the Internet.

Experiment 1: Political Parties

Experiment 1 tested the impact of spatial organization and note-taking cues on note taking with paper and pencil from a Web source. To do so, four experimental groups were created in a 2 × 2 factorial design. The first dimension in the design (matrix vs. freeform) was the presence or absence of matrix organization for the note-taking sheet, and the second dimension was the presence or absence of note-taking cues. Note-taking cues, when present, were inserted into the first column of the matrix organizer or listed at the top of the note-taking sheet (in the freeform condition). For example, in the freeform condition with note-taking cues present, instructions at the top of an otherwise blank page might read: "For each theory, find the following characteristics: definition, assumptions, impact,..." Students were instructed to use one of the four randomly assigned note-taking sheets to gather ideas from text delivered to them via the Internet.

The teachers and two of the current authors together constructed a 2,750-word text addressing differences and similarities among four political parties: Democrat, Libertarian, Republican, and Reform. The text contained 84 meaningful units of information (or *propositions*; see Anderson, 1995) comparing and contrasting the parties. Because there was a national election underway and the school district's curriculum mandated that the students learn to distinguish each party from the others, the experimental content was timely.

Study participants were 108 high school freshmen. Students met in one of the school's media labs for one period of their American government class and were assigned computers and given note-taking materials (all note-taking sheets were 8.5 × 11). Then the students were directed to (1) gather as much of the relevant information as they could on the sheet they were given, (2) work for the entire class period, and (3) ask for assistance if they had any problems. The URL of the Web page containing the teacher-prepared text and other peripheral information (pictures and famous quotes) was written on the media lab dry erase board. The students found the Web page and took notes for the entire class period. Their notes were then collected.

The students' notes were analyzed using a 2 × 2 analysis of variance (ANOVA) for the number of propositions (of 84 possible, see means in Table 4.1) they contained. There were significant differences among the experimental groups. First, students who used the matrix framework gathered more propositions ($M = 45.9$) than students with the freeform framework ($M = 29.3$), $F(1, 104) = 20.68$, $p < .01$ (Table 4.1). Similarly, students given note-taking cues found more propositions ($M = 43.5$) than students without cues ($M = 32.1$), $F(1, 104) = 5.39$, $p < .05$ (Table 4.1). Finally, there was a significant interaction between framework and cues as students who used a cued matrix framework gathered the most propositions ($M = 64.2$), $F(1, 104) = 4.96$, $p < .05$ (Table 4.1). These findings were consistent with the existing research on matrix organizers, but extend the previous findings to include paper-and-pencil notes gathered from online sources.

Table 4.1. Means and Standard Deviations by Group for Experiment 1

Note cues	Matrix	Freeform	Total
Present			
M	64.23	43.50	43.50
SD	22.47	27.10	27.10
Absent			
M	38.25	25.00	32.31
SD	28.07	16.39	24.13
Total			
M	45.90	29.29	
SD	28.55	15.46	

It is important to note that a 50-minute class period does not equal 50 minutes of instructional time. Teachers must take roll, answer questions, and attend to numerous other tasks before the day's lesson begins. We anticipated such time constraints and designed a text from which it would be demanding but not impossible to complete note taking. A 2,750-word text is relatively brief, but can be challenging when the goal is to understand and remember a significant portion of the information presented. The length of the text, including the 84 propositions, was designed to require 40–45 minutes of note-taking time. Because we wanted to know which note-taking frameworks would lead to the gathering of more propositions, it was critical that the time available for taking notes be at a premium in order to avoid ceiling effects. In that sense, the experiment was a success. However, our attempts to measure learning were less successful. We administered multiple-choice measures of factual and relational learning, but both had reliabilities too low to permit their utilization.

Still, the large differences among the groups in the number of propositions gathered was compelling, providing us with motivation to continue developing the online tool with a matrix organization, as well as the capacity to insert instructional cues into the frames (cells) of the matrix. The experimental findings were further supported by the teachers' observations; they noted that typical off-task student behaviors apparent in the traditional classroom also had occurred during the experiment. The teachers were impressed by the experimental results because several of the typically off-task students had been assigned randomly to the matrix or cued groups—the groups with the highest performances. Thus, intermittent student "clowning," while present, did not seem to confound the experimental findings as differences in performance were found in the presence of actual classroom dynamics—a successful design study. Our results, however, did lead to new questions. Although providing the students with an organized note-taking framework seemed to be beneficial, only one type of organization (a matrix) was used. Might a different note-taking organization provide similar benefits? What impact on learning might those different organizations have? Experiment 2 was designed to answer these questions.

Experiment 2: Political Party Development

Based on the results of our first experiment, our programmers increased the pace of the development of *InfoGather*. Meanwhile, our research team was preparing a second experiment that would provide additional information about the efficacy of the matrix framework of *InfoGather*. Experiment 1 had provided enough evidence to move ahead in designing the tool with a cued-frames feature. However, we had tested only one type of organized framing system—matrices, which were shown to be of more benefit than freeform notes. Perhaps organizations other than matrices would prove to be beneficial as well. Experiment 2 moved beyond the previous experiment to compare linear (or outline) organization of notes to the matrix format and to examine measures of learning in addition to note-taking measures.

The teachers helped us create a new experimental text for Experiment 2. The 2000 presidential election was still in the news, and the students were required by the curriculum to understand how the two dominant American political parties—Republican and Democrat—had changed during the 20th century. This became our new topic. Because our goal was to examine learning as well as note taking in this study, the materials needed to be brief enough to allow the students to finish note taking on the topic. Our teachers approximated the length of text that, given their impressions of the students' capabilities, would allow students to finish note taking and still have at least 10 minutes in which to study their notes (1,400 words containing 20 important propositions).

Like Experiment 1, Experiment 2 was conducted in the high school's media labs, and included a second day on which students were given two quizzes covering the material from the note-taking session. The experiment began with 44 high school freshmen meeting in one of the school media labs for their American government class. Each student was given randomly either a paper matrix note sheet or a paper outline note sheet (see Figure 4.2). Each type of note system was cued, prompting students to find specific information.

As in Experiment 1, students received instructions, found the appropriate Web pages, and took notes. When the students completed the note-taking activity, they were prompted to study their notes for 10 minutes. After studying, the notes were collected, and students were allowed to surf the Internet as time permitted. As was expected, virtually all students completed the note-taking activity in time for 10 minutes of study.

On the following day, the American government classes began with two quizzes over the content studied the previous day: (1) a quiz of cued, factual recall and (2) a multiple-choice quiz of relationships between the Democratic and Republican parties. Students completed the quizzes in approximately 15 minutes and handed them in to the researchers.

Table 4.2 shows the mean performances for groups in Experiment 2. Analyses showed significant differences between the two note-taking groups. Two ANOVAs indicated that students in the matrix condition scored higher on each of the two quizzes, $F(1, 48) = 7.66$, $MSE = 90.87$, $p < .01$ for the cued recall of facts and $F(1, 48) = 10.27$, $MSE = 50.82$, $p < .01$ for multiple-choice relationships. The strength of the relationships between note-taking organization and test performances were high as assessed by eta squared, with note-taking organization (linear vs. matrix) accounting for 26% of the variance in recall performance, and 12% of the variance in multiple-choice performance. As can be seen in Table 4.2, the average recall of students in the linear condition was fewer than six propositions (out of a possible 20) on the measure of cued-recall, whereas the matrix group averaged 8.75. On the relationship measure, the linear group averaged 2.54 correct answers (out of a possible 9), whereas the matrix group averaged 4.70.

These results confirmed the findings from previous matrix research. Consistent with prior findings, the matrix group performed significantly

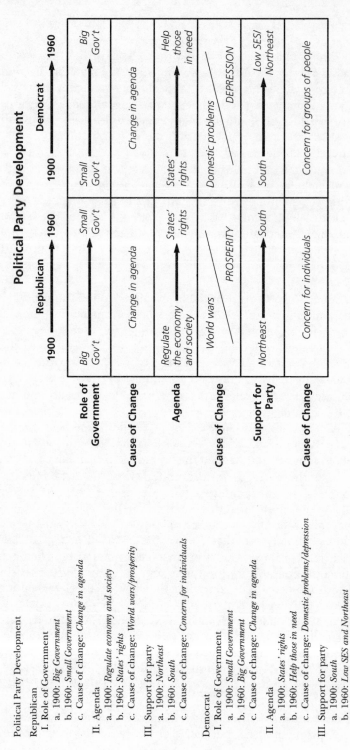

Figure 4.2. Examples of cued outline (left) and matrix (right) from Experiment 2. Student-filled information is in italics.

Table 4.2. Means and Standard Deviations by Group for Experiment 2

Note framework	Cued recall facts	Multiple-choice relationships
Linear		
M	5.87	2.54
SD	3.18	1.88
Matrix		
M	8.75	4.70
SD	3.71	2.43

better than the linear group on tests of facts and relationships (Kiewra et al., 1988, 1999; Robinson & Kiewra, 1995). The current results were based on students gathering the information from the Internet, not from text or lecture, and thus extend previous work. Further analyses of the students' notes revealed that each student in both the matrix and outline groups gathered all 20 propositions; the note-taking cues thus provided effective data-gathering prompts for both groups. However, the matrix group demonstrated the best learning on the tests.

Together, our results from Experiments 1 and 2 suggest that students who use a matrix to gather information from the Web will gather more information (Experiment 1), and that later they will have an advantage in learning from the notes they gathered (Experiment 2). Generally, these two initial studies helped guide the early development of the *InfoGather* tool. They supplied us with enough empirical evidence to design the first version of the tool with a cued frame, or matrix, capacity. Now, we were also ready to move completely into a Web-based environment, with students gathering information from Web sources using the Web-based *InfoGather* tool.

FIRST TESTS OF A WEB-BASED TOOL

The findings from Experiments 1 and 2 increased our confidence in the tool's cued matrix design. Not only were students prompted by a matrix to gather more of the correct information from the Web, but also the framework itself promoted more learning after note taking was completed. The time seemed appropriate to make the Web-based *InfoGather* tool available for student use.

Experiments 3 and 4: The New Deal and the Great Society

While our programmers were completing an operational version of the *InfoGather* tool, we were designing Experiments 3 and 4. The teachers had suggested a move in topics away from American government to American history, which meant that our students were going to be high school juniors, not freshmen. The spring semester of 2001 had begun and the American history classes now were covering important events of the 20th century. The teachers suggested that we create lessons covering The New Deal (the 1930s) and The Great Society (the 1960s), as each topic encompasses important American social and economic programs with features that needed to be compared and contrasted.

Experiments 3 and 4 were the first direct tests of the *InfoGather* tool. As we have indicated, we believed that we had obtained enough empirical support to warrant a matrix design for the tool and to move the note taking itself online. To our knowledge, this was the first time online matrix note taking had been explored experimentally. We designed Experiments 3 and 4 with the belief that the outcomes would mirror those from Experiments 1 and 2. However, this proved not to be the case.

In preparation for Experiment 3, the students received brief training on the use of the *InfoGather* tool on the day before the experiment. Most students were already familiar with word processing programs so the data gathering techniques (typing, copy and paste) required little instruction. Each student also created a user account that allowed us to save and print his/her notes. On the day of the New Deal experiment, 60 high school juniors were assigned randomly to either an online cued matrix notes condition or an online cued freeform condition (i.e., a chart with cues listed down the left side vs. a blank screen with instructional cues listed across the top, similar to the cued conditions in Experiment 1). Then students were given the URL of the Web page containing text on which they were to take notes. They visited the site and took notes for most of a 50-minute period. Some students completed the activity more quickly than others, but, in general, the discrepancy in engagement time was minimal (students finished approximately 25–35 minutes after beginning). When the students finished, they saved their completed notes to our server and were allowed to surf the Internet.

On the following day, the researchers returned to the school, gave the students printed versions of their notes, and asked them to study their notes for 10 minutes. Then the students were distracted by being asked to complete a survey and engaged in conversation to negate rehearsal effects. They then completed two multiple-choice assessment instruments designed to measure factual and relational learning.

Analyses of the dependent measures yielded no group differences. An ANOVA of the fact test was not significant, $F(1, 58) = 1.21$, with the means of the matrix and freeform groups approximately 11 and 10 (of a possible 13), respectively. The ANOVA for the relationships test likewise was not significant, $F(1, 58) = .97$, with the respective means of the matrix and freeform groups approximately 5 and 5.5 (of a possible 7). This was unexpected. Reliabilities for both dependent measures, however, again were very low ($_ < .50$), suggesting that, even if effects had existed, our measures may not have been able to detect them.

Experiment 4, completed approximately one month later, employed the use of different experimental text (addressing the Great Society) and dependent measures, but with experimental conditions and procedures identical to those in Experiment 3. On the first day, 58 students found the Web pages, read the text, and took notes with the *InfoGather* tool. On the following day, they studied their notes and then completed a quiz of facts and a quiz of relationships.

Again, no differences were found between the performances of the matrix group and the freeform group, and the reliabilities of our measures continued to be unacceptably low ($_ < .50$). An ANOVA of the fact test was not significant, $F(1, 56) = .22$, with the means for the matrix and free form groups being 11.8 and 11.6 (of a possible 14), respectively. The ANOVA for the relationships test also was not significant, $F(1, 56) = .74$, with the means for the matrix and freeform groups being 3.8 and 3.6 (of a possible 7), respectively. Thus, our first two online experiments showed no evidence in support of *InfoGather*'s matrix frames capacity. Our belief that the findings of previous paper-and-pencil research would generalize to experiments with an online information-gathering tool did not materialize. Perhaps this was due to faulty measures—but, perhaps not.

There was more to our data than our statistical analyses had revealed, however. As we more closely studied the conditions and findings of Experiments 3 and 4, especially the performance of individual students, we noted that Experiment 4 had included 18 participants from an advanced placement (AP) class, outstanding students who were receiving college credit for American history while still in high school. As we analyzed student notes, we saw that nearly all of these AP participants chose to *type* their notes instead of using the copy and paste function of the tool. We also noted that these students performed very well on the quizzes irrespective of the experimental version of the tool they had received.

In light of this information, we began a qualitative analysis of the student notes gathered in both Experiments 3 and 4. We soon noted that students formed themselves into two distinct groups of information gatherers: typists and copy-and-pasters. Students typically displayed one preference over the other and rarely mixed the two data-gathering approaches. Furthermore, students who chose to type their notes were much more likely to paraphrase or summarize ideas from text instead of typing the text verbatim. Typists outperformed copy-and-pasters on the two quizzes as well, although there were too few typists to perform statistical analyses. This was true of AP and traditional students alike. Clearly, such a distinction was interesting to us as designers of the *InfoGather* Web-based application and as educational researchers.

We thus began to suspect that regardless of experimental placement (freeform vs. matrix organization), some students likely were engaging in deeper processing than others (Craik & Lockhart, 1972). These processing differences may have overpowered and hidden the effects of our experimental conditions, eliminating group differences in our statistical analyses. As a result, we made a major change in our design study approach, shifting our focus in the next two experiments to varying the modes available to students for entering information into the *InfoGather* tool.

A CHANGE IN DIRECTION

With new insights into our findings, we began to design two new experiments in which we had our programmers vary the kinds of information entry options available in the *InfoGather* tool. It was now summer and our high school research participants were on vacation, so we shifted our studies to the University of Nebraska, which was still in session. Our new experiments focused on the ways that students entered data into *InfoGather*, examining conditions in which students either typed notes (Experiment 5) or pasted notes (Experiment 6) into the *InfoGather* tool.

Experiment 5: The New Deal (Type Only)

In the summer and fall of 2001, we conducted a variation of the New Deal experiment in which we controlled the fashion by which the students could insert information into their notes. The copy and paste feature of *InfoGather* was disabled. Students could only enter information into the tool by typing. The experimental text was rewritten to be at an appropriate level for university participants and better dependent measures were constructed and pretested. On the technology side, our programmers created two new note-taking conditions: freeform typing (FFT) and matrix typing (MT). In the FFT condition, the *InfoGather* tool appeared as a frame with instructional note-taking cues at the top of the frame and blank space below. Meanwhile, the MT condition included a cued matrix in the note-taking frame. In both conditions information could be entered only by typing (not pasting). Experiment 5 thus compared two spatial layouts of *InfoGather* in a manner analogous to our initial experiments, where typing into one of two forms of the *InfoGather* tool was analogous to writing notes into one of two paper-and-pencil note-taking frames.

Sixty-eight students met in one of two university computer labs and were assigned randomly to either the FFT or MT group. Participants first created user accounts and were shown how to use the *InfoGather* tool. They then were instructed to find the Web pages (the home URL was written on a dry erase board) and to take notes over the material on the pages by typing into their *InfoGather* tool. The students completed the note-taking activity and saved their notes to our server. Next, the students' notes were printed and handed to them and they were asked to study the notes for 10 minutes. Following study, the students were asked to complete a survey and were distracted with conversation to prevent rehearsal effects. Three dependent measures of learning then were completed: a quiz of cued factual recall, a multiple-choice quiz of facts ($\alpha = .72$), and a multiple-choice quiz of relationships ($\alpha = .83$).

Analyses of the dependent measures (see Table 4.3) revealed differences in learning between the groups on two of the three quizzes. On the cued recall of facts measure, the MT group outperformed the FFT group $F(1, 66) = 49.00$, $MSE = 52.29$, $p < .001$. The strength of the relationship between note organization and recall performance was robust as assessed by η^2, with note organization accounting for 42% of the total variance. The MT group also outperformed the FFT group on the multiple-choice measure of relational learning, $F(1, 66) = 22.90$, $MSE = 428.24$, $p < .001$. Again, the strength of the relationship between note organization and relationships learning was high assessed by η^2, with note organization accounting for 26% of the total variance. No significant differences were found on the multiple-choice measure of facts, however. These results were congruent with both the existing matrix research and our initial findings from Experiment 2.

Table 4.3. Means and Standard Deviations by Group for Experiment 5

Typed notes	Multiple-choice facts	Multiple-choice relationships	Cued recall
Matrix			
M	16.56	9.94	16.28
SD	2.87	1.63	3.74
Freeform			
M	15.78	8.19	11.25
SD	1.43	1.35	2.66

The findings of Experiment 5 suggest that the lack of significant results in Experiments 3 and 4 may have been due in part to individual differences in how students choose to enter information into *InfoGather*. Recall that students in Experiments 3 and 4 were allowed to type notes or to copy and paste notes or to combine the two input processes in building their notes. The differences in processing required to type (paraphrase) notes and paste notes might have influenced learning performances between the freeform and matrix groups to such an extent as to negate the spatial benefits of a matrix. In Experiment 5, where the *InfoGather* tool controlled the type of data entry used by the student, results congruent with previous note-taking research emerged.

To help further explain the results of Experiment 5, we again analyzed the students' notes. The analysis revealed that almost all of the students used a paraphrasing strategy to some degree—a strategy that was evident in the notes generated by type-preference students in the previous two experiments. Presumably, the processing required to simply recognize an important piece of information and then copy and paste the information into a set of notes may be different than the processing required to paraphrase or summarize key ideas in one's own words (Craik & Lockhart, 1972; King, 1992; Kintsch, 1990). By forcing a similar type of data entry among all students in Experiment 5, we may have controlled depth of processing differences among participants in the previous two experiments that could have overridden our expected experimental effects. If that was so, the differences in learning found between the MT and FFT groups likely were due to the different versions of the *InfoGather* tool the students were given and the different kinds of notes constructed with each.

By the end of Experiment 5, we believed we had accumulated evidence supporting the frames capability of the tool. Given our observation that pasters seemed to perform worse than typists, however, one might ask, "Why include the copy and paste function at all, if this feature requires a lower level of processing and, in turn, promotes less learning while taking notes?" Our response to this question would be that copy and paste itself is not inherently a low-level activity. Like any learning exercise, it can be performed effectively or ineffectively. Student choices about *how* they use the copy and paste function may affect its benefits, suggesting that imposing the right constraints on their use might influence them to use it more effectively. Experiment 6 thus examined variations in degree of student control of *InfoGather's* copy and paste function.

Experiment 6: Learning Theories (Copy and Paste)

Because the previous experiments had supported the frames, or matrix, version of the tool, we began to focus on the copy and paste function of *InfoGather.* Interestingly, a search of the existing research literature yielded few empirical investigations of copy and paste, which is a function widely used in the Internet environment. In general, the copy and paste functions of most word processing programs work the same way, with users selecting information from one document, temporarily saving the information, and then adding it to another document where it can be stored. Although our search for research literature addressing copy and paste was not fruitful in helping us propose hypotheses, other related literature is applicable.

Based on our analysis of the text learning literature, we proposed that copy and paste might function as a hybrid of underlining and summarizing. Students underline text information that they judge to be valuable, much like the selecting that happens in copying and pasting. Many students make poor underlining decisions, however. For example, they often underline far too much information (Anderson & Armbruster, 1984). That is not to say that underlining is always ineffective. For instance, students whose underlining is restricted by some instructional guidelines (e.g., find the main idea) learn more (Snowman, 1984), because such restrictions help them to create manageable idea units representing main ideas (Hidi & Anderson, 1986). Like students who underline, students using copy and paste need to find summary representations from a given text. In using copy and paste, however, they can combine words that do not appear in the same sentence, taking them a step beyond simple underlining. Summarization techniques can help students learn (King, 1991; Wittrock, 1991), but they are not always beneficial (Anderson & Armbruster, 1984; Wittrock & Alesandrini, 1990). Again, some level of decision making seems to be the key (Snowman, 1984). An important question, however, is why might making decisions while underlining or summarizing lead to more learning? Perhaps deciding what is valuable and what is not valuable requires deeper mental processing, leading to deeper learning (Craik, 1979; Craik & Lockhart, 1972). If so, data gathering assignments or tools should be designed to prompt students for decisions whenever possible.

In Experiment 6, we assigned students to either a restricted or an unrestricted copy and paste note-taking condition. Restricted pasters were limited to placing seven words or fewer for every cell in a cued note-taking matrix. *InfoGather* thus prompted them indirectly to make more note-taking decisions. In contrast, other students were able to paste unrestricted amounts of information—words, sentences, or paragraphs—into each cell. Members of this group could make deep decisions, but their version of *InfoGather* did not require them to do so. The effects of the note-taking conditions then were assessed with a cued recall test of facts, a multiple-choice concepts test ($\alpha = .82$), and an essay question about relationships (interrater reliability = .91).

The procedures of Experiment 6 were similar to those in previous experiments. Undergraduates ($N = 71$) receiving course credit to participate were placed randomly into either the restricted or unrestricted condition. On the first day, students created user accounts, were informed of the features of the *InfoGather* tool (e.g., that they could paste in a maximum of seven words into a cell), and then took notes on a 2,300-word text describing three learning theories: behavioral, social, and constructivist. They then saved their notes in *InfoGather* and turned in consent forms. Two days later, the researchers visited the students' educational psychology classes and administered the three dependent measures; the students completed the measures and turned them in to the researchers.

We conducted three separate one-way analyses of variance (ANOVAs) testing the effect of manipulating copy and paste restrictions on each of the three dependent measures (see Table 4.4). All three of the ANOVAs were highly significant. First, the restricted copy and paste group ($M = 6.06$, $SD = 3.15$) recalled more from their notes than the unrestricted copy and paste group ($M = 2.24$, $SD = 1.71$, $F(1, 69) = 41.135$, $p < .001$). The strength of the relationship between the level of copy and paste restriction and recall performance was strong as assessed by η^2, with level of restriction accounting for 37% of the total variance. Requiring students to make more specific decisions about which information to include in their notes apparently enabled them to remember much more information than those making less specific decisions. Second, the restricted copy and paste group ($M = 6.44$, $SD = 1.86$) answered more concept quiz items correctly than the unrestricted copy and paste group ($M = 4.86$, $SD = 2.53$, $F(1, 69) = 8.813$, $p < .01$), with level of restriction accounting for 11% of the total variance. Thus, limiting the amount of information that students could paste into their notes was associated with more correct answers to items designed to measure conceptual learning. Finally, on the relationships essay quiz, the restricted copy and paste group ($M = 3.74$, $SD = 1.69$) included many more idea units than the unrestricted group ($M = 1.49$, $SD = 1.12$, $F(1, 69) = 44.206$, $p < .001$), with level of restriction accounting for 39% of the total variance. Thus, students whose copy and paste capability was restricted showed a greater understanding of the relationships among the main ideas of the text. It appears that by adjusting the copy and paste feature it may be possible to prompt deeper decision making and learning.

Table 4.4.   Means and Standard Deviations by Group for Experiment 6

Copy and paste	Cued recall facts	Multiple-choice concepts	Essay relationships
Restricted			
M	6.06	6.44	3.74
SD	3.15	1.86	1.69
Unrestricted			
M	2.14	4.86	1.49
SD	1.71	2.53	1.12

EDUCATIONAL IMPACT AND CONCLUSIONS

This chapter has described a research and development process leading to the current design of *InfoGather*, an Internet-based tool, providing evidence of the tool's educational possibilities. At a time when American students increasingly are relying on the Internet as a source of information (Lenhart et al., 2001), a tool like *InfoGather* may make the synthesis of information from different Web pages more likely. Prior to Web-based note taking, a teacher or student could select an organizing framework for *InfoGather* that can assist in the gathering of relevant information (Experiment 1) and promote learning later (Experiments 2 and 5). In addition to the tool's organizational capabilities, category cues may be inserted to help guide a student's search for information and increase the efficiency with which his/her time is spent on the Web (Experiment 1). Students also can create and insert their own categories for information to be gathered, adding a further dimension of meaning making. Finally, a teacher could promote students' processing of Web-based information by requiring them to summarize main points in their notes with the type function (Experiment 5) or with a restricted copy and paste function (Experiment 6). Both note-taking methods appear to promote deeper processing.

In conclusion, *InfoGather* may also provide a promising mechanism for further theory-based research in learning from Web-based materials. Of particular interest to us is the relationship between conditions that can be created within a tool such as *InfoGather* and learners' own preferred strategies for information gathering. The ability to experimentally control how students process information and to easily save the information they gather for further analysis provides researchers with many possibilities for fine-grained studies of the cognitive processes involved in learning from Web-based resources.

AUTHOR NOTE

This research was made possible by a grant from the U.S. Department of Education to the CLASS project, University of Nebraska–Lincoln. Opinions expressed are those of the authors and not necessarily those of the funders. We thank teachers Leland Jacobs, Joel Cornwell, and Russ Raatz of Lincoln Northeast High School for their invaluable help in the design and implementation of these experiments. We also are grateful to Sara Moshman and David Short of Metalogic, Inc., for their outstanding work in designing and refining the *InfoGather* tool.

Correspondence concerning this chapter should be addressed to L. Brent Igo, Department of Educational Psychology, Teachers College, University of Nebraska, Lincoln, NE 68588. Email: bigo@unlserve.unl.edu

REFERENCES

Anderson, J. R. (1995). *Cognitive psychology and its implications*. San Francisco: Freeman.

Anderson, T., & Armbruster, B. (1984). Studying. In D. Pearson (Ed.), *Handbook of reading research*. New York: Longman.

Bonk, C. J., & Cummings, J. A. (1998). A dozen recommendations for placing the student at the center of Web-based instruction. *Educational Media International, 35*, 82–89.

Brown, A. L. (1992). Design experiments: Theoretical and methodological challenges in creating complex interventions in classroom settings. *Journal of the Learning Sciences, 2*, 141–178.

Brown, A. L., Bransford, J., Ferrara, R., & Campione, J. (1983). Learning, remembering and understanding. In P. Mussen (Ed.), *Handbook of child psychology* (Vol. 3, pp. 77–166). New York: Wiley.

Craik, F. I. M. (1979). Human memory. *Annual Review of Psychology, 30*, 63–102.

Craik, F. I. M., & Lockhart, R. S. (1972). Levels of processing: A framework for memory research. *Journal of Verbal Learning and Verbal Behavior, 11*, 671–684.

Dreher, M. J., & Guthrie, J. T. (1990). Cognitive processes in textbook chapter search tasks. *Reading Research Quarterly, 25*, 323–339.

Glover, R. A., Bruning, R. H., & Plake, B. S. (1982). Distinctiveness of encoding and recall of text materials. *Journal of Educational Psychology, 74*, 522–534.

Hidi, S., & Anderson, V. (1986). Situational interest and its impact on reading and expository writing. In K. A. Renninger, S. Hidi, & A. Knapp (Eds.), *The role of interest in learning and development*. Hillsdale, NJ: Erlbaum.

Kiewra, K. A. (1991). Aids to lecture learning. *Educational Psychologist, 26*, 37–53.

Kiewra, K. A., & Dubois, N. F. (1998). *Learning to learn: Making the transition from student to life-long learner*. Needham Heights, MA: Allyn & Bacon.

Kiewra, K. A., Dubois, N. F., Christian, D., & McShane, A. (1988). Providing study notes: Relation of three types of notes for review. *Journal of Educational Psychology, 80*, 595–597.

Kiewra, K. A., Kauffman, D. F., Robinson, D. H., Dubois, N. F., & Staley, R. K. (1999). Supplementing floundering text with adjunct displays. *Instructional Science, 27*, 373–401.

King, A. (1991). Effects of training in strategic questioning of children's problem solving performance. *Journal of Educational Psychology, 83*, 240–245.

King, A. (1992). Comparison of self-questioning, summarizing, and note taking as strategies for learning from lectures. *American Educational Research Journal, 29*, 303–323.

Kintsch, E. (1990). Macroprocess and microprocesses in the development of summarization skills. *Cognition and Instruction, 7*, 161–195.

Lenhart, A., Simon, M., & Graziano, M. (2001). *The Internet and education: Findings of the Pew Internet & American Life Project* [Online]. Retrieved June 10, 2002, from http://www.pewinternet.org/reports/toc.asp?Report=39

Loranger, A. L. (1997). Comprehension strategies instruction: Does it make a difference? *Reading Psychology, 18*, 31–68.

Robinson, D. H., & Kiewra, K. A. (1995). Visual argument: Graphic organizers are superior to outlines in improving learning from text. *Journal of Education Psychology, 87*, 455–467.

Snowman, J. (1984). Learning tactics and strategies. In G. Phye & T. Andre (Eds.), *Cognitive instructional psychology* (pp. 18–32). Orlando, FL: Academic Press.

Wittrock, M. C. (1991). Generative teaching of comprehension. *Elementary School Journal, 92,* 169–184.

Wittock, M. C., & Alesandrini, K. (1990). Generation of summaries and analogies and analytic and holistic abilities. *American Educational Research Journal, 27,* 489–502.

CHAPTER 5

THINKABOUTIT

A Web-Based Tool
for Improving Critical Thinking

Steve Lehman
Utah State University

Roger Bruning
Christy A. Horn
Center for Instructional Innovation,
University of Nebraska–Lincoln

ABSTRACT

Two studies testing a Web-based application aimed at promoting critical thinking are reported in this chapter. In this application, called *ThinkAboutIt*, learners are asked to make choices and justify them. A database then graphically displays the frequency of their and other learners' choices, and lists the learners' rationales. In two experiments, teacher education students were randomly assigned to different versions of *ThinkAboutIt* embedded in online instruction on the topics of norm-referenced testing and classroom motivation. All students in both studies made choices and justified them in writing.

Web-Based Learning: What Do We Know? Where Do We Go?, pages 79–103

Depending on experimental conditions, some students simply moved on to new content after justifying their choices, while others received graphical feedback on frequency of others' choices. Still others additionally reviewed and interacted with others' rationales. Findings showed that all conditions in both studies produced significant gains in learning and self-efficacy, but did not differentially affect learning, motivation, or critical thinking outcomes. In general, results demonstrated the utility of the tool's feature requiring students to reason about cases, but not of features allowing students to interact with each other's rationales. Data from these studies suggest new possibilities for design of online applications for promoting deeper learning.

The two studies reported in this chapter examine a Web-based tool, called *ThinkAboutIt*, designed to promote deeper learning and critical thinking. *ThinkAboutIt* includes both an individual and a social-cognitive dimension. The individual dimension draws primarily on research relating self-explanations to the development of mental models (e.g., Chi, 2000; Chi, de Leeuw, Chiu, & LaVancher, 1994), while the social cognitive dimension draws on research on knowledge building communities (e.g., Bransford, Brown, & Cocking, 1999; Hewitt & Scardamalia, 1998). In this research (see also Igo, Bruning, McCrudden, & Kauffman, Chapter 4, this volume), which was conducted in connection with our formative evaluation of the CLASS (Communications, Learning, and Assessment in a Student-Centered System) project, we focused on experimentally testing principles drawn from cognitive and social-cognitive theory in the design of a Web-based application.

THE *THINKABOUTIT* TOOL

ThinkAboutIt is aimed at promoting learner engagement and critical thinking in online instruction. It consists of an authorable module that can be linked to Web-based content to encourage learners to engage more deeply with new information and critically reflect on it. In a typical implementation, the tool is inserted into Web-based instruction at points where learners should engage in evaluation, application, or synthesis of instructional content.

The *ThinkAboutIt* activity takes place in two distinct phases: *choice + explanation* and *display + interaction*. In a typical *ThinkAboutIt* application, content is presented via any format available on the Internet. (e.g., text, pictures, video, audio, etc.). In the first phase, *choice + explanation*, learners are required to use what they have learned to first make a choice about how the content should be interpreted or applied. In addition to making a choice, learners provide justification or rationale for their choice. In the second phase, *display + interaction*, the tool (1) returns a dynamic graphical display of the frequencies of all choices in the group of learners working on this application and (2) lists the learner's own rationale and those of all other learners in the population, sorted according to the choices that the learners have made. This permits learners to compare their judgments and rationales to those of their fellow learners. The tool also can (3) promote learners' interaction with the rationales of fellow learners by requiring them to select the best rationales, rate a subset of rationales for their quality, e-mail comments to authors of particular rationales, or simply read the rationales.

Theoretical Frameworks

The two phases of *choice + explanation* and *display + interaction* correspond to the two theoretical frameworks that have figured prominently in *ThinkAboutIt*'s design. The first of these relates self-explanations to the development of integrated mental representations (e.g., Chi, 2000; Chi et al., 1994). For example, Chi and colleagues (1994) asked 8th grade readers to self-explain information as they read information about the circulatory system. Control students simply read the text twice, while the self-explainers described what each sentence meant as they read it. Self-explaining produced a deeper understanding of the concepts and their interrelationships, resulting in enhanced recall and improved mental models, as assessed by complex relational and inferential questions. Chi and colleagues suggest that self-explanation produces deeper learning in part because it "encourages the integration of newly learned materials with existing knowledge" (p. 471). These findings are consistent with Halpern's (1998) recommendation to ask learners questions provoking them to make meaningful causal explanations of events, which can elicit critical thinking. Kuhn's (1991) research on human reasoning further suggests that the explanations individuals use as reasons for their beliefs reflect the extent to which they have generated causal inferences from the instructional material and formed integrated mental representations. Overall, this kind of deeper processing is associated with connected knowledge structures and more integrated representations of the information in text and instructional materials (Graesser, Singer, & Trabasso, 1994; Halpern, 1998).

The second theoretical dimension informing *ThinkAboutIt*'s design traces back to the work of Collins, Brown, and Newman (1989), who argued that social interactions can have positive effects on cognitive growth, as learners reflect on their own conclusions in light of others' thoughts. Such reflection facilitates learner metacognitive activities (Brown & Campione, 1996), which in turn can promote reevaluation and information restructuring. Increased metacognitive activity is particularly apparent in instances in which learners use the material to be learned in the context of solving real world problems. Stahl (2000) has suggested that participation in social interaction also may expose inconsistencies in how learners are representing new information, so that the disequilibrium caused by these inconsistencies stimulates cognitive restructuring. As individuals interact with others about the information to be learned, they have the opportunity to reevaluate their own understanding and construct more useful, internalized representations of the concept.

The social-cognitive perspective has strongly emphasized the role of discourse in knowledge construction, stressing the importance of social interactions in developing knowledge and thought. Cognitive growth is seen as resulting from social and cultural processes, regardless of whether it occurs in home, classroom, or technology-based contexts (Barron, 2000; Cognition and Technology Group at Vanderbilt, 1997; Gauvain, 2001). Thus, exchanges between teachers and students and between students and their peers are seen as central to learning.

During the past dozen or so years, social cognitive theory as described above has been used as a basis for designing a number of large-scale projects in which technology plays a central role. Such applications typically support peer-to-peer interactions and integrate various forms of discourse. Students focus on common problems and interact extensively with each other, sharing references, sources, observations, and ideas as they try to come to a problem solution or a common understanding. According to Hewitt and Scardamalia (1998), the challenge of coming to a shared understanding places a demand on students to "clarify ideas, refine theories, answer each others' questions, and negotiate meaning with one another" (p. 88). Students' interactions also promote awareness of other students' contributions, as they are encouraged to work together as a community, building on and extending each other's ideas through discussion. Interaction with peers leads to deeper content understanding and to a greater appreciation of others' knowledge.

Research Approach

The focal point of the current studies was *ThinkAboutIt*'s feature of learners looking at their own and others' explanations. The efficacy of the making and explaining choices design feature also was of interest and is the focus of continuing empirical work in our Center, but was held constant in the studies reported here. That is, all users of the *ThinkAboutIt* tool were required to complete activities in which they chose a solution to a problem and then explained why their solution was the best option. In this study, evidence of the effectiveness of making and explaining choices was gathered by measuring performance before/after learning. Meanwhile, we experimentally varied the extent to which *ThinkAboutIt* allowed users to interact with others' choices and explanations. Depending on experimental condition, after users had made their own choices and explanations, *ThinkAboutIt* presented various combinations of (1) a summary graphic (a histogram displaying frequencies of each choice) and (2) a list of other users' explanations or rationales. Our goal in presenting this information was to enable users in those conditions to reflect on their own views in light of others' viewpoints and to evaluate their own solutions and thinking processes (Collins et al., 1989). The specific features of the four experimental conditions controlled the extent to which information about others' viewpoints were accessible.

We tested the effects of varying levels of user-to-user interaction on learning in two Web-based instructional units. One unit focused on norm-referenced tests (NRT unit) and the other focused on classroom motivation (MOT unit). We posited that increasing user-to-user interaction should facilitate knowledge construction by presenting users with ideas and perspectives from others who are thinking about the same issues. From this perspective, the tool's display and interaction capabilities represent a form of dialogue in which the learner must consider new or opposing ideas. Some evidence exists to support this perspective. For example, the ability of classroom interactions to promote deeper learning is well known (e.g., Brown & Campione, 1994). Similarly, Scardamalia and Bereiter's (1996) research with CSILE (Computer Supported Intentional Learning Environments) and its successor, Knowledge Forum, and the work of the Cognition and Technology Group at Vanderbilt (1997) has shown that sharing ideas in technology-based communities can promote learning. Furthermore, Lehman, Kauffman, White, Horn, and Bruning (2001) have shown that certain kinds of exchanges between distance-learning teachers and at-risk students can improve motivation and performance of these students in Web-based courses.

Whether the focused interactions in the tutorial environment of *Think-AboutIt* would promote deeper learning was unknown, however. An alternative possibility was that asynchronous electronic user-to-user interaction as operationalized in *ThinkAboutIt* would fail to capture enough of the critical features of face-to-face communication—such as immediacy, nonverbal communication, and communication pragmatics (Grice, 1975)—to affect learning and critical thinking outcomes.

In the two studies conducted to test the efficacy of *ThinkAboutIt's* interactive features, we gathered data from Web-based units offered as part of an undergraduate teacher education course. We specifically tested whether learners' knowledge and understanding of concepts presented in our online instructional units would increase as a result of higher levels of interaction with other users' ideas. Our experimental manipulation consisted of providing users with one of four levels of access to other users' responses in the *ThinkAboutIt* application. Experiment 1 involved content from the NRT unit, and Experiment 2 content from the MOT unit.

EXPERIMENT 1

Method

Participants

Participants were college undergraduates enrolled in one of the four sections of an introductory educational psychology course at a large Midwestern university. All students completed a Web-based instructional unit as a course requirement, but chose whether or not to contribute their data to the research study. All but 2 of the 94 students chose to participate in the study. Students were randomly assigned to one of four levels of user-to-user interaction. Total time to complete the NRT unit was approximately 1.5 hours.

Materials

The core content of the NRT Web site provided students with information on the concepts of reliability and validity as they relate to interpreting norm-referenced tests. The Web site unit consisted of pre-unit measures, instructional material, and post-unit measures. The unit content was composed of four sections (6,895 total words). For this experiment, the sections consisted primarily of text, supplemented by tables, diagrams, and an interactive test report form, which presented a fictitious person's standardized test results. In this interactive form, users could obtain detailed information about each score type (e.g., stanine, percentile, grade equivalent, etc.) by clicking on that column in the graphic, which explained the score type using the person's score as an example for the explanation.

Students thus learned content by reading material, by interacting with the test report form, and by answering and obtaining feedback on the thought questions presented by the *ThinkAboutIt* tool. This cycle was repeated for each of the four sections. Dynamically activated hyperlinks guided users though the four sections of the Web site sequentially so that order of presentation of material was controlled. Each section concluded with the *ThinkAboutIt* application, which required participants to use concepts from the instructional materials in making and justifying a choice about real-life situations. For example, the *ThinkAboutIt* question after the section on reliability read as follows:

Generally, a single norm-referenced (standardized) test will be more reliable than any single assessment that a classroom teacher can construct (e.g., a quiz, assignment, unit test). If you wanted to have the most reliable measure of what a student had achieved during a semester or year in, say, world history, biology, or algebra, which would you choose as your measure?

a. a norm-referenced test given at the end of the semester or year
b. the total number of points earned by the student during the semester or year, based on the sum of all the quizzes and assignments s/he has completed
c. can't decide based on the information given

Participants chose one of the three options (a, b, or c) and then wrote a brief (2–5 sentences long) justification of their choice. When the student submitted this information, the Web site returned a dynamically generated "View Responses" page constituting the experimental manipulation. Depending on the experimental condition, this page provided users with one of four different levels of user-to-user interaction: At Level 1 of the manipulation, the page displayed only the participant's own choice and rationale. At Level 2, the lowest level of interaction with other's rationales, participants viewed their own choice and rationale, plus a dynamically generated graph displaying what percentage of other users had chosen "a," "b," or "c." At Level 3, participants viewed all features of Level 2, plus the rationales other users had given to justify their answers. At Level 4, participants viewed all features of Level 3; they additionally were asked to rate the quality of five rationales and comment on at least one. This condition was considered to be the highest level of interaction because participants were exposed to a variety of rationales and had to actively evaluate their merits. Figure 5.1 shows an example of a page that users at Level 4 might have viewed.

Dependent Measures

Pre-unit measures

Pre-unit measures consisted of an eight-item self-efficacy pretest questionnaire, an eight-item Web experience questionnaire, and a 10-item multiple-choice pretest of content knowledge. The *self-efficacy* instrument measured users' perceived confidence in interpreting norm-referenced test results. The *Web experience* questionnaire asked users to rate their experience in Web-based activities ranging from sending and receiving e-mail to constructing and maintaining a Web site. This instrument was given to measure the potential effects that experience with the World Wide Web might have on motivation and learning in the various experimental condi-

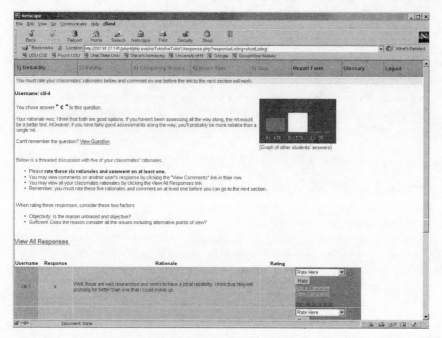

Figure 5.1.   Screen capture of Level 4 display of responses.

tions. The 10-item multiple-choice *knowledge pretest* measured users' understanding of basic concepts necessary for interpreting norm-referenced tests. Questions on the multiple-choice pretest were generally written using nontechnical language and less difficult distracters to avoid floor effects.

Post-unit measures

Three post-unit measures were obtained: a post self-efficacy questionnaire, a post knowledge test, and an essay question designed to measure critical thinking/deep understanding of concepts. The post-unit self-efficacy questionnaire and multiple-choice knowledge quiz paralleled the pre-unit measures so that changes resulting from the experimental conditions could be observed within subjects. More specifically, the *post self-efficacy* measure was identical to the 8-item self-efficacy measure given at the beginning of the unit. *Post-unit knowledge* was measured using a 20-item multiple-choice knowledge test. The questions covered factual information about norm-referenced tests that was presented in the instructional unit. The 20-item knowledge test consisted of two items that were identical to pretest items (used to assess within-subject change), eight items that were parallel to pretest items, and 10 new items that had not appeared on the pretest. Items on the posttest included both fact-recognition and higher-order application questions.

The essay question assessing users' critical thinking and deeper level of understanding of unit content asked users to apply information from the unit to decision making about the appropriate use of a norm-referenced test. This *critical thinking* measure, which took the form of a *ThinkAboutIt* question and justification, asked participants to take a position on whether or not University of California officials should continue to use the SAT as an entrance requirement and to write an essay explaining why their choice was better than the other alternative. Two independent raters blind to the experimental conditions graded the critical thinking essay responses on the extent to which users had produced evidence to justify their claims. Raters were trained to use a rubric based on Kuhn's (1991) and Toulmin's (1969) work on assessing the quality of thinking and argumentation, including the number of supported claims that were made, reasons supporting the claims, and evidence supporting the claims. Variations of this rubric have been used successfully to measure readers' deeper comprehension of text (Lehman & Schraw, 2002) and critical thinking (Stapleton, 2001). Interrater reliability after preliminary scoring was initially moderate ($r = .61$). After conferring with the trainer and each other, raters independently rerated all essays with scores that differed by more than one point. After rerating, interrater reliability was acceptably high ($r = .87$).

In addition to the rating of critical thinking (argumentation), raters also assigned each essay a *holistic score* based on the extent to which raters judged the essay to be convincing, accurate, and coherent. This scale, which ranged from 1 (poor) to 5 (exemplary), was taken to enable a check on the effectiveness of the critical thinking rating (argumentation rubric). Interrater reliability was moderately high for the holistic score ($r = .67$ in Experiment 1 and .74 in Experiment 2), and was highly correlated with the critical thinking score ($r = .81$ in Experiment 1 and .93 in Experiment 2).

Ancillary data

Beyond the three outcome measures, ancillary data gathered into the site's database included the amount of time spent in the unit and users' perceptions of the Web site. A rough measure of *time spent* in the unit was obtained by time stamping the submission time of each *ThinkAboutIt* question. This enabled an estimation of the amount of time users had spent on the site between submissions. A final questionnaire also was administered to assess users' impression of the Web site. This 14-item survey, which users completed after working through the content of the unit, included 10 Likert-scale *Web site rating* items asking users to rate the Web site in terms of their engagement, learning, and judgment of the overall value of the site. The remaining four survey items were open-ended essays, included to provide qualitative feedback. These questions asked users to comment on (1) what they liked about the *ThinkAboutIt* feature, (2) what could be done to make the *ThinkAboutIt* feature more effective, (3) what they thought was the most interesting part of the Web site, and (4) any suggestions they had for improving the Web site.

Procedure

Users received preliminary instructions for logging into the units from their instructors and were informed that the server would save their work so that they did not have to complete the unit in a single sitting. Students could access the Web site at their convenience within a 3-week period using any computer connected to the Internet. To access the site users created an account and completed the online pre-unit questionnaires of self-efficacy, Web experience, and knowledge. Users then worked through the first set of unit materials, answered a thought question, and received information (as dictated by their experimental condition) on their responses to the thought question. This cycle of reading, answering questions, and receiving feedback was repeated for each of the four sections of the unit. After completing the four sections, users checked out by completing the final questionnaire concerning their impressions of the Web site unit, the post-unit self-efficacy measure, and the knowledge posttest. Information regarding the performance in the unit was sent from the experimenters to the student's instructor, who then assigned credit based on whether the student completed the activities in the unit.

Results

Preliminary analyses confirmed the initial equivalence of the experimental groups on pretests of self-efficacy and knowledge, supporting the success of our randomization procedures. Analyses of variance (ANOVA) tests were conducted next to examine effects of varying the level of user-to-user interaction on measures of user learning and motivation, including learner self-efficacy, knowledge, and critical thinking, plus the amount of time users in the four conditions spent studying in the Web site. Significance levels were set at .05 for all analyses and post hoc tests. Additionally, users' comments on the final questionnaire were analyzed for evidence of impact of user-to-user interaction. Table 5.1 presents correlations among pre- and post-measures, and Table 5.2 presents the means and standard deviations of the scores obtained by the users in each of the four experimental conditions.

Table 5.1. Correlations among Dependent Variables for Experiment 1 (NRT)

	Self-efficacy posttest	Web experience	Knowledge pretest	Knowledge posttest	Critical thinking	Time spent	Web site rating
Self-efficacy pretest	.302**	.140	.088	-.127	-.049	-.218	-.246*
Self-efficacy posttest		-.032	.378**	.453**	.228*	.312**	3.27*
Web experience			-.121	-.165	-.077	-.313**	-.086
Knowledge pretest				.513**	.064	.220	.084
Knowledge posttest					.446**	.500**	.329*
Critical thinking						.390**	.109
Time spent							.251*

** Correlation is significant at the 0.01 level (two-tailed).

* Correlation is significant at the 0.05 level (two-tailed).

Table 5.2.   Means and Standard Deviations for Experiment 1 (NRT)

Variable		1	2	3	4	Total
		Level of interaction with other students' explanations				
Knowledge pretest	M	6.10	6.30	6.82	6.24	6.36
	SD	1.87	1.68	2.06	1.85	1.85
Knowledge posttest	M	13.10	12.56	13.55	12.12	12.78
	SD	2.81	3.80	4.01	4.06	3.71
Web experience	M	26.05	24.93	23.77	25.08	24.95
	SD	5.00	6.24	5.71	5.16	5.55
Time total (sec.)	M	2020	2223	2184	2909	2358
	SD	1125	2355	1533	1863	1825
Self-efficacy pretest	M	25.33	24.93	26.82	27.16	26.04
	SD	4.61	5.50	5.66	4.91	5.21
Self- efficacy posttest	M	34.04	33.26	35.31	33.32	33.93
	SD	3.93	6.67	3.60	4.62	4.96
Critical thinking	M	2.88	2.54	2.73	2.57	2.67
	SD	1.36	1.06	1.18	.98	1.13
Holistic score	M	5.43	4.96	5.31	4.83	5.11
	SD	1.72	1.96	1.74.	1.36	1.71

Note. Data is from the unit on norm-referenced tests (NRT). Levels of interaction 1 to 4 represent increasingly more intensive interactions with other students' rationales, as described in text.

Correlations

Correlations among dependent measures indicated that time spent in the unit was significantly positively related to post-unit self-efficacy, knowledge about norm-referenced tests (as reflected in the multiple-choice test), and level of critical thinking, but negatively related to users' pre-unit Web experience (see Table 5.1). These relationships are consistent with a view that Web-based units can be effective means of developing professional knowledge, given that users spend adequate time using the materials. Those with higher levels of Web experience tended to spend less time on the site, which may indicate that those individuals familiar with the Web can learn more efficiently in Web-based settings than those who lack Web experience. An alternative explanation for this negative correlation, however, is that experienced Web users spend less time on the site because they are accustomed to rapidly skimming Web pages rather than studying online materials.

Correlations also showed that post-unit knowledge about norm-referenced tests was associated with self-efficacy posttest scores, but not with self-efficacy pretest scores. Users who rated the Web site highly also tended to score better on measures of knowledge, critical thinking, and self-efficacy. They also spent more time in the Web site. Those who had high self-efficacy coming into the Web site gave the Web site lower ratings, possibly indicating that those with lower confidence felt that the Web site was more helpful than those who felt they already knew the material.

Self-efficacy

Self-efficacy scores (see Table 5.2) were obtained by summing the eight items on the self-efficacy measure (possible range of 8 to 40). Factor analysis confirmed that all items loaded on a single factor, and reliability analysis indicated a high level of internal consistency (α = .91). The pre– and post–self-efficacy measures were taken to assess the affective and motivational effects of the treatment on users. At pretest, there were no differences among users in the four conditions. A within-subjects comparison of pretest to posttest indicated that the instructional materials presented by the unit increased self-efficacy for interpreting norm-referenced tests. Across all experimental conditions, user self-efficacy measures for interpreting norm-referenced tests increased from 26.0 on the pre-unit measure to 33.9 on the post-unit measure ($F(1, 93)$ = 159.43, p <.01, MSE = 33.78, η^2 = .63). Analysis of variance revealed, however, that the level of user-to-user contact did not influence self-efficacy posttest scores ($F(3, 93)$ < 1, p = .57, MSE = 22.73, η^2 = .02).

Knowledge test

Knowledge of the basic concepts taught in the unit was assessed using an online 20-item multiple-choice quiz administered at the completion of the unit. Reliability for the measure was acceptable (α = .77). An initial within-subjects test comparing performance on items occurring in both the pretest and the posttest revealed that working through the unit significantly increased users' knowledge of interpreting norm-referenced tests ($F(1, 93)$ = 14.80, p < .01, MSE = .19, η^2 = .14). However, different levels of user-to-user contact (see Table 5.2) again did not affect users' ability to recognize facts taught in the unit ($F(3, 94)$ < 1, p = .66, MSE = 10.49, η^2 = .02).

Critical thinking/deeper processing

Essays measuring responses to the critical thinking question were scored using an argumentation rubric that tallied the number of supported claims, warrants, and evidence and required the assignment of a holistic score. Interrater reliability was high (r = .87) for the rubric-based (critical thinking/argumentation) score and moderate for the holistic score (r = .67). An

ANOVA test of critical thinking scores revealed no effects (see Table 5.2) for user-to-user interaction ($F(3, 92) < 1$; $p = .72$, $MSE = 1.31$, $\eta^2 = .02$). An additional test of the holistic rating score also showed no differences ($F(3, 67) = 1.24$, $p = .30$, $MSE = 2.94$, $\eta^2 = .06$) (see Table 5.2).

Time spent in units

Time spent in units was obtained by adding the number of seconds between submissions of *ThinkAboutIt* activities. This measure obviously provided only an approximation of time spent, because we had not yet added the tracking features enabling us to determine whether users were working in the Web site during the time they were logged on. To eliminate users who were not continuously working on units between *ThinkAboutIt*s, all adjacent time stamp differences greater than 30 minutes were eliminated prior to analysis. As might be expected, the mean time of the highest level of user interaction was substantially higher than the means of other conditions (see Table 5.2). However, due to high within-group variability in amount of time spent, the effect of the four different levels of user-to-user interaction ($F(3, 74) < 1$, $p = .46$, $MSE = 3.35 \times 10^6$, $\eta^2 = .04$) was not statistically significant.

Users' written comments

Comments on the post-experimental survey assessing student reactions to the Web site were predominantly positive. For example, on the questions asking what could be done to make the site better, 21% ($n = 23$) of responders stated that the site needed no changes. On the question asking what the most interesting part of the site was, 31% ($n = 29$) of the users cited *ThinkAboutIt* and viewing other users' comments as the most interesting part of the Web site.

Regarding what users liked most about the *ThinkAboutIt* feature, the largest proportion (40%, $n = 38$) of users liked the ability to add a rationale to their choices. Over a third ($n = 32$) stated that they liked having to give a rationale for their choice because this caused them to think about why they had chosen an answer. The second most frequent response was that of liking the ability to share opinions and view others' responses (11%). This proportion significantly underestimates the opinions of our sample, of course, because only one-half of our participants were able to view other users' rationales.

Suggestions to improve the unit clustered into four general categories: content, activities, formatting, and navigation. The most common suggestion for improving the site occurred in the "content" category where users suggested reducing the length of the text materials (33%). Users also suggested incorporating more activities (7%), reformatting to make reading online easier (6%), and clarifying how to navigate the site (7%).

Discussion of Experiment 1

Overall, findings from Experiment 1 suggest that the interactive dimension of Web-based instruction, as operationalized in levels 2 through 4 of the present study, produced minimal differential effects on learning, but that an application that has learners make choices and explain them can produce engagement and significant gains in students' knowledge and self-efficacy. We were somewhat surprised by the findings that having access to other students' reasoning produced no effects on self-efficacy, fact learning, or critical thinking/deeper processing. One possible explanation for these no-differences findings for levels of user interaction may have been that features of face-to-face interaction were missing (Grice, 1975), such that even our highest level of interaction did not positively influence learners' deeper processing. Another was that four instances of user-to-user interaction did not constitute enough opportunities for user-to-user interaction. Given that many participants spontaneously noted that their most-preferred instructional dimension was the ability to see other users' comments, we increased the amount of user-to-user interaction in the second experiment, and made access to this information easier.

EXPERIMENT 2

To further investigate possible effects for social interaction, we applied *ThinkAboutIt* to a second Web-based instructional unit focusing on a new topic, classroom motivation (the MOT unit). In this unit, we intensified the user-to-user interaction and improved user ability to monitor what others were saying about their explanations.

Method

Participants

Seventy-two college undergraduates enrolled in one of four sections of an introductory educational psychology course at a large Midwestern university completed a version of the "Increasing Motivation" Web unit as a course requirement. All who completed the unit chose to participate in the research. Participants again were randomly assigned to one of four levels of user-to-user interaction as they logged onto the Web site. Total time to complete the motivation unit was approximately 1.5 hours.

Materials

The Web-based materials used in the experiment were designed to help preservice and inservice teachers better understand ways of increasing intrinsic motivation in the classroom. As with the NRT unit, the motivation (MOT) unit consisted of pre-unit measures, instructional material, and post-unit measures. The instructional materials consisted of 4,298 words. In contrast to the NRT site, the MOT site did not provide materials completely new to the students; all sections of the educational psychology course in which they were enrolled had covered at least some motivation-related content by the time users entered the site.

Compared to the NRT site, the MOT site intensified student–student interaction in two ways. First, the number of subsections was doubled, from four to eight, so that users completed more *ThinkAboutIt*s. The additional *ThinkAboutIt*s provided users in high interaction conditions with more opportunities for making choices, giving explanations, and reviewing others' explanations. Second, users were provided with an additional resource page that logged all their rationales to *ThinkAboutIt*s as well as any comments that other users had made on their rationales. Our intent here was to increase users' ability to monitor their ideas and responses to their ideas.

Dependent Measures

Dependent measures paralleled those of the NRT site. We assessed pre- and post-unit knowledge about motivation and pre- and post-unit self-efficacy, and administered the post-unit critical thinking/deeper processing essay measure. For this unit, self-efficacy was assessed using an eight-item self-efficacy scale parallel to the one used for the NRT site (with a range from 8 to 40 points), but focusing on self-efficacy for increasing students' classroom motivation. A 20-item online multiple-choice quiz was used to assess basic understanding of motivation concepts taught in the unit. As with the NRT site, the pre-unit multiple-choice quiz was written with non-technical language and with relatively easy distracters. Four questions from the pretest were identical to those on the post-test measure. Internal reliability for the post-unit multiple-choice test was marginally acceptable ($\alpha = .58$). Interrater reliability was moderately high on first rating of the critical thinking/deeper processing measure ($r = .73$), and increased further after consultation and rerating ($r = .88$).

Results

Table 5.3 presents correlations among dependent variables, and Table 5.4 the means and standard deviations, for student scores in the four experimental conditions. Initial analysis of pre-unit measures showed no differences among experimental groups on either self-efficacy or knowledge of

Table 5.3. Correlations among Dependent Variables in Experiment 2 (MOT)

	Self-efficacy posttest	Web experience	Knowledge pretest	Knowledge posttest	Critical thinking	Time spent	Web site rating
Self-efficacy pretest	.549**	.171	-.109	-.303**	-.235	-.093	-.446*
Self-efficacy posttest		.045	-.147	-.093	.080	.097	.503*
Web experience			-.089	-.199	-.080	.067	-.129
Knowledge pretest				.466**	.121	-.018	-.044
Knowledge posttest					.364**	.100	.214
Critical thinking						.477**	.332**
Time spent							.181

** Correlation is significant at the 0.01 level (two-tailed).

Table 5.4.   Means and Standard Deviations for Experiment 2 (MOT Unit)

Variable		Level of interaction with other students' explanations				
		1	*2*	*3*	*4*	*Total*
Knowledge pretest	M	7.46	7.65	6.93	7.42	7.41
	SD	1.45	1.72	1.28	1.17	1.45
Knowledge posttest	M	13.00	12.92	13.00	12.73	12.90
	SD	2.58	3.35	3.23	2.28	2.89
Web experience	M	21.62	25.00	24.27	23.42	23.84
	SD	4.59	6.92	3.10	4.87	5.42
Time total	M	1326	1234	1115	1749	1369
	SD	501	711	935	698	744
Self-efficacy pretest	M	31.62	31.46	30.00	30.53	30.94
	SD	3.55	3.59	4.90	3.85	3.92
Self-efficacy posttest	M	36.15	34.19	34.07	33.11	34.23
	SD	3.65	4.23	3.73	4.11	4.05
Critical thinking	M	3.23	2.78	2.64	2.39	2.74
	SD	1.33	1.20	1.00	1.44	1.27
Holistic rating	M	6.00	5.42	5.32	4.81	5.35
	SD	1.83	1.56	1.68	1.86	1.73

Note. Data is from the unit on student motivation (MOT). Levels of interaction 1 to 4 represent increasingly more intensive interactions with other students' rationales, as described in text.

motivational constructs ($p > .05$). Four ANOVA tests were conducted to examine potential effects of different levels of user-to-user contact on user learning and motivation. Dependent measures included post-unit measures of learner self-efficacy, performance on the knowledge test (multiple-choice quiz), and performance on the post-unit critical thinking/deeper processing measure. Differences in the amount of time users spent studying in the Web site and users' written comments were also analyzed for evidence of impact of user-to-user interaction.

Correlations

Correlations among dependent measures indicated that high levels of critical thinking were associated with users spending more time in the units as well as performing at higher levels on the multiple-choice test measuring knowledge of motivational concepts (see Table 5.3). These relationships provide evidence consistent with the idea that Web-based instruction can promote critical thinking. In contrast to the NRT unit, however, time spent in the MOT unit was not related to users' knowledge of concepts covered in the unit, nor was it related to post-unit self-efficacy. This may not be surprising, however, given the fact that all users previously had completed a section on motivation in their educational psychology course. It is also possible that users who were confident that they understood the concepts may not have attended as well to the content, a conjecture supported by the fact that self-efficacy pretest was negatively related to post-unit knowledge.

Self-efficacy

As in Experiment 1, a comparison of self-efficacy between pretest and posttest showed that students' self-efficacy increased significantly, from a mean score of 30.9 on the pre-unit measure to 34.2 on the post-unit measure $(F(1, 71) = 55.45, p < .01, MSE = 7.03, \eta^2 = .44)$. Analysis of variance comparing post-unit self-efficacy across levels of the treatment, however, again showed the differing levels of contact among learners having no effect on post-unit self-efficacy scores $(F(3, 72) = 1.62, p = .19, MSE = 15.72, \eta^2 = .07)$.

Knowledge test

Consistent with Experiment 1, within-subject differences on content knowledge items shared by the pretest and posttest showed a significant increase $(F(1, 71) = 10.44, p < .01, MSE = .48, \eta^2 = .13)$. Also consistent with Experiment 1, an ANOVA test revealed no differences between the four levels of user-to-user interaction on users' post-unit understanding of basic unit concepts $(F(3, 72) < 1, p = .89, MSE = 8.04, \eta^2 = .01)$.

Critical thinking/deeper processing

Critical thinking/deeper processing in Experiment 2 was again measured using a *ThinkAboutIt*-like question, with the question focusing on responding to a classroom motivation challenge. Interrater reliability was high $(r = .88)$ for the rubric-based scoring and moderate $(r = .74)$ for a holistic scoring. An ANOVA test of scores on the argumentation rubric showed no effects for level of user-to-user interaction $(F(3, 67) = 1.14, p = .34, MSE = 1.61, \eta^2 = .05)$ or holistic rating score $(F(3, 93) < 1; p = .61, MSE = 2.95, \eta^2 = .02)$.

Time spent in units. Time spent in units (see Table 5.4) was obtained by calculating the number of seconds between submissions of successive *ThinkAboutIt* activities. No reliable differences were found among the four different levels of user-to-user interaction $(F(3, 47) = 1.76, p = .17, MSE = 5.28 \times 10^5, \eta^2 = .11)$. As in Experiment 1, those users exposed to the highest condition appeared to have spent more time in the unit (see Table 5.4), but effects may have been masked due to the high variability in the time sample data.

Users' written comments

User's written comments regarding the effectiveness of the instructional unit were taken from four questions on the final survey that were identical to the questions for the NRT site. Reactions again were predominantly positive, with 49% (*n* = 35) of comments on the "suggestions to make the site better" question stating that the site needed no changes. Half of the students (*n* = 36) cited *ThinkAboutIt* and viewing other students' comments to be the most interesting part of the Web site. Regarding what they liked most about the *ThinkAboutIt* application, the greatest proportion (38%, *n* = 27) of students cited providing a rationale for their answers because it caused them to think about why they had chosen an answer. Thirty-two percent (*n* = 23) mentioned either the ability to see others' responses to the question or the ability to share opinions as being a feature that they liked. Suggestions to improve the unit clustered into three general categories: content, activities, and navigation. Despite the fact that the MOT text was half as long as the NRT text, the most common suggestion for improving the site, other than "no improvement necessary," was to reduce text length (11%, *n* = 8).

Discussion of Experiment 2

Our findings in Experiment 2 closely paralleled those from Experiment 1, where work in the unit produced significant gains in learning and self-efficacy for applying unit-related content, but did not show effects of varying levels of interaction with other students' explanations. Given that we had increased the level of student-to-student interaction with other students' explanations, these findings could suggest that such interactions may have limited utility in Web-based contexts. At the same time, however, given the high proportion of users who found the user-to-user interaction to be the most interesting part of the unit, the findings also point toward a valuable motivational function of such interactions in Web-based instruction.

GENERAL DISCUSSION

As part of an overall research program examining a Web-based tool based on concepts of self-explanation and social interaction, we conducted two experiments in which student interactions with other students' explanations of choices were varied. We proposed that increasing user-to-user contacts (i.e., increasing social interaction) in online settings would enhance constructive processing. In contrast, we entertained the possibility that user-to-user online contacts would not enhance constructive processing, because of the recognition that Web-based interactions lack components of face-to-face communication such as immediacy and nonverbal communication.

Results from both experiments showed no significant effects linked to interactions with others' explanations. That is, increased levels of interactivity with others' explanations produced no differences in knowledge, critical thinking, or self-efficacy for using information provided by the unit. At the same time, however, significant increases in knowledge and self-efficacy in two different content areas were observed as a result of student participation in these Web-based units. Students also cited the ability to see others' explanations as a positive feature of these instructional units.

The lack of learning and critical thinking differences between levels of interaction was somewhat puzzling, however. It may be that online interaction is not as compelling as face-to-face interaction and generally may have limited effectiveness for promoting learning. It may also be, as Jarvela and Hakkinen's (2000) analysis of social interaction on the Web suggests, that part of the power of accessing others' perspectives on the Web depends on the expectation of response and the opportunity for dialogue, both of which were limited here. They propose that dialogue may be hindered in Web-based interactions because of the reduced number of social cues (e.g., facial expressions, inflection, nonverbal cues) and increased social distance. Users also may need more personal information from discussion participants in order for this interaction to develop a baseline level of social cues needed for a profitable discussion. Our findings suggest that creating Web-based social interactions that reliably enhance learning may be a challenging task.

Contextual Factors and Future Research

In interpreting the current results, several contextual/motivational factors that may have affected learning and critical thinking in the experimental treatments should be noted. First, both instructional units were presented as ancillaries to undergraduate courses, with credit assigned on the basis of completing the unit rather than on level of performance in the unit. Previous pilot work, which involved teachers and administrators using *ThinkAboutIt* to interact about norm-referenced testing in their schools, had produced notably high levels of interest in viewing and engaging with others' rationales. Under the current conditions, however, with completion a course requirement but quality of response not an evaluative criterion, course instructors reported that participant motivation focused more typically on unit completion than on performing well. Second, although students found viewing each other's responses interesting, there was no immediate benefit or reward for their interacting with others. In fact, Levels 3 and 4, which required students to review each other's explanations, may even have been construed as mildly punishing because their interactive components required more time to be spent in the unit. Finally, the design of the experimental conditions may have reduced motivation at the higher levels of interaction by constraining participant choice. Participant choices were somewhat controlled in Level 3, where students were required to read other's justifications, and even more highly constrained at Level 4, where students were required to rate others' explanations and write a response to them. In some studies, constraints on choice have been found to reduce motivation of participants (see Deci & Ryan, 1987).

Despite these limitations, our data showing overall gains in participants' knowledge and self-efficacy for using the constructs have encouraged us to continue to include the dimension of self-explanation in our Web-based applications. The opportunity to view others' explanations also was very positively received, with this feature rated in both experiments as the unit's most interesting feature. The correlational data also were encouraging in their showing a relationship between time spent in Web-based learning environments and level of critical thinking. In Experiment 1, students who spent more time in the Web site performed better on measures of knowledge and critical thinking about norm-referenced tests, while those in Experiment 2 who spent more time in the MOT module produced essays exhibiting higher levels of critical thinking. These data suggest that Web-based instruction may not only be profitable for knowledge acquisition, but may also provide a means to promote critical thinking. These data align closely with a broad body of research on facilitating learners' understanding of cause–effect relationships in text and instructional materials (e.g., Chi, 2000; Graesser et al., 1994; Willoughby, Wood, Desmarais, Sims, & Kalra, 1997). The unanimous consensus of this literature is that understanding "why" one idea leads to another determines the degree to which the learner understands the information.

One of the primary benefits of these studies to us is that they have yielded important information about what it takes to produce a Web site that promotes learning and enhances motivation. We have been particularly interested in the challenges presented in conducting experimental studies with random assignment, dynamically generated variation of instructional material, and automated data gathering, while at the same time attempting to deliver an educationally viable intervention. We continue to believe that experimental-educational units such as ours have the potential for helping researchers develop an empirically based understanding of learning processes in Web-based contexts, while simultaneously providing instructional designers with design principles for improving their instructional materials.

Based on our findings, we are revising both units to improve their functionality in regard to context, instructional design, and social interactive characteristics. We have modified the contextual frame in which our studies take place to situate the instructional units more integrally within courses (e.g., assigning some portion of credit to performance on unit assessments). *ThinkAboutIt*'s navigation has been simplified and we have attempted to make improvements in content (e.g., by replacing text with visual and interactive instructional materials) and in the quality of the *ThinkAboutIt* questions. We also are seeking to more closely align the social interaction conditions with those known to be productive in face-to-face settings (e.g., Bonk, Daytner, Daytner, Dennen, & Malikowski, 1999; Brown & Campione, 1994; Scardamalia & Bereiter, 1996). These modifications include structuring the social interaction to more closely simulate a cognitive apprenticeship (Collins et al., 1989), where the unit includes expert viewpoints and uses metacognitive modeling to explicitly demonstrate warranted assertability of explanations. We are exploring features for tagging higher-level responses made by peers so that users can readily compare their own ideas with reasoning judged to be at a high level. Although our initial attempts to promote interactions around each other's explanations did not produce differences, comments from users indicate they are well received and have potential for promoting integrated understanding of concepts and principles. We thus are continuing to explore ways to enhance this feature of *ThinkAboutIt*.

We are currently testing several new uses for *ThinkAboutIt*. In one, *ThinkAboutIt* is being used for teacher professional development in connection with the Nebraska Statewide Writing Assessment. Beginning in 2001 and concluding in 2003, the Nebraska Statewide Writing Assessment is evaluating the writing of approximately 75,000 fourth-, eighth-, and eleventh-grade students in Nebraska. This writing will be hand-scored by a subset of teachers who have been trained in the 6-Trait Writing Model. Included in this assessment is a significant professional development opportunity for Nebraska teachers focusing on writing across the curriculum. A Web site organized around the *ThinkAboutIt* tool provides the chance for teachers to rate multiple fourth- and eighth-grade writing samples using the 6-Trait Writing Model, explain their ratings, and compare their ratings and explanations to those of other teachers. For this use, we have added two significant features to *ThinkAboutIt*—a "Coach," which provides audio and video input from expert teachers about criteria that might be used to rate specific papers, and an "Expert," which provides expert teachers' ratings and explanations after the teachers have made their ratings and explanations. Another version of *ThinkAboutIt* that focuses on case studies in teaching currently is being developed and tested for use in our undergraduate teacher education classes. In this implementation, students can review written or video cases on a variety of topics ranging from classroom discipline to test use, receive scaffolding and coaching from experienced teachers, make and explain their choices, look at their peers' choices and explanations, and receive feedback from experts. We expect that results from these studies will provide more detailed information on the effectiveness of both self-explanation and user interaction in promoting deeper learning.

REFERENCES

Barron, B. (2000). Problem solving in video-based microworlds: Collaborative and individual outcomes of high-achieving sixth-grade students. *Journal of Educational Psychology, 92*, 391–398.

Bonk, C., Daytner, K., Daytner, G., Dennen, V., & Malikowski, S. (1999). *Online mentoring of preservice teacher with Web-based cases, conversations, and collaborations: Two years in review.* Paper presented at the annual meeting of American Educational Research Association, Montreal.

Bransford, J., Brown, A. L., & Cocking, R. R. (1999). *How people learn: Brain, mind, experience, and school.* Washington, DC: National Academy Press.

Brown, A., & Campione, J. (1994). Guided discovery in a community of learners. In K. McGilly (Ed.), *Classroom lessons: Integrating cognitive theory and classroom* (pp. 229–270). Cambridge, MA: MIT Press.

Brown, A. L., & Campione, J. C. (1996). Psychological theory and the design of innovative learning environment: On procedures, principles, and systems. In L. Schauble & R. Glaser (Eds.), *Innovations in learning: New environments for education* (pp. 289–325). Mahwah, NJ: Erlbaum.

Chi, M. (2000). Self-explaining expository texts: The dual process of generating inferences and repairing mental models. In R. Glaser (Ed.), *Advances in instructional psychology: Educational design and cognitive science* (pp. 161–237). Mahwah, NJ: Erlbaum.

Chi, M., de Leeuw, N., Chiu, M., & LaVancher, C. (1994). Eliciting self-explanations improves understanding. *Cognitive Science, 18*, 439–477.

Cognition and Technology Group at Vanderbilt. (1997). *The Jasper project: Lessons in curriculum, instruction, assessment, and professional development.* Mahwah, NJ: Erlbaum.

Collins, A., Brown, J. S., & Newman, S. E. (1989). Cognitive apprenticeship: Teaching the craft of reading, writing mathematics. In L. B. Resnick (Ed.), *Knowing, learning, and instruction: Essays in honor of Robert Glaser* (pp. 453–494). Hillsdale, NJ: Erlbaum.

Deci, E.L., & Ryan, R.M. (1987). The support of autonomy and control of behavior. *Journal of Personality and Social Psychology, 53*, 1024–1037.

Gauvain, M. (2001). *The social context of cognitive development.* New York: Guilford Press.

Graesser, A. C., Singer, M., & Trabasso, T. (1994). Constructing inferences during narrative text comprehension. *Psychological Review, 101*(3), 371–395.

Grice, H. P. (1975). Logic and conversation. In P. Cole & J. L. Morgan (Eds.), *Syntax and semantics* (pp. 41–49). New York: Academic Press.

Halpern, D. F. (1998). Teaching critical thinking for transfer across domains. *American Psychologist, 53*, 449–455.

Hewitt, J., & Scardamalia, M. (1998). Design principles for distributed knowledge building processes. *Educational Psychology Review, 10*(1), 75-96.

Jarvela, S., & Hakkinen, P. (2000). Levels of Web-based discussion: Theory of perspective-taking as a tool for analyzing interaction. In B. Fishman & S. O'Connor-Divelbiss (Eds.), *Fourth international conference of the learning sciences* (pp. 22–26). Mahwah, NJ: Erlbaum.

Kuhn, D. (1991). *Skills of argument.* Cambridge, UK: Cambridge University Press.

Lehman, S., Kauffman, D., White, M., Horn, C., & Bruning, R. (2001). Teacher interaction: Motivating at-risk students in Web-based high school courses. *Journal of Research on Technology in Education, 33* [Online]. Retrieved from http://www.iste.org/jrte/33/5/lehman_s.html

Lehman, S., & Schraw, G. (2002). Effects of coherence and relevance on shallow and deeper levels of text processing. *Journal of Educational Psychology, 94*, 738–750.

Scardamalia, M., & Bereiter, C. (1996). Computer support for knowledge-building communities. In T. Koschmann (Ed.), *CSCL: Theory and practice of an emerging paradigm.* Mahwah, NJ: Erlbaum.

Stahl, G. (2000). A model of collaborative knowledge building. In B. Fishman & S. O'Connor-Divelbiss (Eds.), *Levels of Web-based discussion: Theory of perspective-taking as a tool for analyzing interaction* (pp. 70–77). Mahwah, NJ: Erlbaum.

Stapleton, P. (2001). Assessing critical thinking in the writing of Japanese university students. *Written Communication, 18*, 506–548.

Toulmin, S. (1969). *The uses of argument.* Cambridge, UK: Cambridge University Press.

Willoughby, T., Wood, E., Desmarais, S., Sims, S., & Kalra, M. (1997). Mechanisms that facilitate the effectiveness of elaborative strategies. *Journal of Educational Psychology, 89*, 682–685.

AUTHOR NOTE

This research was made possible by a grant from the U.S. Department of Education to the CLASS project, University of Nebraska–Lincoln. Opinions expressed are those of the authors and not necessarily those of the funders. We would like to express our appreciation to several individuals who contributed significantly to the success of the project: to Sara Moshman and George Krueger of Metalogic, Inc., for exceptional programming and database management of the current sites; to Mary Jane White, Brent Igo, and Chad Buckendahl, for their contributions to the content of the units; and to Jeremy Sydik and Bill Udell, for their programming of early prototypes of the NRT unit.

Correspondence regarding this chapter should be sent to Steve Lehman at the Department of Psychology, 2810 Old Main Hill, Utah State University, Logan, UT 84322-2810, or by email at slehman@coe.usu.edu

CHAPTER 6

TEACHERS, TECHNOLOGY, AND STUDENTS AT RISK

Lisa M. PytlikZillig
Christy A. Horn
Center for Instructional Innovation,
University of Nebraska–Lincoln

Mary Jane White
University of Minnesota, Twin Cities

ABSTRACT

Little is known about how teachers use technology with at-risk students. To investigate technology use as it pertains to students at risk, we conducted a survey of teacher observations and recommendations. Teachers also reported numerous individual-difference variables, including their extent of experience working with students characterized by different types of risks. Results revealed three major findings. First, despite current thinking about how to best motivate at-risk students, teacher-reported observations implied the use of simple and remedial (rather than more complex) technologies by at-risk students. Second, teacher recommendations emphasized simple and remedial technology with special education and other students at risk, but teachers were more likely to recommend complex computer-mediated func-

Web-Based Learning: What Do We Know? Where Do We Go?, pages 105–127
Copyright © 2003 by Information Age Publishing

tions for gifted and general education students. Third, teacher observations and recommendations were generally unrelated, and there were few predictors of the extent to which teachers were likely to make complex recommendations. We discuss potential reasons for the discrepancies between research-based recommendations and teacher recommendations for the use of technology with at-risk students, as well as the need for future research.

The test of our progress is not whether we add more to the abundance of those who have much; it is whether we provide enough for those who have too little."

—Franklin D. Roosevelt

Given the ubiquitous presence of technology in our world today, it makes sense that teachers who are concerned with helping *all* students succeed—regardless of background, disability, or current environment—might like to use technology to assist students at risk for academic failure (see, e.g., Enwefa & Enwefa, 2002). The importance of the effective use of technology with at-risk students is illustrated by the quote above, which suggests that the true measure of the success with which we use technology in education lies not in the learning gains of average or gifted students, but in the learning gains achieved by at-risk students.

Are educators using technology in a manner that enhances the learning of students at risk? Before that question can be resolved, two other questions must be answered: How *should* teachers use technology with students at risk? And how *are* teachers using technology with such students? This chapter is concerned with both of these questions. In addition, this chapter is concerned with the teacher, environment, and student characteristics that may contribute to the variety of ways teachers use technology with students at risk, and that may help us understand why teachers do or do not use technology in a manner that is consistent with current research-based recommendations.

In this chapter, we highlight some of the findings from prior studies of teacher technology use—especially regarding technology use with students at risk—and we present the results of a survey designed to build on that research. We emphasize three themes throughout this chapter. First, we describe teacher technology use patterns and note a discrepancy between those use patterns and current research-based recommendations for teaching students at risk. Second, we observe that prior studies have investigated teacher use of technology, but have not examined teacher technology use *recommendations*. Examinations of teacher recommendations, however, could help pinpoint why teacher technology use patterns sometimes conflict with research-based recommendations. Third, we note that research on students at risk often does not give detailed consideration to the diverse impacts that different risk characteristics may have on students. We examine the possibility that teachers do differentiate between different types of risk, and we explore whether different levels of experience with different types of students at risk affect teacher observations of and recommendations for technology use with at-risk students.

PRIOR STUDIES OF TEACHER USE OF TECHNOLOGY IN THE CLASSROOM

Currently, very little is known about how teachers use technology in their classrooms, whether it be with students in general, or with at-risk students in particular. In 1999, Levin, Stephens, Kirshstein, and Birman declared that "empirical data about current uses and outcomes of technology are woefully lacking" (p. 23). Following that declaration, a few surveys and reports such as the "Teachers' Tools for the 21st Century" published by the National Center for Education Statistics (NCES) in 2000, have focused on a variety of factors relating to teacher use of technology, and have provided a partial remedy to that lack of research.

The NCES (2000) report and other studies have found several interesting predictors of teacher classroom technology use. For example, teacher use of technology sometimes depends on school-level factors such as poverty level and racial composition (Durán, 2002), as well as on class-level factors such as grade level and student achievement level (e.g., Durán, 2002; Pierson, 2001). Studies have also implicated the importance of teacher individual differences. Some researchers have found that technology use is influenced by teacher pedagogical experience, attitudes toward information technology, and experience and training with technology (e.g., Monaghan, 1993; NCES, 2000; Pierson, 2001).

Because technology can be used in a variety of ways that may variably impact learning, some specific attention has focused on the factors that predict teacher choice of different computer applications. In decisions concerning the use of complex software, teachers appear to rely on judgments of technology utility that take into account both the subject matter and student ability or potential (Durán, 2002; Ravitz, Becker, & Wong, 2000). Becker and Riel (2000), for example, found that teachers working with high-achieving students reported using more high-level software (e.g., spreadsheets, presentation software) than teachers working with lower achieving students. Meanwhile, teachers working with lower achieving students reported the greater use of game software. In addition, teachers have been found to use technology in more constructivist-oriented ways if they perceive themselves to be working with a high-achieving class of students. However, this is less true if teachers are working in high-poverty schools.

Importantly, it has been noted that this last finding may be due to the fewer resources available in high-poverty schools, rather than teachers having a different perception of students in high-poverty schools (Durán, 2002). It is common for researchers and others to wonder if lack of access might explain demographically related variations in technology use (e.g., see Durán, 2002; Jolly & Horn, Chapter 3, this volume; NCES, 2000). However, there is evidence that even when access is not an issue, teachers in high-minority and high-poverty schools use the computer in a less diverse manner (NCES, 2000). Students in such schools also are generally less likely to be asked by their teachers to use the Internet for the complex tasks of research, visual presentations, simulations, or multimedia projects (Durán, 2002; Meyer, 2001).

More recently, however, Durán (2002) has persuasively asserted that more specific and detailed reports are still needed before we can say that we have really described technology use in various areas and, more importantly, that we really understand its impact on the learning of at-risk students. One reason why Durán argues that additional investigations of classroom technology use are needed is that prior, large-scale surveys have sometimes revealed complex and confusing relationships between technology and other variables. For example, Wenglinsky (1998) reported the surprising finding that a greater frequency of computer use negatively predicted achievement on National Assessment of Educational Progress (NAEP) math tests after controlling for important background variables. However, Durán observed that teacher use of computers to teach lower-level skills also predicted lower NAEP math scores, and speculated that teachers may have chosen software focusing on lower-level skills in order to accommodate their lower achieving students. Unfortunately, without data on student prior achievement, it could not be determined whether student characteristics or computer use was driving the relationship. Large-scale survey studies, although useful for uncovering technology's broad mediating effects, may sometimes hide as much as they illuminate (Durán, 2002)—especially if they fail to assess important specific characteristics of the teachers, students, learning environment, and technology use in that environment. Therefore, in the present study, we assessed numerous teacher and student characteristics as part of our investigation of technology use by students at risk versus not at risk for academic failure.

RESEARCH-BASED RECOMMENDATIONS FOR TECHNOLOGY USE WITH AT-RISK STUDENTS

Findings such as those reviewed above, indicating the lesser use of complex technologies and the greater use of simple technologies in schools comprised largely of students labeled as "at risk," are important in light of current recommendations for teaching at-risk students. For example, it has been noted that lower-level tasks such as those typically associated with skill and practice software can fail to motivate students and fail to promote complex cognition (e.g., DiCintio & Gee, 1999; Means & Knapp, 1991). To the extent that a "basic" task is low level, teacher controlled, and routine, it may place at-risk students at even higher risk for failure by undermining their motivation, presumably by boring them and thwarting their needs for autonomy and higher levels of valued competence (Deci & Ryan, 2000). Other studies further suggest that the overuse of technology for basic skill and practice exercises may negatively impact teacher–student and student–student interactions that might otherwise facilitate motivational and learning processes (see, e.g., Horn, PytlikZillig, Bruning, & Kauffman, Chapter 7, this volume; Lehman, Kauffman, White, Horn, & Bruning, 2001).

In general, research-based recommendations currently suggest that teachers should assign higher level tasks that at-risk students can personalize, and that integrate basic skills learning with the opportunity to exercise higher-order thinking skills. Other suggestions for working with at-risk students include the assignment of authentic, real-world tasks offering choices and challenges in a context that facilitates the collaboration of students of varying ability levels (DiCintio & Gee, 1999; Means, 1997). Meanwhile, the overuse of technology for simple or remedial tasks has been criticized, especially for students who may be at risk due to motivational, not learning, deficits (e.g., DiCintio & Gee, 1999).

TEACHER RECOMMENDATIONS FOR TECHNOLOGY USE WITH STUDENTS AT RISK

One question that is not often investigated is whether or not teacher recommendations are consistent with research-based recommendations. Just as intention can be distinguished from behavior (e.g., Ajzen, 1996), teacher beliefs and preferences (e.g., as reflected in their recommendations for the use of technology with students) may be distinguished from observations of teacher behavior (e.g., use of technology with their students). A divergence between research-based recommendations and the observed use of technology by students at risk could be attributable to a large number of factors. An investigation of teacher recommendations could rule out or implicate the role of teacher beliefs. If teacher recommendations are consistent with research, the divergence between those recommendations and actual use of technology with students at risk may be due to access, choices made by students, institutional barriers, or other factors. Meanwhile, findings that teacher recommendations are inconsistent with research-based recommendations may imply teachers' lack of awareness or rejection of current recommendations.

Rejection of or disregard for research-based recommendations could occur for a variety of reasons. For example, teachers could feel that the research-based recommendations are not relevant because they rarely think of themselves as working with "at-risk" students in general. As some have noted, it is very difficult to characterize a typical member of any group of students at risk (Payne & Payne, 1991; Rumberger, 1987). Thus, teachers may conceptualize their work with at-risk students at a more fine-grained level, and see themselves as working with individual students who may be specifically classified as learning disabled, undermotivated, physically challenged, and so on. If teachers conceptualize at-risk students at this more fine-grained level, their recommendations for technology use by students at risk may also vary depending on the nature of the risks that they see as most characteristic of their students.

RESEARCH-BASED CONCEPTUALIZATIONS OF THE TERM "AT-RISK"

Researchers, on the other hand, typically have made little effort to systematically distinguish between different categories of risk characteristics in their studies. The concept of *academic risk* has been used quite broadly by educational researchers as a way to identify and address the needs of students facing a wide variety of educational, social, and familial difficulties that impede academic success (Council of Chief State School Officers, 1987; Mendrinos, 1997). Some experts characterize the at-risk population by factors such as the lack of basic academic and literacy skills, lack of a stable and non-turbulent home life, and feelings of alienation at school (e.g., Gentile & McMillan, 1991). Others have focused on the nature of other barriers to academic success, defining at-risk students as those in danger of failing to complete their education with the skills necessary to function in a modern technological society (e.g., Slavin, Karweit, & Madden, 1989). Still others have asserted,

> Students are not "at risk," but are placed at risk by adults.... Students are placed "at risk" when they experience a significant *mismatch* between their circumstances and needs, and the capacity or willingness of the school to accept, accommodate, and respond to them in a manner that supports and enables their maximum social, emotional, and intellectual growth and development. (Hixson, 1993, emphasis added; see also Bruner, 1996)

Given the variability of potential academic risk factors, it would seem that the first step in the accommodation of "mismatched" students at risk should be the clarification of who they are and what specific factors place them at risk for which academic problems. In fact, the most appropriate and effective response to students at risk may vary and depend upon the risk factors that pertain to different students, suggesting that the recommended uses of technology may vary depending on students' unique risk characteristics. For example, while students at risk due to factors affecting their motivation may benefit from the application of the research-based recommendations discussed above, perhaps different technological applications are more appropriate for students at risk due to learning disabilities or due to a lack of access to technology. Currently, however, there is a tendency to treat academic risk in a rather stereotypical fashion. For example, politicians, administrators, and others often automatically categorize students attending rural schools as at risk (e.g., Dean, 2000; Sack, 1999), in part because of the lack of support services in many rural areas.

THE PRESENT STUDY

The present study was designed to help address the lack of research on classroom technology use with and by students at risk. We surveyed teachers from across Nebraska in order to examine three major questions. First, we examined teacher-reported observations of at-risk student use of technology in order to see if previous patterns of technology use (i.e., the use of simpler technologies with and by students at risk) would be found in our sample, and to explore predictors of those observations. Second, we examined teacher-reported recommendations for the use of technology by at-risk and not-at-risk students in order to assess whether their recommendations were consistent with teacher-reported observations and/or current research-based recommendations. When investigating teacher recommendations, we also specifically differentiated special education students from other students at risk. Finally, we focused on risk categories at an even more fine-grained level. Using factor analyses, we examined the possibility that teachers distinguish between different major categories of risk, and we explored whether teacher observations and recommendations of technology use were related to individual differences in teachers' levels of experience with different *types* of students at risk.

METHODS

Our first step was to clarify what it means, according to youth professionals, to be an "at-risk" student in Nebraska. In June and July of 1998, we held five focus groups across the state, involving a total of 27 teachers and community service workers with experience working with at-risk youth. Prior to attending, participants were asked to independently brainstorm answers to the question, "What are the factors that create barriers to educational success?" Participant answers were collected and individually printed on cards before the focus group meeting, at which participants received the stack of risk characteristics generated by the members of their group. Individuals were then asked to sort the cards into categories and to assign a descriptor to each pile that would capture the essence of the similarities of the risk characteristics it contained. The focus group meetings resulted in the compilation of a list of over 100 risk characteristics that provided the basis for the formation of 32 risk characteristic categories.[1]

Survey Measures

We next created a seven-page survey to assess teacher observations of the use of technology by and with students at risk, teacher recommendations for technology use with students at risk, and teacher experience with different types of students at risk. In addition, the survey assessed a variety of other teacher individual-difference variables that have been found to predict technology use in prior studies.

Teacher observations of technology use by students at risk

Based on prior literature distinguishing between complex and basic technology use (e.g., DiCiento & Gee, 1999; Durán, 2002; Means, 1997), our survey included questions pertaining to a list of 13 computer-mediated functions (hereafter, CMFs) of varied complexity.[2] Specifically, teachers were asked to report (a) the extent to which they observed students at risk using each CMF, and (b) whether or not they had observed students at risk using the computer for each function while they were working with them on the computer. Response options for the first question ranged from never observed = 1, observed 1–5 times per year = 2, observed 1–5 times per month = 3, observed 1–5 times per week = 4, to observed 1–5 times per day = 5. For some analyses, we used variables reflecting the mean *extent of observed simple* (five items, Cronbach's α = .81) and *complex* (eight items, Cronbach's α = .87) *CMF use* by students at risk.

Teacher recommendations of technology use for at-risk and other students

Using the same list of 13 CMFs that were used for the observation data, teachers also were asked to report their personal recommendations of the CMFs that would most benefit different students (identified as special education, at-risk, gifted, or general education students). Specifically, teachers were asked to write a check mark next to the CMFs (presented in list form) that would most benefit students in each of the four student categories. In addition to examining specific teacher recommendations, we also created variables reflecting the *number of complex technologies recommended* for each category of student (at risk, gifted, general education, and special education; mean Cronbach's α of these scales was .83). However, it is important to note that there was unintended ambiguity in the wording of this survey question. First, the question instructed respondents to "identify the five computer-mediated functions" that would most benefit students in each category. Meanwhile, the end of the instruction read, "check all that apply." As discussed in the results section, we dealt with this issue by conducting separate analyses for teachers who chose five or fewer recommendations for each category, and for teachers who chose more than five recommendations for one or more student categories.

Teacher-reported experience with different types of students at risk

We used the 32 risk characteristic categories obtained from the focus groups to construct a measure of teacher-reported levels of experience with different types of students at risk. Specifically, teachers were given the following instruction: "Using the following scale from 0 (no experience) to 100 (extensive experience), please rate your level of experience working with students identified by or exposed to these risk factors." Following this instruction was the list of 32 risk characteristics and a 0–100 anchored response scale. The anchoring descriptors for the scale were as follows: "no experience" (corresponding to ratings of 0), "little experience" (corresponding to ratings of 20–30), "average experience" (ratings of about 50), "above average experience" (ratings of 70–80), and "extensive experience" (100).

Other survey scales and items

In addition to the above measures, our survey included multi-item scales assessing the following teacher individual differences:

- *Technology experience* was assessed by asking teachers to rate their level of experience with 14 different types of technology, and then averaging across items ($\alpha = .88$).
- *Positive attitudes toward technology* (e.g., "I like working with computers"), including the use of technology for instructional purposes (e.g., "The use of computers enhances teacher effectiveness"), were

assessed by averaging across teacher-rated agreement with eight items ($\alpha = .89$).

- *Self-efficacy for teaching with technology* (the extent to which teachers felt able to use technology in the classroom) was assessed with three items (e.g., "I successfully incorporate computer-based educational technology in my classroom," $\alpha = .93$).

- *Self-efficacy for working with students at risk* was assessed with four items (e.g., "I am successful when working with students at risk," $\alpha = .94$).

- *Positive and negative observations of at-risk student technology use* were assessed by measuring teacher agreement with statements of positive observations (seven items, $\alpha = .84$) and negative observations (four items, $\alpha = .66$), using questions in the following form: "In general, when students at risk use computer-based technology in my classroom, they" (stem): "Have difficulty understanding how to use technology" (example negative item), "Seem determined to learn" (example positive item).

- *Perceived administrative support for the use of technology* was assessed with four items (e.g., "I have received adequate training for using computer-mediated instructional technology in my classroom" and "My administrator listens to teachers' concerns regarding computer-mediated instruction," $\alpha = .55$). However, the low reliability for this scale suggested caution in its use.

Finally, the survey included individual items designed to assess the following other teacher-level variables:

- *Background/demographics* (e.g., gender, race/ethnicity, teaching grade level, years teaching, subjects taught, position, level of formal education).

- *Extent of home, school, and classroom computer use* (e.g., "Approximately how often do you use the computer at home?" This item had response options ranging from "Once or more daily" to "I don't have a computer at home").

- *Approximate level of in-school involvement with students at risk* (in terms of hours per week spent with students at risk).

- *Rated accessibility of computer-based technology* for at-risk and other groups of students at their school (response options ranging from 1 = no access to 5 = easy access).

- *Approximate number of Internet-ready computers* available at school.

Procedures

Postcards inviting participation in an online version of the survey were distributed to over 1,500 Nebraska teachers in August 1999. Only 86 teachers responded to that first call, and their data were used to make revisions and additions to the survey prior to a second mailing (in October) to all participants who had not responded to the initial invitation. In the second survey administration, in which teachers were given the option of either responding online or on paper, response rates increased to 20%.

All teachers were asked to complete the portion of the survey that assessed background/demographic characteristics, computer experience and use, beliefs about technology, experience with students at risk, and number of Internet-ready computers. Directions within the survey asked participants to complete the other survey items only if they had some experience working with students at risk and if they had worked with some form of computer-based technology. This resulted in 36 teachers who refrained from answering the remainder of the survey questions.

Participants

A total of 306 teachers responded to the second survey. Most respondents (97%) were full-time teachers. A total of 35 submitted their information online, while 271 responded by mail. The teachers represented 41 of Nebraska's 93 school districts and had 1 to 42 years ($M = 18$ years, $SD = 9.3$) of teaching experience. The vast majority (97%) were white, approximately half (52%) were female, and 64% were from rural schools.

RESULTS AND DISCUSSION

In this section we present and discuss the major results from our survey, as they pertain to the three themes reviewed in the introduction. First, we find that in spite of current research-based warnings and recommendations for the use of technology with at-risk students (e.g., DiCiento & Gee, 1999; Means, 1997), teachers observe students at risk to be using simple computer-mediated functions (CMFs) more than complex CMFs. Second, independent of these observations, teachers offer recommendations that generally favor simple technology use by students at risk. Meanwhile, teachers recommend that other (gifted and general education) students use more complex CMFs. Third, teachers do seem to distinguish between different categories of students at risk. In this study, however, neither those distinctions, nor teacher observations, nor other teacher individual differences were strongly related to technology-use recommendations.

Descriptive Results

Teacher observations of technology use by students at risk.

It is no longer taken for granted that students must learn "basic" knowledge such as facts and definitions before they are able to engage in and practice "advanced" complex thinking skills such as evaluation and problem solving (Means & Knapp, 1991). Means (1997) notes, for example, that technology could be used to help at-risk students complete more complex and meaningful tasks, thereby enhancing student motivation, as well as complex thinking (e.g., as described by Durán, 2002). Despite these research-based recommendations, teachers in our sample reported observing students at risk using simple and remedial CMFs significantly more often than complex ones. As shown in Table 6.1, teachers tended to report more observations of students at risk engaging in simple applications (i.e., written text and organization functions, see Enwefa & Enwefa, 2002) or remedial computer-mediated activities, as opposed to complex applications (e.g., gathering data, creating models or simulations).[3] Furthermore, a paired *t*-test comparing the average complex and simple mean levels of observations revealed a significant difference: On average, teachers reported observing at-risk students using the simple CMFs somewhat more than one to five times per year, but using the complex CMFs (especially the creation of visual models and displays) fewer than one to five times per year. In addition, compared to observations of complex function use, teachers reported that the observations of basic computer activities occurred more often while the teacher was working with the student on the computer.

Teacher technology use recommendations

Consistent with the observational data, teacher recommendations for the use of technology with students at risk showed an overall pattern that was inconsistent with current research-based recommendations. As shown in Table 6.2, teachers tended to recommend simpler or remedial CMFs for at-risk and special education students, but more complex CMFs for general education and gifted students. At times the differences were striking. For example, an additional 50% of the teachers in our sample recommended the use of technology for remedial purposes when working with at-risk students (even though special education students were rated separately) than when working with gifted students. If one looks at the number of highly endorsed CMFs, one sees that seven of the eight complex CMFs were

**Table 6.1.   Teacher Observations of Computer Use
by At-Risk Students**

Teacher-observed computer-mediated functions (CMFs)	Mean[a]	SD	% obs. while working with student(s)[a]
Visual models and displays (complex)			
Create models or simulations	1.52	0.78	7%
Create graphics, diagrams, or pictures	1.95	0.87	19%
Create visual displays of data/information	1.93	0.83	20%
Create visual presentations	1.77	0.81	15%
Data and results (complex)			
Collect data/perform measurements	2.02	0.94	22%
Manipulate/analyze/interpret data	2.04	0.89	24%
Communicate results of investigations	2.23	0.88	26%
Perform calculations	2.07	1.22	14%
Writing and organizing (simple/basic)			
Written text functions (plan, draft, proof)	2.37	0.97	37%
Organize and store information	2.29	0.97	27%
Compensation (simple/remedial)			
Support individualized learning	2.19	1.07	23%
Remediation of basic skills	2.18	1.17	24%
Compensate for a disability or limitation	2.06	1.15	20%
Mean across all eight complex CMFs	1.94[b]	0.66	18% [c]
Mean across all five simple CMFs	2.21[b]	0.80	27% [c]

Notes. $N = 258$ to 263. CMF = Computer-mediated function.
[a] Ordinal response options were 1 = never observed, 2 = observed 1–5 times per year, 3 = observed 1–5 times per month, 4 = observed 1–5 times per week, and 5 = observed 1–5 times per day. The last column, "% obs while working with student," denotes percent of teachers who affirmed that their reported observations of a CMF occurred while he/she was working on the computer with an at-risk student.
[b] Paired $t(254) = 6.76$, $p < .001$.
[c] Paired $t(261) = 4.97$, $p < .001$.

endorsed by at least 60% of the teachers as beneficial for gifted students and five complex CMFs were endorsed at this level as beneficial for general education students, but *none* of the complex CMFs were endorsed at this level for either the at-risk or the special education students. Comparison of the number of complex technologies recommended for each group (see bottom of Table 6.2) also revealed that the greatest number were recommended for gifted students, followed by general education students and students at risk, with the fewest complex technologies recommended for special education students. Paired *t*-test comparisons between student types were all highly significant (p < .001).

Table 6.2.   Teacher Recommendations for Technology Use by Different Classes of Students

Teacher-recommended computer-mediated functions (CMFs)	Gifted	Gen. ed.	At risk	Spec. ed.
Visual models and displays (complex)				
Create models or simulations	**72%**	49%	40%	32%
Create graphics, diagrams, or pictures	**61%**	54%	53%	42%
Create visual displays of data/information	**72%**	**66%**	58%	46%
Create visual presentations	**71%**	**63%**	53%	43%
Data and results (complex)				
Collect data/perform measurements	**60%**	**66%**	53%	40%
Manipulate/analyze/interpret data	**76%**	**64%**	50%	31%
Communicate results of investigations	**71%**	**74%**	59%	41%
Perform calculations	46%	49%	50%	49%
Writing and organizing (simple/basic)				
Written text functions (plan, draft, proof)	**67%**	**81%**	**72%**	**64%**
Organize and store information	55%	**84%**	**74%**	**69%**
Compensation (simple/remedial)				
Support individualized learning	58%	59%	**70%**	**72%**
Remediation of basic skills	19%	46%	**69%**	**77%**
Compensate for a disability or limitation	22%	34%	50%	**80%**
Mean number of complex recommendations [a]	5.30	4.83	4.17	3.35
SD number of complex recommendations	(2.33)	(2.56)	(2.85)	(2.71)

Notes. Items under the same heading loaded on the same factor in a principal components factor analysis with varimax rotation (factor analysis of teacher observations from Table 6.1). Percentages above 60% are in bold. Gen ed. = General education, Spec. ed. = Special education.
[a] Paired *t*-tests of number of complex recommendations were all significant (*t*s > 4.9, df = 258, *p* < .001).

The reader will recall that the teacher recommendation data in Table 6.2 were obtained by asking teachers to simply write a check mark next to the CMFs (presented in list form) that would most benefit students in each of four categories: gifted, general education, special education, and at-risk students. The unintended ambiguity in the wording of this question (see "Methods"), however, could have influenced the patterns of data just described. Therefore, we conducted additional analyses to see if the pattern of recommendations was consistent across respondents who made "up to five" recommendations versus those who checked next to "all that apply." Supporting the generalizability of our results, the pattern of recommendations was very similar across both groups. In fact, the recommendations made by each group were highly correlated ($r = .81$).[4]

Our finding—that teachers recommended a greater number of complex technologies for gifted and general education students than for students at risk or in special education programs—builds on prior research conducted at the school level. Our findings are consistent with other research (e.g., Becker & Riel, 2000) suggesting that teachers who teach in schools with greater proportions of students at risk are likely to use technology for simpler purposes. In addition, our findings suggest that within schools or classrooms teachers may recommend that their at-risk students use technology for simpler, more basic, and remedial purposes than their gifted or general education students. In contrast, research-based recommendations support motivating students at risk with the use of complex CMFs, and warn against the overuse of remedial and potentially demotivating CMFs. The potential motivational detriment associated with overly simple technology use is important in light of the fact that most of the risk factors obtained from the focus groups seemed more relevant to student motivation than ability.

It is possible, however, that the general patterns of teacher observations and recommendations that we found might be moderated by other factors such as specific experience with different types of students at risk or technology access. Indeed, as shown in Table 6.2, the tendency to recommend more simple CMFs and fewer complex CMFs was more accentuated for "special education" students than for generally "at-risk" students. Therefore, we next discuss teacher-reported experiences with students at risk. Following that discussion, we report those variables found to be predictive of teacher observations and recommendations.

Teacher experience with different types of students at risk

To explore teachers' experiences with different categories of students at risk, we examined both the factor structure and mean levels of teacher-reported levels of experience with the 32 different categories of risk. Due to space constraints, we only briefly summarize those results here.

First, a principal components factor analysis of teacher ratings of the 32 risk category items revealed only one general factor according to the scree plot, but six factors with eigenvalues > 1. Thus, there was evidence both that teachers tended to perceive themselves as having more versus less experience with students *generally* at risk (evidenced by the general factor observed in the scree plot), and that teachers make at least some distinctions between *specific* types of students at risk. An examination of the varimax rotated six-factor solution revealed that major risk categories included characteristics associated with (1) students' home environments or personal histories (e.g., divorce, abuse), (2) social-environmental factors (e.g., homelessness, gangs), (3) limited school/community resources, (4) disabilities (including learning, behavioral, and physical disabilities), (5) teacher–student factors (e.g., high student–teacher ratios, overworked teachers), and (6) student–student factors (e.g., excessive competition, prejudice). While future research is needed to determine the utility and replicability of such risk factors, simple correlations between these at-risk experience factor scores and other study variables did reveal preliminary support for the validity of the scores. For example, higher experience with students at risk due to relative lack of school and community resources was negatively correlated with the reported number of Internet-ready computers available ($r = -.21$, p < .001), and higher experience with students at risk due to teacher–student factors (e.g., high student–teacher ratios, overworked teachers) was negatively related to perceived administrative support for technology use ($r = -.16$, p < .05). Thus, the orthogonal regressed factor scores for each of the six at-risk experience factors were saved as new variables for use in subsequent analyses.

Next, we examined teacher endorsement of specific risk characteristics. Teachers reported moderately high experience with students exposed to individual-level and family-related risk factors that might place students at risk for failure by interfering with their motivation. In fact, some of the most highly endorsed characteristics included characteristics relevant to student home environment/personal history, disabling factors, and teacher–student factors. On the other hand, teachers reported less experience with social-environmental, school/community, and student–student risk factors; and teachers reported the highest levels of experience with risks stemming from learning disabilities ($M = 65$ on the 100-point scale) and exposure to overworked teachers ($M = 67$). Paired t-tests revealed that the teachers rated experience with learning disabilities significantly higher than each of the other risk factors except for exposure to overworked teachers. Meanwhile, experience with other ability-related factors such as low IQ ($M = 42$) and illiteracy ($M = 34$) were given lower ratings.

This pattern of mean ratings suggests that teachers in our sample often saw themselves as struggling to meet the needs of a great variety of at-risk students, including both students faced with risks due to motivation-affecting factors and those at risk due to learning and other disabilities. When thinking about students at risk, teachers may see themselves, at least in part, as focused on finding ways to efficiently remedy the learning of students with learning disabilities and/or students who are academically behind their peers. Perhaps it is no surprise then that teachers in our sample recommended and observed at-risk students using simpler CMFs. After all, simple skill and practice software often promises, or may be assumed to promise, both time-saving and remedial advantages. However, the fact that teachers on average both observe and recommend that students at risk use simpler CMFs does not automatically mean that those observations and recommendations are related. Nor does it mean that their recommendations and observations are caused by certain experiences with at-risk students rather than other factors. To explore these possibilities we needed to look at the relationships among variables, not merely at the descriptive results. We turn to those results next.

Correlational Results

Teacher observations of technology use by students at risk

Table 6.3 shows the correlations between teacher observations, teacher recommendations of complex CMFs for at-risk and other students, teacher experience with different risk factors, and other study variables. While our data could not definitively answer "why" teachers observe students at risk using simple CMFs more than complex ones, some insight might be gained by examining the relationships in Table 6.3. Do the correlational results suggest that teachers who observe simple CMF use by at-risk students are recommending such use? No. While teachers who observed at-risk students more frequently using simple CMFs were also likely to observe them using complex CMFs ($r = .63$), those teachers most highly recommending that students at risk use complex computer-mediated functions were no more likely than other teachers to observe high levels of simple or complex technology use by their students at risk ($rs < .10$, $ps > .60$). These findings suggest that teacher recommendations are not being directly translated into student behavior.

Several other variables did predict teacher observations. As shown in the far left columns of Table 6.3, both the observed complex and simple use of technology by students at risk were positively predicted by variables such as teacher experience with technology, positive attitudes toward technology, experience with students at risk due to home/environment factors, and efficacy for working with technology and students at risk. In addition, higher levels of perceived administrative support and involvement with students at risk positively predicted observed simple CMF use. Meanwhile, the number of Internet-ready computers available for use in the school slightly and positively predicted observed complex computer use by at-risk students,

Table 6.3. Correlations between Teacher Observations, Teacher Recommendations, and Other Study Variables

Variables	Observed CMF use		Complex CMF recommendations			
	Complex (at risk)	Simple (at risk)	Gifted	General ed.	At risk	Special ed.
Teacher observations of at-risk students						
Observed complex CMF use	—	.63**	−.03	.03	.05	.03
Observed simple CMF use	.63**	—	−.03	−.03	.02	−.01
Complex CMF recommendations						
For gifted students	−.03	−.03	—	.81**	.79**	.65**
For general education students	.03	−.03	.81**	—	.85**	.72**
For at-risk students	.05	.02	.79**	.85**	—	.79**
For special education students	.03	−.01	.65**	.72**	.79**	—
Orthogonal risk experience factors						
Home environment/personal history	.16*	.28**	.01	−.01	.11	.03
Social-environmental factors	.08	.01	−.06	−.03	−.05	−.06
Limited school/community resources	.07	.02	.11	.07	.05	.00
Student disabilities	.08	.14*	.09	.08	.05	.08
Teacher–student factors	−.06	−.02	−.02	−.02	−.01	−.02
Student–student factors	.12	.09	.16*	.17*	.19*	.17*
Other teacher individual differences						
Computer experience	.40**	.28**	.00	.12	.09	.12
Positive attitudes toward technology	.29**	.25**	.02	.08	.06	.08
Efficacy for using technology	.40**	.40**	−.01	.07	.06	.08
Efficacy for teaching at-risk students	.22**	.29**	.01	.00	.02	.02
Level of in-school involvement with at-risk students	.09	.15*	−.04	−.05	.03	−.04
Positive observations of at-risk technology use	.15*	.19**	−.11	−.08	−.06	.03
Negative observations of at-risk student technology use	−.14*	−.10	.03	−.03	−.08	−.12
Perceived administrative support	.12	.26**	.04	.04	.12	.16
Number of Internet-ready computers available	.14*	.08	−.09	−.01	.02	.02

Notes. Pairwise *N* = 235 to 275. Though overall results are shown here, correlations involving teacher recommendations are only starred if significant for both the "all that apply" and "up to five" instructional groups. CMF = Computer-mediated function.
** *p* < .01; * *p* < .05

but negative observations of at-risk students' use of technology negatively predicted these observations. Thus, teacher attitudes and efficacies do seem to be related to their observations, and may impact teacher use of complex and simple CMFs with at-risk students. However, those attitudes are not mediated by teacher recommendations for technology use as measured here. This suggests that it may not be enough for teachers to believe or recommend that at-risk students should use technology to enhance learning. In addition (or perhaps instead), teachers must have the administrative support and technology experience necessary to employ complex technologies with their at-risk students.[5]

Teacher technology use recommendations

If it were the case that teacher assumptions about technology and different types of students at risk were driving teacher recommendations for technology use, it might be expected that other teacher individual differences, such as attitudes toward technology or positive and negative observations of at-risk student use of technology, might predict teacher recommendations. However, our investigation of teacher individual differences found no variables robustly and highly predictive of teacher recommendations. While the recommendations themselves were substantially intercorrelated (rs generally above .50[6]), there was little support for the hypothesis that teachers may alter their recommendations based on different levels of experience with these different types of students. Only reports of high levels of experience with student–student risk factors generally (but slightly) predicted higher recommendations for the use of complex CMFs (rs = .16 to .19, ps < .05). Among the few other predictors of recommendations that emerged, there were different predictors for teachers who checked "five or fewer" versus "all" beneficial CMFs. For example, among teachers recommending five or fewer CMFs per group, teachers were somewhat more likely to recommend complex CMFs for at-risk students if they reported higher levels of experience with students at risk due to home environment/personal history risk factors ($r(108) = .19, p < .05$). While this seems positive in the sense that some teachers may be recommending that complex technology be used to motivate such students at risk, the effect size was small and was not significant among teachers who followed the "check all that apply" instruction.

Study Limitations

Because our survey provided only correlational data, alternative explanations for various patterns of results exist. For example, the independence of teacher recommendations and observations may be partly attributed to the fact that the survey question regarding teacher observations asked about students at risk in general, while the question regarding teacher recommendations explicitly asked teachers to make separate recommendations for special education students and students generally at risk. In addition, the observation data were retrospective reports. Retrospective data can be biased or inaccurate. Furthermore, it could be that teachers who have more experience with technology might report more computer use by *all* students, perhaps because they pay attention to, notice, and remember student use of technology to a greater extent than other teachers. Also, note that in order to make sure that the survey was of manageable length, the observation and recommendation questions referred to students at risk in general rather than to numerous specific categories of students at risk. It may be that teacher-reported observations and recommendations would have varied more predictably if the survey had explicitly asked teachers to consider specific categories of students at risk. Finally, with regard to teacher perceptions of student risk characteristics, it should be noted that the analysis of more objective measures of student risk characteristics might reveal a different structure (with different predictive abilities) than the current analysis of teacher-perceived risk characteristics.

CONCLUSION

The results of this study provide a valuable contribution to the current need for additional research on technology use in the classroom. One important finding is that students at risk may not be using technology in a manner that maximally enhances their motivation and learning, with many teachers not recommending that students at risk use complex CMFs to the same extent as other students. If teacher recommendations for and observations of technology use for students at risk are indeed unrelated, then remedies for the current situation may need to be multifaceted. To change teacher recommendations of technology use, it may be useful to increase teachers' awareness of current theory and research. However, because teacher recommendations may not automatically translate into actual technology use with students at risk, it may be necessary to provide additional administrative support and training for teachers that can increase their experience with technology and self-efficacy for working with students at risk. With the present results as a guide, the next steps for future research should be to conduct more formal observations of the use of technology with at-risk and other groups of students, to more clearly identify categories of risk having different implications for teaching and learning with technology, and to begin to study the actual outcomes of specific uses of technology with specific groups of students at risk.

REFERENCES

Ajzen, I. (1996). The social psychology of decision making. In E. T. Higgins & A. W. Kruglanski (Eds.), *Social psychology: Handbook of basic principles* (pp. 297–325). New York: Guilford Press.

Becker, H., & Riel, M. (2000). Teacher professional engagement and constructivist-compatible computer use. In *Teaching, learning, and computing: 1998 national survey* (Rep. No. 7). Irvine, CA & Minneapolis, MN: Center for Research on Information Technology and Organizations.

Bruner, J. (1996). *The culture of education*. Cambridge, MA: Harvard University Press.

Council of Chief State School Officers. (1987). *Characteristics of at risk students*. Washington, DC: Author.

Dean, K. (2000, April 12). *Kerrey's online learning torch* [Online]. Retrieved September 18, 2002, from http://www.wired.com/news/politics/0%2C1283%2C3554 7%2C00.html

Deci, E. L., & Ryan, R. M. (2000). The "what" and "why" of goal pursuits: Human needs and the self-determination of behavior. *Psychological Inquiry, 11*, 227–268.

DiCintio, M. J., & Gee, S. (1999). Control is the key: Unlocking the motivation of at-risk students. *Psychology in the Schools, 36*, 231–237.

Durán, R. P. (2002). Technology, education and at-risk students. In S. Stringfield & D. Land (Eds.), *Educating at-risk students* (pp. 210–230). Chicago: University of Chicago Press.

Enwefa, S. C., & Enwefa, R. L. (2002). The role of technology in the education of all children. In F. E. Obiakor, P. A. Grant, & Dooley, E. A. (Eds.), *Educating all learners: Refocusing the comprehensive support model* (pp. 166–178). Springfield, IL: Charles C Thomas.

Gentile, L. M., & McMillan, M. M. (1991). Reading, writing and relationships: The challenge of teaching at risk students. *Reading Research and Instruction, 30*, 74–81.

Hixson, J. (1993). *Redefining the issues: Who's at risk and why* [Online]. Retrieved September 18, 2002, from http://www.ncrel.org/sdrs/areas//issues/students/atrisk/at5def.htm

Lehman, S., Kauffman, D. F., White, M. J., Horn, C. A., & Bruning, R. H. (2001). Teacher interaction: Motivating at-risk students in Web-based high school courses. *Journal of Research on Technology in Education, 33*(5) [Online]. Retrieved September 18, 2002, from http://www.iste.org/jrte/33/5/lehman_s.html

Levin, D., Stephens, M., Kirshstein, R., & Birman, B. (1999). *Toward assessing the effectiveness of using technology in K–12 education*. Washington, DC: U.S. Department of Education, Office of Educational Research and Improvement.

Means, B. (1997). *Critical issue: Using technology to enhance engaged learning for at risk students* [Online]. Retrieved September 18, 2002, from http://www.ncrel.org/sdrs/areas//issues/students/atrisk/at400.htm

Means, B., & Knapp, M. S. (1991). Cognitive approaches to teaching advanced skills to educationally disadvantaged students. *Phi Delta Kappan, 73*, 282–289.

Mendrinos, R. B. (1997). *Using educational technology with at risk students: A guide for library media specialists and teachers*. Westport, CT: Greenwood Press.

Meyer, L. (2001, May). New challenges. *Education Week, 20*(35) [Online]. Retrieved September 18, 2002, from http://www.edweek.org/sreports/tc01/tc01article.cfm?slug=35challenges.h20

Monaghan, J. (1993). IT in mathematics initial teacher training: Factors influencing school experience. *Journal of Computer Assisted Learning, 9,* 149–160.

National Center for Education Statistics (NCES). (2000). *Teachers' tools for the 21st century* (NCES 2000-102) [Online]. Retrieved September 18, 2002, from http://nces.ed.gov/pubsearch/pubsinfo.asp?pubid=2000102

Payne, B. D., & Payne, D. A. (1991). The ability of teachers to identify academically at-risk elementary students. *Journal of Research in Childhood Education, 5,* 116–126.

Pierson, M. E. (2001). Technology integration practice as a function of pedagogical expertise. *Journal of Research on Computing in Education, 33*(4), 413–430.

Ravitz, J., Becker, H., & Wong, Y. T. (2000). *Constructivist-compatible beliefs and practices among U.S. teachers: 1998 National Survey* (Rep. No. 4). Irvine, CA: Center for Research on Information Technology and Organizations.

Rumberger, R. W. (1987). High school dropouts: A review of issues and evidence. *Review of Educational Research, 57*(2), 101–121.

Sack, J. L. (1999, June). Gifted students in rural schools often overlooked, according to new report. *Education Week, 18* [Online]. Retrieved September 18, 2002, from http://www.edweek.org/ew/vol-18/38gift.h18

Slavin, R. E., Karweit, N. L., & Madden, N. A. (1989). *Effective programs for students at risk.* Boston: Allyn & Bacon.

Wenglinsky, H. (1998). *Does it compute? The relationship between educational technology and student achievement in mathematics.* Princeton, NJ: Educational Testing Service, Policy Information Center.

AUTHOR NOTE

This work was made possible by a grant from the U.S. Department of Education to the CLASS Project, University of Nebraska–Lincoln. Opinions expressed are those of the authors and not necessarily those of the funders. We would like to express our appreciation to several individuals who contributed significantly to the success of this project: to Kathleen Barrett for her assistance with the focus groups; to Bill Udell for his programming work; to Roger Bruning, Mary Bodvarsson, and Xiongyi Lui for their assistance in the writing and editing of this article; and finally, our sincere appreciation to the teachers and community service workers who participated in our surveys.

Correspondence concerning this chapter should be addressed to Lisa PytlikZillig or Christy Horn at 209 TEAC, Center for Instructional Innovation, University of Nebraska–Lincoln, Lincoln, NE 68588-0384; or by email to lpytlik@unlserve.unl.edu or chorn@nebraska.edu

NOTES

1. List of risk categories are available from the authors.

2. The 13 computer-mediated functions (CMFs) are listed later in Tables 6.1 and 6.2.

3. The complex versus simple item groupings in Tables 6.1 and 6.2 were supported by a principal components factor analyses of the observation data reported in Table 6.1. A varimax-rotated four-factor solution revealed the first two factors (accounting for 21% of the variance each) as being defined by complex CMFs, with the highest loading items pertaining to the creation of visual models and displays (factor 1), and items relevant to data analysis and results (factor 2). The last two factors were primarily defined by the compensation/remediation and writing/organizing items (factors 3 and 4, respectively, accounting for 19% and 12% of the variance).

4. Note that in all subsequent analyses involving this survey item, we always checked for differences between the two groups of teachers (those following the "all that apply" vs. "up to five" instruction). Hereafter, we only note when the pattern of results differed between the groups. When the pattern was the same, we simply report the overall results.

5. Nonetheless, regression analyses examining the relationship between teacher recommendations and observations while controlling for variables such as computer experience and/or efficacy for using technology and working with students at risk never revealed a significant association between recommendations and observations.

6. For teachers recommending five or fewer technologies, correlations were lower because choice of one CMF reduced the probability that another CMF would be chosen.

CHAPTER 7

AT RISK IN CYBERSPACE

Responding to At-Risk Students
in Online Courses

Christy A. Horn
Lisa M. PytlikZillig
Roger Bruning
Center for Instructional Innovation,
University of Nebraska–Lincoln

Douglas F. Kauffman
University of Oklahoma

ABSTRACT

The primary goal of this chapter is to offer a set of preliminary recommendations for effective technology use with at-risk students. In two studies, one including in-depth observations and the other incorporating experimental methodology, we derive a set of recommendations and illustrate how they might be empirically tested and clarified. Results from the observation study indicate that technology can be used to effectively engage students but that at-risk student course engagement needs to be closely monitored, and stu-

Web-Based Learning: What Do We Know? Where Do We Go?, pages 129–152
Copyright © 2003 by Information Age Publishing

dents need to be provided with feedback on their self-regulatory activities. We also found that technology frustration and student expectations can have an impact on the learning environment. The results from our experimental study suggest that both invested/caring and motivating communications can have positive effects upon student engagement, motivation, and performance. These recommendations are preliminary and further research needs to be conducted to elaborate on these initial findings.

The primary goal of this chapter is to provide evidence leading to a set of preliminary recommendations for effective technology use with at-risk students. In two studies, one including in-depth observations and the other incorporating experimental methodology, we derive a set of recommendations and illustrate how they might be empirically tested and clarified. Although technology offers the promise of engaging, interactive environments that can be individualized to meet student needs, there are currently very few specific, research-based recommendations educators can use to guide their work with at-risk students. While general recommendations have been offered—including the use of technology by at-risk students to complete meaningful and complex tasks that require the use of higher-order thinking skills—the observation that teachers apparently do not widely follow those recommendations suggests the need for more specific guidance (see PytlikZillig, Horn, & White, Chapter 6, this volume). As Durán (2002) has noted, despite the positive outcomes sometimes associated with technology, "the application of technology as a means of implementing instruction or skills training does not guarantee positive student outcomes" (p. 217).

Our recommendations, based largely on case study data, are necessarily preliminary and in need of further empirical scrutiny. Nonetheless, a focus on case studies is strategically in line with counsel recently offered by others. Durán (2002), for example, upon reviewing the complex and sometimes convoluted patterns of results found in large survey studies, advised the following:

> In order to develop additional and important forms of understanding about how technology does or does not facilitate learning, we need to examine how technology affects authentic, everyday learning activities, using an approach that is more direct and detailed…. For this purpose, we should consider the use of situated case studies. (pp. 218–219)

Although Durán (2002) focused primarily on the way that student development of technology-related skills affects and interacts with other learning outcomes, his main point—that aggregate data may fail to reveal important underlying processes—applies broadly. Like Durán, Russell (1997) has noted that "no significant difference" findings may be masking interactive effects, such as when the same factors affect some students positively and others negatively. Russell argues that it is critical that educators identify and acknowledge learning differences and make "maximum use of the technology to serve them accordingly" (p. 1).

THE PRESENT STUDIES

In Study 1 we used case study data to begin to identify the effects of technology on social and motivational processes likely to affect learning outcomes for a specific student subgroup: students at risk for academic failure. Study 2 then was designed to follow up certain case study observations and to clarify more precisely the sometimes complex and interactive effects of multiple variables that operate in specific contexts. These studies were conducted at the University of Nebraska–Lincoln (UNL) over two summers (1997-98) and involved students enrolled in online Web-based courses produced by the CLASS (Communications, Learning, and Assessment in a Student-Centered System) Project. As described in more detail in the introduction to this volume (see also Zygielbaum, Chapter 8, this volume), the overall goal of the CLASS Project was to develop and operate a Web-based system that would provide online, nationwide access to high school education.

In Study 1, both at-risk and not at-risk students were observed for approximately 5 weeks as they participated in pilot versions of the CLASS online courses, accessed from an on-campus computer lab. Data from Study 1 included daily measures of student attendance, engagement, frustration, and progress through the course; results from in-depth focus groups conducted with the at-risk students; and student and instructor interviews. Study 1 therefore provided a variety of case study data pertaining to the effects that a specific form of technology (online courses) has on social and motivational processes of students at risk and their learning outcomes.

Study 2 was planned based on patterns observed in Study 1 and used experimental methodology to clarify our understanding of teacher–student communication in online courses. Based on the Study 1 observation that certain kinds of online communication seemed to be having detrimental effects on the motivation of at-risk students, Study 2 investigated whether theoretically derived interventions might counteract such effects. Thus, a different sample of at-risk students were randomly assigned to groups receiving carefully designed "motivational" and/or "caring" enhancements to online communications in order to see if such conditions would affect subsequent student engagement and achievement. As illustrated throughout the rest of this chapter, this case study plus empirical follow-up approach was fruitful both in enhancing our understanding of some of the processes by which technology was likely affecting at-risk student learning, and in devising a promising intervention.

STUDY 1: CASE STUDIES OF STUDENT AND TEACHER TECHNOLOGY USE IN PRELIMINARY WEB-BASED COURSES

In the summer of 1997, we conducted in-depth pilot studies of four different online high school courses developed by the CLASS project. The purpose of these pilot studies was to better understand the issues involved in delivering multimedia, Internet-based courses to high school students and to uncover any technology-related issues in a controlled environment where such issues could be readily addressed. The courses—geometry, chemistry, writing composition, and social studies (a course focused on Bosnia)—were taught by five different teachers. In these courses, multimedia content was delivered across the Internet, and students submitted their assignments and interacted with teachers via email. Students were paid for their participation, and required to come to the lab to work on their courses regularly, for about two hours a day, Monday through Friday, for about 5 weeks.

A diverse set of 15 students participated in the study, including 8 students who were classified as at risk according to their eligibility for free or reduced-price lunches. The sample was predominately female, with one male participant in the not at-risk group, and two males in the at-risk group. The most notable differences between the at-risk and not at-risk students were that the at-risk students included more ethnic minorities (50% vs. 14% of the at-risk and not at-risk students, respectively), and had lower grade point averages (2.5 vs. 3.8 on a 4-point scale). In addition, 100% of the not at-risk students indicated plans to attend college, compared to 75% of the at-risk students. More than 70% of students in both groups indicated some prior experience with the Netscape Web browser. However, 63% of the at-risk students reported that their experience with technology was "minimal," compared to only 29% of the not at-risk students, who were more likely to report either "moderate" or "high" levels of technology experience.

As much as possible, students' interests and grade levels were used to assign them to one of the four courses. For the duration of the course, students were provided on-campus computer lab space and access to onsite *lab facilitators* (CLASS project research assistants). The primary purpose of the lab faciliators was to answer technical and computer-related questions as they arose and to record their observations of students. Thus, lab facilitators had daily face-to-face contact with the students. Meanwhile, the *course instructors* communicated with students about their work in the course via email. The instructors were certified teachers with prior experience teaching distance-education courses in a print-based, independent study high school environment.

In-depth data were gathered from a number of sources. Students were asked to complete feedback forms after each session, as well as daily exit ratings of their day's activities, learning, motivation, and various aspects of the course. Tracking forms were also completed daily by the lab facilitators. At the end of the study, students and instructors were interviewed and five of the at-risk students participated in an at-risk focus group. It should be noted that, unlike the lab facilitator, instructors were not research assistants and were not given any research-related directions with regard to their responses to students. Thus, instructor interviews shed some light on a variety (albeit a more limited variety) of teacher responses to the novel experience of being immersed, for the first time, into an online Web-based course.

Findings

Presented next are the major themes or issues, relevant across courses, from which most of our preliminary recommendations were derived. Only key findings are highlighted here. Our extensive data revealed a number of other course-specific issues that are beyond the scope of this chapter and are reported elsewhere in technical reports related to the CLASS Project (e.g., Bruning et al., 1997; Bruning, Horn, Reisetter, & Lehman, 1997).

Technology and engagement. First, there was substantial evidence that the technology used in the online courses successfully elicited student interest. For example, students noted,

> The graphics and some videos and things like that, that you know, kept your attention rather than—they kind of took away from reading for a while. (chemistry student, 1997)

> It was interesting and it kept you going and there was a whole variety of ways of learning. It wasn't just all the same. I mean there was a visual and then you could also hear them [the authors] talk and you could see stuff. (writing student, 1997)

While technology's ability to enhance interest and attention is commonly noted and likely applies to students in general, it may be especially important for students who are at risk due to factors potentially undermining their motivation. Interestingly, although neither of the two at-risk social studies students completed the course, their ratings of the course overall and of its specific activities indicated that they viewed it positively. Some of their positive reactions were attributable to a feature of the course, titled "talking heads," which involved hearing and seeing individuals from Bosnia describe the conflict from different perspectives. In response to this component, the at-risk students wrote,

> It was a pretty fun class most of the time. Lot of interesting stuff, pictures and sites and all that stuff, and actually getting to listen to people talk to you. (social studies student, 1997)

> ...it was exciting to like, mainly learn about the life of the different leaders and hear what people had to say and that lived through the hard times in Bosnia. (social studies student, 1997)

As shown in Table 7.1, evidence for at-risk student engagement also was found in student ratings. When students rated the courses overall on a scale ranging from 0 ("really bad") to 100 ("really good"), at-risk student ratings were about as high as or higher than those of not at-risk students. Similarly, at-risk student ratings of the appropriateness and helpfulness of different aspects of the courses were modestly positive, and not strikingly different from not at-risk students.

At-risk student disengagement

Despite the positive evidence for student engagement found in student self-reported ratings, a different story was suggested by student performance data and lab facilitator reports. As shown in Table 7.1, a number of indicators suggest that the at-risk students disengaged from course content more readily than students not at risk. On average, both groups of students participated for more than 5 weeks. However, 75% of the at-risk students, versus 0% of not at-risk students, attended irregularly. At-risk students also attended the lab fewer total days, completed fewer course activities, and spent fewer hours on the course. The activities the at-risk students did complete were also given lower average grades.

Lab facilitator reports also indicated at-risk student disengagement. Lab facilitators, who knew only general information about each student,[1] rated the at-risk students as exhibiting less on-task behavior than the not at-risk students. Students in the online courses were monitored, but still worked largely independently while in the lab, providing them considerable opportunity to engage in off-task behaviors. Observed off-task behaviors included writing emails not relevant to the course, visiting online chat rooms, and socializing with others in the lab. Students exhibited varying degrees of these behaviors, which obviously could affect the quality and/or quantity of their work. For example, one at-risk chemistry student was observed to frequently engage in these behaviors and, despite earning high grades on completed work, only completed 16 of the 37 assessments.

Table 7.1.   Course Evaluation and Course Involvement by At-Risk and Not At-Risk Students

Measure	At-risk (n = 8)	Not at-risk (n = 7)
Student ratings		
Overall course rating (0–100 scale)	77	61
Activity appropriateness (1–5 scale)	3.24	3.40
Appropriateness of readings (1–5 scale)	3.25	3.29
Helpfulness of multimedia (1–5 scale)	3.32	3.41
Helpfulness of Web sites (1–5 scale)	3.43	3.50
Student performance		
Mean number of weeks on course	5.6	5.5
Percent irregular attendees	75%	0
Mean days of attendance on record	8.37	11.00
Mean percent activities completed	59%	65%
Mean hours spent on course	35.6	43.9
Mean performance on completed activities	74%	89%
Lab facilitator reports		
Mean on-task behavior (1–5 scale)	3.87	4.57
Mean frustration level (1–5 scale)	2.10	2.10
Mean amount of assistance (1–5 scale)	1.92	2.07
Mean frequency of assistance per visit	1.84	2.44

Note. For the student ratings, higher numbers reflect more positive ratings and a rating of "3" on the 1 to 5 student rating scales indicates a neutral opinion. Lab facilitators used slightly different 1 to 5 scales anchored with descriptors such as "none" to "very much."

Interestingly, as also shown in Table 7.1, at-risk students did not report greater frustration with the courses, and seemed to request less assistance from the lab facilitators. Therefore, it seems unlikely that at-risk students were disengaging due to frustration with course technology. It still may have been, however, that they engaged in off-task behaviors when they were delayed by malfunctioning technology. Regardless, technology-related concerns were prominent in the interview and focus-group data and, to the extent that substantial numbers of at-risk students only have minimal experience with technology, such problems may disproportionately affect at-risk students and are worthy of note.

Technology-related problems

As would be expected in the first "live" offerings of complex, multimedia-based courses, instructors and students alike reported a variety of technology-related problems and concerns. Interviews suggested that those instructors and students who lacked technology experience encountered a greater number of frustrations, perhaps resulting from that lack of experience. For example, one teacher noted,

> The technical part of it has been most challenging to me, I think because it involves more than just being the teacher. It involves finding different things.... It may not be a challenge to a newer teacher because many new teachers have more computer and technological experiences than I've got. (teacher, 1997)

Similarly, many of the student emails in the writing course involved problems with technology rather than course content; and student interviewees from the writing course also noted problems that might have been overcome with additional instruction and familiarity with the course-specific technology. For example, students wrote,

> Well, I had a bit of a problem at the beginning.... I was sending in papers and not getting responses for a couple of days. But that was partly my fault because I didn't understand where to email it to. I got the wrong address.... I also had a problem with publishing. I was saving it instead of publishing it.... And...in the writing course you are supposed to go through the pre-writing and then go to your journal page for that exploration. And instead...I was opening up just a fresh journal page.... And so my teacher...she would open up Exploration 3 and there would be nothing there.... So that could be specified clearer.... (writing student, 1997)

> I'd lose whole assignments just because the notebook got confusing. (writing student, 1997)

Comments like these suggested that at-risk students with less technology experience might benefit from additional instruction or clarification of course-related technology. However, some problems were purely technical, such as when Web links were broken or certain course components would not open. Interestingly, some of the students with the most technological experience reported a very high level of frustration when the technology did not function as they expected. This observation suggests that, although the at-risk and not at-risk students did not differ in the amount of frustration experienced, the sources of their frustration may have varied.

In general, however, frustration levels were not unduly high (averaging about "2" on the 1 to 5 scale). Frustration levels also did not differ between at-risk and not at-risk students when examined over time in the course.

Such differences, however, might have been expected if high frustration at the beginning of the course had led the at-risk students to disengage in order to eliminate subsequent frustration. We turn next to other observations potentially relevant to at-risk student disengagement.

Student expectations

The case studies suggested a less direct way in which technology might undermine the motivation of at-risk students—by altering and thwarting their expectations. For example, one instructor suggested that technology-related stereotypes may encourage students to expect online courses to be more fun and less work. This instructor said,

> They don't have to approach it as seriously as other courses and I just didn't see a lot of effort...maybe the medium is what gives them the impression that they really don't have to do much. (teacher, 1997)

This instructor's comment is consistent with the observations of others (see Clark, Chapter 1, this volume; Salomon, 1984), and was backed by student comments indicating unmet expectations. Despite appreciating the interest value added by the multimedia aspects of the course, both students at risk and not at risk sometimes complained that there was not *enough* interest value:

> ...the course was fun through most of it, but then 25% of the time I was having difficulty here and there and it got kind of boring sometimes through the whole two hours you were sitting there... (at-risk chemistry student, 1997)

> There were some that was fun, but it was kind of boring, all the reading and looking for stuff, like going off the course and looking in the Internet and stuff.... Because you'd like read one page then you'd think you'd be done and then there'd be a whole other page that you'd have to read, and it's, like, really small words so that's, like, more than a regular written-out page. (not at-risk chemistry student, 1997)

Reflecting upon these comments, one might wonder if students in a less technology-enriched course would have "rejoiced at" rather than "complained about" a course in which 75% of the content was *not* boring, and which required reading *only* a little more than a couple of pages of reading at a time. Though this issue affected all students, it is worth noting because of the greater extent that at-risk students might be affected by such demotivating factors.

The technology also may have influenced some students to expect very rapid feedback, even when such expectations were not warranted. In one extreme case, an at-risk student, frustrated by a problem with her assignment, emailed her instructor several times over a period of a few hours.

This student, evidently expecting an immediate response, used an increasingly large font size with each successive email (along with color and capital letters), illustrating her increasing frustration. Much education software, of course, provides immediate feedback; instant messaging software also allows two parties to "converse" in real time, provided they are online at the same time. However, CLASS teachers were providing feedback primarily via email, and were not online at the same time as students.

Generally, instructors attempted to provide feedback as rapidly as possible, often within one to three days of a student-initiated contact. Nonetheless, student interviewees frequently indicated that teacher responses were not as rapid as they would like, and that delayed feedback sometimes impacted their ability to proceed in the course. In these cases, technology may not have been creating unwarranted student expectations so much as it was failing to meet common student expectations found in more traditional courses. In traditional courses, students typically are able to ask their instructor a simple question in class, and get an immediate response that then allows them to immediately return to their assignment. Clearly, technology was impacting communication in the course, above and beyond its influence on student expectations.

Communication, interaction, and class community

Online courses are obviously unique in that students are distanced from teachers and other students, and need to communicate electronically rather than face to face. In the present study, this distance seemed generally to contribute to a lack of class community. For example, the only course evidencing substantial student–student interaction was the writing course, in which there were a variety of planned activities requiring students to interact (i.e., peer reviews of papers). Even in the writing course, however, the students generally did not interact with each other beyond the required peer reviews, in spite of efforts by the writing teacher encouraging them to post messages to the discussion area.

With regard to teacher–student communication, some have suggested that the lack of face-to-face contact and time lags in teacher–student communication might beneficially decrease the potential for teacher–student conflict (Birch & Ladd, 1996). Indeed, the instructor who had received the rapid succession of frustrated emails in our earlier example expressed great appreciation for the opportunity that the lagged email communication format provided for thinking carefully about how to respond.

Overall, however, our results suggested that the lack of teacher–student face-to-face contact may not have been beneficial. First, the lack of contact sometimes made it difficult for teachers to monitor student progress, especially when assignments did not clearly and explicitly require student–teacher communication. For example, neither of the students enrolled in the social studies course (both of whom were at-risk students) completed the course. The social studies course was different from other courses in that, after completing some preliminary mastery-oriented assessments, students primarily engaged in Internet exploration and research tasks. The tasks were intended to help students acquire Internet research skills and to allow them, through their explorations, to become experts on self-chosen topics. Once students began the explorations, they spent the majority of their time researching, and did not communicate with their instructor. As a result, the instructor was largely unable to judge student progress, and students received little feedback. In an attempt to remedy this situation, the instructor did send emails to students asking them to report on their progress. Without being able to observe the students' research activities, however, it was difficult for the instructor to provide appropriate support or feedback.

Second, there was suggestive evidence that the lack of teacher–student face-to-face contact may have contributed to a lack of class community detrimental to at-risk student engagement. The interviews suggested that students, especially the at-risk students, felt they had a closer relationship with the lab facilitators, whom they saw daily, than with the instructor. In the interviews, students often used the term "teacher" to describe both the lab facilitator and the instructor. At-risk students were especially likely to express appreciation for the lab facilitators' help, and to speak about them as if they were the primary rather than secondary course instructors. This happened despite the fact that the lab facilitators consistently directed the students to interact with their online instructor. At the end of the course, the interviewers asked questions specifically distinguishing between the "instructor" and "lab facilitator." During these interviews, students (two at risk, and one not at risk) from three of the four courses made statements that might be paraphrased as, "Instructors should be physically present while we are working." In other words, the students perceived their interactions with the course instructors to be lacking. Additional evidence from findings concerning teacher roles, discussed next, added weight to these student comments.

Teacher roles

The findings discussed above suggest several roles that instructors may play in online courses. During interviews involving four of the five course instructors, questions were explicitly asked regarding the roles of an online instructor. The instructors identified four different teacher roles that they played: (1) as *assessors/evaluators,* instructors graded assignments and monitored and judged student progress; (2) as *managers,* they coordinated student interactions with other students, assisted students with technical problems, kept track of grades, and responded to student queries; (3) as *teachers*, they provided students with structure, assignments, feedback, and assistance in order to ensure that students learned the course material; and (4) finally, as *motivators*, they attempted to promote student engagement in the course and with course materials by providing support and a sense of community.

The instructors reported difficulty meeting the demands of all these roles, however, with individual teachers differing in their perceptions and opinions about the extent to which they should emphasize each role. All of the instructors agreed on the importance of the "evaluator" role, and noted the surprisingly large amounts of time it took to manage interactions with students and the computer. Communications intended to "manage" and "evaluate" may not enhance student feelings of community as much as "motivating" and "teaching" communications. Due to time pressures, however, teachers varied in the extent to which they took on teaching and motivating roles, as exemplified by the following instructor comments:

> I'm really in the mode of being the evaluator...as long as the information is there; the student learns the material and has the necessary motivation. (teacher, 1997)

> Well, my main goal is to make sure that the student understands what he's supposed to understand in the lesson...and evaluate it in terms of a grade and quality of work, ...beyond that I'm not sure that I really play much of a role. (teacher, 1997)

> There may be other roles that the teacher can play; the problem seems for me to be finding the time to do those things. Because, at least at this point, it just often seems overwhelming to manage the workload that I have. (teacher, 1997)

In part, the extent to which teachers embraced the roles of teaching and motivating students seemed related to the strategies they used to cope with the course workload. One instructor, for example, was unable to keep up with the multiple student assignments that were part of the course design. As a consequence, the instructor provided extremely slow feedback, sometimes as late as 1 to 4 weeks after the assignment was handed in. A total of 55% of this instructor's emails were sent to students after the course had ended. Another instructor coped with the volume of assignments by sending both late emails and short responses. Often, this teacher's communications may have been motivating in the sense that they were very positive and encouraging (e.g., "You are off to a fine start! Try to relax and have fun in this course"); however, they contained very little directive or corrective feedback that might have improved student performance. Meanwhile, students praised the writing instructor for providing helpful and detailed feedback. The writing course, however, incorporated the use of peer review, which reduced, at least slightly, the amount of feedback needed from the instructor.

Discussion

Consideration of these findings in the context of other research and theory led us to develop several of the preliminary recommendations listed in Table 7.2. Note that these recommendations generally assert that course designers and instructors should take into account the impact of technology on student motivation and engagement, as well as upon student cognition. These recommendations give special attention to the "motivator" role, the role that seemed to be most difficult for the instructors in the pilot courses.

First, like others (e.g., Symonds, 2000), we found that technology can be used to effectively engage students. Course designers can capitalize on the interest-generating features of technology, using it to bring information "to life," and to break up the long sections of text such as those that our participants reported undermined their motivation. Use of these technology capabilities may be especially important for students at risk due to motivation-affecting factors and may show up in higher overall course ratings.

Technology can be used ineffectively, however. Although less of an issue in CLASS courses, which were specifically designed to involve higher-level, real-world tasks and information, research generally recommends that at-risk students not be overloaded with simplistic technology-mediated skill and practice tasks (see PytlikZillig et al., this volume, for a review). The overuse of technologically mediated skill and practice exercises may not only bore at-risk students, but may also negatively impact teacher–student interactions. That is, if the computer is providing the questions, answers, and feedback, students will be interacting less with their teachers and each other. To the extent that both "interesting tasks" and "relationships" are important motivators for at-risk students, the use of basic skill and drill programs with at-risk students may be doubly detrimental.

Table 7.2. Preliminary Recommendations for the Use of Technology with Students At Risk

1. Use interest-generating and illustrative technology to engage students.
   - Do not overuse skill and practice software.
   - Use technology in the service of moderately complex tasks that apply to the real world and that students can personalize.
2. Closely monitor and evaluate student engagement using multiple indicators designed to identify points and sources of student disengagement.
   - For example, assess student frustration, interest, time on task, attendance, and other indicators.
3. Offer feedback on student self-regulatory activities.
   - Be willing to seek or develop creative measures in diverse contexts.
4. Pay adequate attention to technical aspects of the course.
   - Test and pilot course-related technologies prior to using in a course.
   - Train students to use specific course-related technologies, especially if they do not have extensive experience with the technology.
   - Train teachers to use the technology and to troubleshoot problems likely to arise.
5. Take into account student expectations.
   - Explicitly identify and illustrate the nature of the course and problems that may arise.
   - Attempt to meet student expectations, especially when they are difficult to alter.
6. Actively foster a sense of course community that includes positive student–teacher and student–student relationships.
   - If possible, incorporation of some face-to-face interaction may be helpful.
   - Use personalized, caring communication when interacting from a distance.
7. In teacher–student communications, use encouraging, informative responses that build self-efficacy and provide corrective direction.
   - Include responses attributing student success to student effort.
   - Help students to see assignments as within their control and abilities.
   - Maintain a focus on the course and its content, even while encouraging and building student efficacy.
8. In general, pay attention to individual student needs and risk characteristics, and provide appropriate directive and corrective feedback.
9. Recognize the time and effort requirements associated with the many roles required by the technology and plan accordingly.
   - This may mean planning in additional staff support, smaller classes, and/or altering aspects of course design.

Second, at-risk student course engagement should be closely monitored as part of the instructor's evaluation activities. Instructors in this study indicated expending considerable effort evaluating student achievement in terms of mastery of course content, but were not prepared for the explicit evaluation of behaviors indicating student engagement or disengagement. Many of these behaviors would be readily apparent in the classroom (e.g., whether or not the student is staying on task, feeling frustrated, etc.), but are less visible—or even invisible—in an online course. Given the specific patterns found in our case studies (i.e., at-risk students were similar to not at-risk students in terms of certain indicators, but different on others), multiple indicators of engagement may be needed in order to determine more precisely points of student disengagement. The learning process involves several steps, and individual at-risk students may disengage at different points. For example, students may get frustrated with the technology, experience difficulty staying on task, have difficulty with other aspects of self-regulated behavior, or all of these.

Our third recommendation is related to the second; when students disengage, instructors should offer students feedback on their self-regulatory activities. Several researchers have noted that students who are academically at risk may lack the high levels of persistent and skilled self-regulation and self-motivation that Web-based courses often require (e.g., Lee & Lehman, 1993; McWhirter, McWhirter, McWhirter, & McWhirter, 1993; Shin, Schallert, & Savenye, 1994). The need for self-regulatory feedback seemed especially acute for the students in the social studies course working on the Internet research activities. Recall that neither of these two students, both of whom were at risk, completed the course.

However, creative, context-specific measures may be required to obtain the information needed to evaluate student engagement, to identify the point at which they disengaged, and to provide helpful feedback on student self-regulatory activities. In the case of the social studies students, additional "milepost" assignments—such as having students list the URLs of the Web sites that they visited, along with highlights relevant to their main topic from each site—might have added structure to their Internet exploration. Such information also would have allowed instructors to give self-regulatory advice concerning when students seemed to have lost track of their focus, or when they failed to recognize that they were finished with a topic. Other measures of student disengagement, however, may be more difficult to obtain. To the extent that a student likes to socialize, the ready availability of Internet chat rooms and conversations with one's classmates may be tempting alternatives to schoolwork. However, students may not inform their instructors that these activities are the real cause of their less-than-optimal performance. Nonetheless, the development of unique and readily identifiable Web pages for in-class activities might allow a simple scan of the computer monitors to indicate whether the student is on- or off-task. In the future, Web pages also might be specially programmed to give instructors feedback on student online activities. In general, course designers should be committed to finding creative solutions for monitoring student self-regulation in different and challenging contexts.

Fourth, though our at-risk students did not report greater frustration than not at-risk students, many students reported some technology-related frustration, and a greater number of the at-risk students did report having "only minimal" experience with technology. Without our on-site lab facilitators to answer technical questions, the frustration of the at-risk students may have been greater. Thus, consistent with the recommendations of others (e.g., Gladieux & Swail, 1999), we recommend that online courses be thoroughly tested and piloted, and that at-risk students be given additional training in the course-specific technology. Teachers, too, may need administrative support to enhance their own familiarity with course technology.

Fifth, we recommend that instructors take into account student expectations. Our finding—that students may expect online courses to be less demanding than traditional courses—is consistent with the observations of others (see Clark, this volume; Salomon, 1984) and suggests that students need to be made explicitly aware of course work requirements. In addition, students need to be aware of potential technical problems. During course orientation, for example, it may be helpful to expose students to some of the problems they are most likely to encounter (e.g., crashing Web sites, down servers). In our studies, care was taken to explain to the students that the courses were being piloted, that there would be "bugs" in the courses, and that they were being hired to help evaluate and fix the courses. Despite this information, however, many students expressed frustration over the technical problems encountered. Thus, there seems to be a limit to which teachers can *change* student expectations. In some cases, it may be more beneficial simply to try to *meet* student expectations. Responding promptly to student queries, for example, not only meets student expectations but also provides students with valuable and timely feedback that can be used to inform their subsequent work in the course.

Sixth, instructors working with at-risk students should give additional attention to motivating students via relationships. Classroom research (e.g., Battistich, Solomon, Watson, & Schaps, 1997; Midgely, Feldlaufer, & Eccles, 1989; see also Dede, 1998, cited in Durán, 2002, p. 219) has shown that a sense of community is an important component of student success. Thus, the limited sense of community evidenced in our students' lack of interaction with each other and in their dissatisfaction with the frequency and timing of student–teacher interactions is a cause for concern. Although a limited sense of community was expressed by both at-risk and not at-risk students, it may be that at-risk students were more sensitive to such factors, resulting in their higher levels of disengagement. When designing or planning technologically mediated courses, special attention may be required to build relationships with and among students, perhaps by including formal assignments specifically designed to acheive these goals. Even in primarily Web-based courses, it might be useful to include some face-to-face interaction, as well as personalized feedback designed to enhance at-risk students' sense of community and relationship with the instructor.

We reiterate and elaborate this last recommendation and formulate a seventh recommendation in Study 2. Study 2 was inspired by the recognition that a more formal intervention could help us better understand key features of communication in online courses. Indeed, there may be an upper limit to the *amount* of interaction and personalized feedback that can be made available in any course. Thus, it might be especially important to consider the *quality* or type of interaction and feedback. For example, if certain types of teacher responses and interactions are perceived as more satisfying and motivating than others, it would be cost efficient and important to include those types of interactions and, for the sake of time, to omit other, less effective forms of interaction. Our second study sought to empirically investigate such issues.

STUDY 2: A STUDY OF CARING AND MOTIVATION-BUILDING ELECTRONIC TEACHER COMMUNICATION

Results from Study 1 strongly suggested that motivational elements needed to be incorporated into the design of online instruction in order to prevent at-risk students' disengagement. A variety of potentially effective motivational interventions appropriate to the traditional classroom have been suggested by the literature (e.g., Bandura & Cervone, 1983; Baumeister & Leary, 1995; Dweck & Leggett, 1988) and are consistent with our observations in Study 1. However, little is known about how to most efficaciously implement such motivational components with technology. Research clearly was needed, and we therefore attempted to operationalize key theory-based concepts and our observations into a systematic, empirical study. Because this experiment is available in published form elsewhere (Lehman, Kauffman, White, Horn, & Bruning, 2001), we only briefly overview it here, primarily focusing upon its relevance to our final recommendations for serving at-risk students with technology.

In this study, we investigated whether teacher communication specifically designed to promote student motivation could effectively reduce at-risk student disengagement. We focused on personalizing teacher–student communications and investigated two potential interventions suggested by the case studies above and by motivational theory. One line of reasoning suggests that student motivation and performance will be enhanced by *caring* that relates to students' needs for belongingness and relatedness (e.g.,

Baumeister & Leary, 1995; Deci & Ryan, 2000). Caring may have specific effects that are especially important for students who are at risk due to factors undermining relationships with significant adults in their lives (Kramer-Schlosser, 1992; McWhirter et al., 1993; Werner, 1984). Some research has found relationships between teacher caring and student persistence, especially for at-risk students (e.g., Kramer-Scholsser, 1992; McWhirter et al., 1993; Rak & Patterson, 1996; Werner, 1984). Caring and invested communications from teachers may create connections with students that then increase the value of the tasks assigned by the teachers (Noddings, 1992).

There also exists substantial literature suggesting that student motivation and performance, in general, is enhanced by *motivational* factors related to (a) student efficacy (i.e., students' beliefs in their course-relevant capabilities (e.g., Bandura & Cervone, 1983, Pajares, 1996), and (b) attributions of assignment controllability and of the role of student effort as contributing to their successes (e.g., Weiner, 1986). Together, (a) and (b) are thought to work to influence students' expectancies of success (e.g., Atkinson, 1964) and their motivation to move toward that success. We expected that communications from teachers enhancing these factors should therefore enhance student motivation and performance.

Study 2 involved 13 female and 3 male (50% minority) students identified as at risk by one or more public institutions (school, social services, etc.). This group of students were at risk primarily due to factors such as the personal history and home environment, social-environmental, and student–student factors, described in PytlikZillig and colleagues (this volume). All of the students also reported limited experience with computers and the Internet. In this study, students participated in an online high school writing course very similar to the one described in Study 1. Because the course was still in pilot form, it was not offered for credit. However, all other conditions paralleled those likely to exist in an online course.

The writing instructor was trained to deliver three types of communication (baseline professional, motivated, and caring/invested) to create the four conditions investigated in this study. All 16 students received baseline professional communication, characterized by standard levels of motivational and caring/invested teacher communication, including clear instructions, timely answers to student questions, and helpful feedback on graded assignments. The manipulated communications included higher (vs. standard) levels of motivating and caring/invested communications, incorporated into a 2 × 2 design. Thus, during the study phase of the course,[2] one-fourth of the students received baseline professional communications. Another one-fourth of the students received baseline professional communication plus enhanced motivating professional communication that involved statements designed to enhance student efficacy and attributions.

For example, the teacher might write, "The last three assignments you have handed in have been stellar. You are doing very well in this section." Another one-fourth of the students received baseline professional communication plus added caring/invested professional statements that focused on relationship building. An example of such a caring/invested statement might be, "If you can't think of a topic, write about a movie you liked. Have you seen any good ones lately?" The final one-fourth of the students received both enhanced motivating and caring/invested professional communications from their teacher in addition to baseline professional communication. An example of such a motivating and caring/invested professional communication is, "The way you put sentences together in that last message seemed very casual without being sloppy or lacking skill. Have you been writing a lot?"

Findings

In small-N studies such as this, effect sizes can be used to complement more traditional tests of significance and as appropriate indices of the impact of the intervention (e.g., Cohen, 1977; Cook & Campbell, 1979; Lipsey, 1990). In Study 2, an examination of the effect sizes associated with the caring/invested and motivating teacher communication factors revealed a robust pattern of positive, small, moderate, and large size effects that, taken together, suggested the importance of these types of teacher communication. For example, student email assignments completed during weeks 2–4 of the course were subjected to blind ratings of length, idea development, and overall completeness of the assignment. Student effort on these email assignments was moderately higher in the motivating professional and in the caring/invested professional conditions than in the baseline professional condition. There was also a sizable interaction effect, with the pattern of mean effort ratings suggesting that caring/investment communications were associated with greater effort only if motivating communication was low. Students with the highest effort ratings were those in the high motivating and low caring/invested professional group.

Similarly, an analysis of overall student performance in the courses (as indicated by mean performance on assignments graded by the course instructor) revealed large effects of enhanced teacher communication. The courses were in their testing phase and were not taken for credit. Thus, students knew that assignment grades would not be a part of their academic record. However, we assumed that graded performance on assignments would reflect student engagement in the course. The mean performance of students in the caring/invested and motivating professional groups were higher than those in the baseline professional group.

However, there was an interaction suggesting that adding caring/invested communication to motivating communication did not incrementally increase student performance. This finding mirrors other findings concerning the importance of appropriate feedback in the writing process (see Bruning & Horn, 2000).

Ratings of student engagement by lab facilitators also indicated enhanced student effort by students in the enhanced conditions. Each day, lab facilitators rated student engagement based on whether the student self-started in the course, persisted in course activities, and refrained from non-course–related activity. The lab facilitator ratings, which were made blind to condition, were higher for students receiving the high caring/invested communications. In addition, there was an interaction effect with those students in the high caring/invested but low motivating communication conditions receiving the highest engagement ratings.

As a test of whether experimental conditions were being delivered as designed, instructor emails were rated by two independent raters blind to the experimental conditions in terms of the amount of motivational communication, caring/invested communication, and content-related feedback they contained. The ratings indicated that students in the motivating professional groups did receive more motivation communication, and that students in the invested professional groups received more caring/invested communication. In addition, however, the high motivating professional students received more caring/invested communication than those in the low motivating professional group, and more content-related feedback than students in the caring/invested professional group. These findings suggest that the relative effectiveness of the enhanced motivating professional communications might be attributed in part to some combination of higher content relevance, and the tendency with which they were perceived as evidencing teacher caring/investment. These positive results were dramatic enough that we made the decision to shift all students to the motivated and caring/invested communication condition (see Footnote 2). All students thus completed the course under conditions that our data and observations were showing us were encouraging higher levels of engagement and performance.

Discussion

The results from Study 2 suggest that both invested/caring and motivating communications can have positive effects upon student engagement, motivation, and performance. Thus, the seventh recommendation listed in Table 7.2 involves the use of encouraging responses specifically designed to enhance self-efficacy. In online communication with students, we recommend that teachers attribute student success to effort and skill (e.g., as opposed to ease of the assignment or luck), and assist students in viewing the assignments as controllable (e.g., by clarifying their mistakes so that they feel their understanding will help them to avoid the same mistake in the future). These communications will naturally include a greater focus on course content, be perceived as more caring, and, as shown in the analysis of student effort on emails and performance on assignments, the motivating communications may have more robust effects than simply caring communications.

CONCLUDING RECOMMENDATIONS AND DIRECTIONS FOR FUTURE RESEARCH

Our eighth recommendation (see Table 7.2) may be viewed as a "meta-recommendation" in the sense that it is implicit in the others. We recommend that instructors be attentive to student individual differences. In any course, students will vary in terms of their interests, sources of frustration, self-regulatory skills, amount and type of engagement or disengagement with the course, experience with technology, expectations, and so on. While some of the recommendations here apply generally (e.g., all students require appropriate and timely feedback), and some may be especially important for at-risk students (e.g., attention to relationships and active efforts at building self-efficacy), the most effective instructors will tailor their approach and feedback to meet individual needs.

However, we recognize that current or future online instructors may read these recommendations with raised eyebrows and wonder, with more than a hint of irony, where they should pick up their "super teacher" cape prior to that first day of online class. Our last recommendation explicitly recognizes that, while technology may simplify some aspects of the teaching and learning process, it does not eliminate many of the challenges of motivating students at risk. Thus, teachers almost certainly will have to make accommodations and adjustments among their various roles. This may mean concentrating on certain kinds of communication, limiting class size, altering course design, and planning for additional staff support.

In conclusion, we reiterate the preliminary nature of these recommendations. They are the product of our experience with specific types of technology (online courses administered in a lab context), and future research is required to verify their utility, determine the breadth of their applicability, and develop the best methods for their implementation. For example, future research is needed to determine the extent to which the inclusion of certain technological features into courses influences students to take them less seriously, to have higher expectations regarding the entertainment value and ease of the courses, and to exert less effort and resilience in the face of normal course challenges. Future research is needed to examine the relative impact of enhanced caring and motivational communications on both at-risk and not at-risk students, and to study the utility of including such factors in automatic computer-generated feedback in addition to human-mediated responses. Research also is needed to investigate methods for altering student expectations about their online experiences, as well as the extent to which students' expectations can be altered by verbal messages. Research comparing the costs and benefits of different methods of coping with online course time demands also will be valuable. Eventually, future research could also examine the impact of various teaching methods and uses of technology for different at-risk groups and begin to identify strategies and technologies especially helpful for various at-risk subgroups. We hope this chapter encourages such research, leading to the development of a more refined and comprehensive set of recommendations and more effective technology-based instruction for at-risk students.

REFERENCES

Atkinson, H. (1964). *An introduction to motivation.* Princeton, NJ: Van Nostrand.

Bandura, A., & Cervone, D. (1983). Self-evaluative and self-efficacy mechanisms governing the motivational effects of goal systems. *Journal of Personality and Social Psychology, 45,* 1017–1028.

Battistich, V., Solomon, D., Watson, M., & Schaps, E. (1997). Caring school communities. *Educational Psychologist, 32,* 137–151.

Baumeister, R. F., & Leary, M. R. (1995). The need to belong: Desire for interpersonal attachments as a fundamental human motivation. *Psychological Bulletin, 117,* 497–529.

Birch, S. H., & Ladd, G. W. (1996). Interpersonal relationships in the school environment and children's early school adjustment: The role of teacher and peers. In J. Juvonen & K. R. Wentzel (Eds.), *Social motivation: Understanding children's school adjustment* (pp. 199–225). New York: Cambridge University Press.

Bruning, R., & Horn, C. A. (2000). Developing motivation to write. *Educational Psychologist, 35*(1), 25–38.

Bruning, R., Horn, C. A., Reisetter, M., & Lehman, S. (1997). *CLASS Project technical report no. 7: 1997 summer pilot teacher interviews.* Lincoln: Center for Instructional Innovation, University of Nebraska–Lincoln.

Bruning, R., Horn, C. A., Shell, D., Barrett, K., Kauffman, D., Lehman, S., et al. (1997). *CLASS Project technical report no. 6: 1997 summer pilot study.* Lincoln: Center for Instructional Innovation, University of Nebraska–Lincoln.

Cohen, J. (1977). *Statistical power analysis for the behavioral sciences* (rev. ed.). New York: Academic Press.

Cook, T. D., & Campbell, D. T. (1979). *Quasi-experimental design and analysis: Issues for field settings.* Dallas, TX: Houghton Mifflin.

Deci, E. L., & Ryan, R. M. (2000). The "what" and "why" of goal pursuits: Human needs and the self-determination of behavior. *Psychological Inquiry, 11,* 227–268.

Durán, R. P. (2002). Technology, education and at-risk students. In S. Stringfield & D. Land (Eds.), *Educating at-risk students* (pp. 210-230). Chicago: University of Chicago Press.

Dweck, C. S., & Leggett, E. L. (1988). A social-cognitive approach to motivation and personality. *Psychological Review, 95,* 256–273.

Gladieux, L. E., & Swail, W. S. (1999). The virtual university and educational opportunity: Panacea or false hope? *Higher Education Management, 11,* 43–56.

Kramer-Schlosser, L. (1992). Teacher distance and student disengagement: School lives on the margin. *Journal of Teacher Education, 43,* 128–140.

Lee, Y., & Lehman, J. (1993). Instructional cueing in hypermedia: A study with active and passive learners. *Journal of Educational Multimedia and Hypermedia, 2,* 25-37.

Lehman, S., Kauffman, D. F., White, M. J., Horn, C. A., & Bruning, R. H. (2001). Teacher interaction: Motivating at-risk students in web-based high school courses. *Journal of Research on Technology in Education, 33* [Online]. Retrieved from http://www.iste.org/jrte/33/5/lehman_s.html

Lipsey, M. W. (1990). *Design sensitivity: Statistical power for experimental research.* Newbury Park, CA: Sage.

McWhirter, J. J., McWhirter, B. T., McWhirter, A. M., & McWhirter, E. H. (1993). *At risk youth: A comprehensive response.* Pacific Grove, CA: Brooks/Cole.

Midgely, C., Feldlaufer, H., & Eccles, J. S. (1989). Student/teacher relations and attitudes toward mathematics before and after the transition to junior high school. *Child Development, 60,* 981–992.

Noddings, N. (1992). *The challenge to care in schools: An alternative approach to education.* New York: Teachers College Press.

Pajares, F. (1996). Self-efficacy beliefs in academic settings. *Review of Educational Research, 66,* 543–578.

Rak, C. F., & Patterson, L. E. (1996). Promoting resilience in at-risk children. *Journal of Counseling and Development, 74,* 368–373.

Russell, T. (1997). Technology wars: Winners and losers. *Educom Review, 32*(2), 44–46.

Salomon, G. (1984). Television is "easy" and print is "tough": The differential investment of mental effort in learning as a function of perceptions and attributions. *Journal of Educational Psychology, 76,* 774–786.

Shin, E., Schallert, D., & Savenye, C. (1994). Effects of learner control, advisement, and prior knowledge on young students' learning in a hypertext environment. *Educational Technology Research and Development, 42,* 33–46.

Symonds, W. C. (2000). Wired schools. *BusinessWeek Online* [Online]. Retrieved from http:// www .businessweek.com/2000/00_39/b3700114.htm

Weiner, B. (1986). *An attributional theory of motivation and emotion.* New York: Sperling-Verlag.

Werner, E. E. (1984). Resilient children. *Young Children, 39,* 68–72.

AUTHOR NOTE

This work was made possible by a grant from the U.S. Department of Education to the CLASS project, University of Nebraska–Lincoln. Opinions expressed are those of the authors and not necessarily those of the funders. We would like to express our appreciation to a number of individuals who contributed significantly to the success of this project: to Kathleen Barrett, John Nietfeld, Steve Lehman, Mary Jane White, and Brent Igo for their contributions as members of the research team to both studies; to Jeremy Sydik and Bill Udell for their programming and troubleshooting expertise; to the engineers, Web developers, and designers from the CLASS Project and Nebraska Educational Television; and to the teachers from the Independent High School for their assistance and support in this project.

Correspondence concerning this chapter should be addressed to Christy A. Horn, 215 TEAC, Center for Instructional Innovation, University of Nebraska–Lincoln, Lincoln, NE 68588-0384, or by email to chorn@nebraska.edu

NOTES

1. The lab facilitators did not have access to the at-risk and not at-risk classifications of students, which were designations made at the end of the study (based on free and reduced-price lunch status) and prior to analyzing the data.

2. For the last 3 weeks of the 7-week course all students were shifted to the motivating invested professional condition, so that they might all reap the maximum benefits possible.

CHAPTER 8

ENGINEERING ISSUES AND PERSPECTIVES IN DEVELOPING ONLINE COURSES

Arthur I. Zygielbaum
National Center for Information Technology in Education,
University of Nebraska–Lincoln

ABSTRACT

From the beginning, the CLASS (Communications, Learning, and Assessment in a Student-Centered System) Project was exciting, highly innovative, and filled with technological challenges. The project, a grant awarded to the University of Nebraska–Lincoln, was funded through the General Services Administration and the U.S. Department of Education Star Schools Program. Participants developed 53 online high school courses, the basis of a complete high school diploma sequence. During the 5-year development period, the project wrestled with and overcame significant unforeseen technical challenges, created a course/learning management system, and utilized instructional design principles in the development of course content. This chapter chronicles the project's technical innovation and the difficulties

Web-Based Learning: What Do We Know? Where Do We Go?, pages 153–168
Copyright © 2003 by Information Age Publishing
All rights of reproduction in any form reserved.

inherent in a project managed as a research and development effort yet weighed with production environment expectations. Although benefited by the availability of skilled and engaged personnel, the project suffered from a lack of engineering and technical management rigor. Because this environment is not unlike that in which many of today's educators work, the final section of the chapter is devoted to the techniques used by software engineers and managers to mitigate the risk inherent in software.

From the beginning, the CLASS (Communications, Learning, and Assessment in a Student-Centered System) Project was exciting, innovative, and filled with technological challenges. The project, was funded through the General Services Administration and the U.S. Department of Education Star Schools Program. Taking seed from ideas planted by the leaders of the University of Nebraska–Lincoln (UNL) Division of Continuing Studies (DCS) and Senator Bob Kerrey (Nebraska), participants in the project developed 53 online high school courses, the basis of a complete high school diploma sequence. The project leadership was assigned to DCS, and the production of Web pages, video, audio, and interactive components was under the aegis of Nebraska Educational Telecommunications. Sarnoff Laboratories, in Princeton, New Jersey, was the original technology partner. Formative evaluation founded in cognitive psychology and educational research were the purview of UNL's Center for Instructional Innovation. During the 5-year development period, the project wrestled with unforeseen technical challenges, created a course/learning management system, and utilized instructional design principles in the development of course content. This chapter focuses on engineering issues in the technology development process. A technical history and background of the project is followed by observations and suggestions based on lessons learned.

CLASS PROJECT TECHNICAL BACKGROUND

When the CLASS Project was initiated in 1996, the intent was to take advantage of the confluence of existing educational content, emerging technology, and the opportunity to reach many high school students through the Internet. The environment at the time seemed right to embark on a pioneering effort to use technology to make high-quality courses available to students no matter their setting—a poor urban housing project or a ranch distant from a major city—and to effectively lower the per-unit cost of education.

As envisioned in the plans for CLASS, the major component of the new venture, educational content, was to be provided by the University of Nebraska–Lincoln (UNL) Independent Study High School. UNL had been operating this highly successful print-based correspondence high school since 1929. Thousands of students had taken high school courses and received high school diplomas issued by UNL. The huge amount of content available through the Independent Study High School, which had been either developed and owned by UNL or licensed for UNL distribution, seemed ripe for conversion to the online environment afforded by the Internet. The pool of teachers who guided and counseled these distant correspondence students would be available to perform those same functions online.

The second component, student tracking, was to be derived from emerging technology developed by the Sarnoff Laboratories. Sarnoff Laboratories had, under federal sponsorship, developed technology to track how individuals were using computers online. These tools seemed to be ideally suited to track a student's progress through courses presented online.

The third component was the Internet, which provided a new opportunity to reach students. In 1996, the year the CLASS Project began, the Internet had about a half-million Web sites. Outside an institutional setting, connectivity to the Internet backbone was provided through modem banks operated by Internet service providers. The typical connection rate was 28.8 Kbs for the home or K–12 school. Text could be downloaded at a reasonable rate—a 500-page book could be downloaded in about 10 minutes. Images, videos, or interactive assets could take an excruciatingly long time, however. For example, a reasonable-quality 60-second video would take 1 hour and 20 minutes to download.

As conceived early in the grant development process, the project was to take the developed content used by the Independent Study High School, move that content to an online environment, introduce online assessments, provide tracking information to teachers, and provide a teacher interface. It was expected that the basic model of the single student interacting with a distant teacher would remain, but be enhanced by adding the advantages associated with recent computer technology. As many information technology–based projects first appear, this one seemed to be relatively straightforward.

The complicated reality of the project struck fairly early. It became quickly apparent that conceiving of the task as just moving text from paper to the screen was much too simplistic. New instructional designs were developed to take advantage of the interactive and multimedia capabilities of computers. The designs included audio tracks and videos specifically produced for the new media, animation, interactive simulations, and both text-based and graphical interactive assessments. Unfortunately, the relatively slow Internet interconnection environment was not compatible with downloading large multimedia assets.

The technology produced by Sarnoff was found to be unsuitable for tracking students in the CLASS Project. Although it could track students, the software initially required several minutes to download and initialize after the user's Internet browser was launched. The redesign to overcome this difficulty was dependent upon close integration with the Netscape browser. In the end, modifications to allow the software to work with other browsers and to add needed functionality proved more significant than funding and time would allow. Nebraska Educational Telecommunications (NET) was assigned to develop the tracking solution required for the CLASS Project.

These were not the only problems. The greatest challenge facing the project was more subtle. Although the endeavor was funded and managed as a research and development effort, the project was expected to produce a core high school diploma curriculum involving more than 50 courses within the 5-year grant period. The marriage of production expectations with research and development processes is at best a shaky proposition, and can become a disaster. Fortunately, as will be described next, the CLASS project tended toward the former.

TECHNOLOGY CHANGES AND CHALLENGES

Research and development is a necessary part of any information technology–based effort. In the case of CLASS, two areas are particularly illustrative of this need. First, significant work was required to define and implement the tracking mechanism that was intended to reveal how students were progressing through the courses. Second, a great deal of work was also required to solve the problem of how to provide large video, audio, and interactive assets to students despite slow modem interconnections.

Tracking Students

Teachers needed student tracking to monitor student progress. This was especially important in courses that did not have regular assignments due (for further discussion, see Horn, PytlikZillig, Bruning, & Kauffman, Chapter 7, this volume). The combination of assessments and knowledge of what the student has studied is a powerful tool to help diagnose student difficulties, should they occur.

The tracking mechanism seemed to be fairly straightforward at first. The World Wide Web is an example of client-server systems. Users access information by first entering a Uniform Resource Locator, or URL, into a Web browser running on their computer—the client machines. The URL is an electronic address to a specific Web page or other resource residing somewhere on the Internet. More particularly, the address includes the name of the computer hosting the Web site, and, optionally, the location of the page or other resource in the host's storage directory structure. The network communications protocol automatically supplies the address of the client (return address) to the host computer, without any direct action on the part of the user. The server uses the return address to direct a response—the requested Web page—to the user. Naturally this is an over-simplification; much additional information, such as the browser type and the operating system, also is transmitted from the user or client machine to the Web server.

To track student progress, a database was created on the server (known colloquially as the "back end") that recorded addresses of the Web pages requested by the students as well as the time of those requests. Ostensibly, one could use that database to present a complete timeline of students' progress, and the amount of time they spent on a particular page. Unfortunately, one of the optimizations inherent to Web browsers, the caching scheme, got in the way.

Caching works as follows: When a Web page is downloaded to a user's computer (i.e., a client), that page may include pictures, text, audio clips, and so on. Without caching, if the user moves to another page and then back again (with the back button, for instance), that original page would have to be downloaded in its entirety a second time. The same holds true if the user shuts the browser down, relaunches it, and revisits the same Web site. Traffic loads on the Internet would obviously be adversely impacted by users redownloading pages because, for example, most users revisit the home page on a site many times during a session. To avoid this burden, Web browsers incorporate a "cache" file. When a Web page is accessed, the contents of that page are written to this file. Whenever a Web page is accessed by the user, the browser first checks to see if that page exists in the cache. If the page does exist in the cache, and if there is not a more recent document on the host computer, the browser presents the "cached" content to the user without redownloading the page. All browsers have a setting that indicates when the cache is "flushed." It can be set to "every session," "once a day," and so on. Note that the cache must be cleared for the browser to automatically redownload a Web page. The "refresh" or "reload" buttons that are included in common Web browsers may also force a new download.

Even more complex, in order to minimize traffic on Internet backbones (high-bandwidth regional, national, and international interconnections), Internet service providers or large users such as schools or businesses might use caching proxy servers. These are computers that cache Web pages accessed by users within that school or business. If a user, for example, requests a page previously accessed by a different user at that institution, the page would be supplied by the proxy computer rather than through a request to the original host. The user has little or no ability to cause the proxy cache to be updated or erased.

In these caching schemes, the tracking mechanism at the server could only record repeated page views if caches were flushed. If not flushed, subsequent views of a page would come from the cache, and not involve a request to the server. Hence the server's tracking mechanism would not be notified. Clearly, any tracking scheme at the "back end" is thwarted and unable to maintain full cognizance of the user's trail.

To remedy this problem, special software was written by the CLASS Project engineers to automatically intercept communications between the browser and the cache. If the Web page request was satisfied through the cache, then a message was generated and sent back to the server to record that action. Hence, the back end was aware of and able to accurately track all student actions. As it turns out, this special software would also prove useful in solving the problem of moving large files over slow Internet connections.

Large File Transfer

As described earlier, for the CLASS Project to succeed, a mechanism needed to be developed to overcome the potentially long download times required by large assets such as multimedia files. The first attempted solution was based on the browser's cache file. Consider that if one were to visit all of the pages on a CLASS course Web site during a session, all of the elements of those pages would be stored in the cache file, as described earlier. The resulting cache file could be written to a CD-ROM and, taking advantage of the fact that most browsers allow specification of where the cache file resides, one could insert the CD-ROM in a user's computer to replace the default cache file residing on a hard drive. The browser would retrieve assets from the CD-ROM rather than from the server. Hence, commercial software was procured that forced creation of a complete cache file for the course Web site. Students were then supplied a cache CD-ROM along with their course materials.

Problem solved? Unfortunately, the solution was flawed. While internationally accepted standards guaranteed the format and sequences of communications between Web clients and servers, no such standards existed for the format of the cache files. A cache file used by Microsoft's Internet Explorer had a different format than a cache file used by Netscape and whenever either browser was updated the cache file specification might change. Hence, the cache CD-ROMs in otherwise well-functioning courses were rendered useless by an upgrade of the browser or one of the ancillary "plug-in" programs. Students who updated their browser or plug-ins were suddenly relegated to long waits while large assets downloaded via their modems. Needless to say, the CLASS engineers were bombarded with phone calls and emails. Because the logistics were overwhelming, the project was unable to generate cache CD-ROMs for all conceivable versions of browser and plug-in combinations.

A new approach was developed involving the invention of the Local Resource Disk (LRD). The LRD is a CD-ROM upon which was written the large assets required in a course, or, in some cases, all of the content of the course Web site. Based on the tracking software mentioned above, special software was created to track all requests for content to the server. When a user requested a Web page from the server, the new software intercepted and analyzed the information contained in the message to the server. If the content requested at the server had a date/time stamp identical to or earlier than the content on the LRD, the software automatically and transparently retrieved the necessary elements from the LRD and supplied them to the browser. If the date/time stamp at the server was later than that for the LRD contents, as might occur if content corrections were made, the request was forwarded intact to the server. The server then supplied the needed elements to the browser. The software, in other words, acted as a communications switch. It selected the latest content either from the LRD or from the Web server. The advantages of this method were (1) independence from the vagaries of the cache file, (2) LRD content identical to that generated for the Web server, and (3) a way to correct any content errors without issuing new CD-ROMs.

Other Technology Challenges

Student tracking and making available large assets represented only two of the challenges met by the software engineers. They are highlighted because they represented significant effort and innovation. The CLASS Project had other needs. For example, teacher grade books had to be created to allow teachers to access and supply records of student accomplishment. The grade books had to automatically access the databases that contained the results of the assessment activities included as part of the courses. The engineers created a student registration system coupled with a computer account management system. Mechanisms also had to be created to allow students to submit homework and other materials to their teachers. Homework included text, images, references to Web sites, and even recorded audio in the case of foreign language courses.

The LRD itself evolved to satisfy the needs of CLASS. The LRD became an integral part of a Course Resource Utility (CRU). Like the LRD, the CRU contained large assets needed by the courses. It also contained an installation program that would advise the user about the configuration of their browser, and supply needed plug-ins that were compatible with the courses.

Changes in Context

In 1998, UNL created a for-profit spin-off, CLASS.COM™, to market and distribute the CLASS Project courses. The new entity was established with the concurrence of the Department of Education in order to facilitate moving project products into the educational marketplace. In this role, CLASS.COM™ applied significant pressure on the project to deliver courses at a market-based pace not necessarily compatible with research and development. Furthermore, CLASS.COM™ determined that selling courses for entire classrooms would be a more lucrative market than individual enrollees. In this market context, the courses were used to augment existing curriculum or to provide a subject that would otherwise not be taught because no qualified teacher was available. Recall that the original goal of the CLASS Project was the design of courses to be used by single individuals connecting to the Internet directly or via modems. The schoolroom environment brought a new set of challenges: firewalls and shared CD-ROM drives. The CRU software was not designed to accommodate the protection mechanisms of firewalls, nor was it designed to deal with anything other than a CD-ROM installed in the client computer. Other technical elements, such grade books, also had to be modified for the new environment. Once again, CLASS Project engineers were called upon to redesign their software to accommodate new conditions and needs.

Clearly, as limitations and faults were discovered, significant resources were required to resolve them. Funding and time originally planned for content and technology development had to be diverted to fix system problems. In essence, courses were being produced and distributed in parallel with needed technology research and development. The situation was not unlike inventing a bicycle while riding it. There were many scrapes and bruises.

THE CHALLENGE OF SOFTWARE DEVELOPMENT

The seminal software engineering paper "No Silver Bullet," written in 1987 by Fred Brooks, indicated that software includes essential and accidental difficulties. *Essential difficulties* are those inherent in the nature of software, while *accidental difficulties* are those inherent in the production of software. Essential difficulties result from complexity, conformity, changeability and invisibility. Software is complex. The interactions of the hundreds or thousands of lines of program code developed for CLASS not only needed to implement required functions, they needed to work correctly under any and all expected conditions. They also needed to conform to the specifications and limitations of Web browsers, international Web standards, and connections to operating systems. Software is inherently changeable, however; as errors are discovered or as requirements change, software is modified. Unfortunately, software is also invisible. Unlike physical machinery, inspection cannot be done visually and interconnections must be understood mainly through the mind of the developer. Accidental difficulties, on the other hand, are those that arise from the creation process. Anything that simplifies the production, testing, and maintenance of software decreases accidental difficulties. Programming language improvements, stable operating systems, and the availability of reusable program code–all of these reduce accidental difficulties. Essential difficulties, however, largely remain.

Brooks's (1987) key thesis—that there is no "Silver Bullet"—is written in acknowledgment of the problems inherent in producing software-based systems. Producing software is a challenging enterprise. Government, industry, and academia have all suffered from projects that significantly overran cost and schedule. For example, major government efforts, such as NASA's Space Shuttle Checkout and Launch Control System, have been canceled due to such overruns. Neither a simple fix nor, indeed, a "Silver Bullet" existed to solve these problems. It is in this context that one should view the challenges faced by the CLASS Project.

There were several symptoms of both essential and accidental difficulties in the CLASS software development. Some of the more prevalent problems included difficulties predicting software cost and schedule. This resulted both from incomplete or ambiguous specification (essential difficulties) and process difficulties such as the inability to achieve expected results from using a particular authoring tool (accidental difficulties). As a result, cost estimates seemed unrelated to actual costs and development schedules were rarely met. Other problems resulted from incomplete specification and testing. For example, software that was declared complete failed to work when sent to students and, frequently, a cascade of new errors was created during repair of earlier problems. CLASS encountered the classical difficulties enumerated by Brooks (1987) and suffered by many software projects over the past half-century.

Additional problems resulted from the research and development environment, wherein software development and maintenance was dependent upon a particular group of extremely talented and dedicated individuals. CLASS was reliant upon this small group of experts because the schedule would not allow freeing the existing staff to oversee training of additional engineers. It was difficult to bring new engineers into the development process without increasing risk and disrupting schedule and cost.

As with many software-intensive systems, the increasing schedule and budget pressure began with inadequate management processes and weak initial project engineering. No systems design was performed at the beginning of this project. To be fair, the technical architecture was generally conceptualized; however, no one had written specifications for the system, identified research and development that was critical to function and performance, or decomposed the system into smaller implementation units. Specifications with respect to the amount of multimedia, video, response times of the servers and network, and so on, were lacking. With no strong documentation at the beginning, or strong resource monitoring throughout the process, instructional designers, software engineers, and graphic artists were left to their own devices in producing products. The benefit and bane of extremely talented people is that they want to produce the best products they can. Well-meaning and highly engaged developers defined and constructed capabilities that were not part of the original specification. Known in the industry as "feature creep," these improvements were high risk, high cost, and occasionally unwarranted. In the absence of strong management control, "desirements" became approved requirements—another instance of essential difficulties.

Further problems arose because technology required for the project—whether developed locally, purchased as part of the development environment, or inherent to browsers and Web servers—was cutting edge and immature. This increased the risk of cost and schedule overruns. Such was the case with the LRD and tracking software.

In addition, the schedules and budgets that were created for specific courses were treated as mere guidelines and gave way easily when the project was confronted with technology problems or delayed production deliveries. Although the project as a whole did not at any time exceed its funding allocation, because there were no planned contingencies identified in either the timeline or resources, it was very difficult to accommodate problems within a course budget. Finally, the project was also hampered by the lack of documentation. Documentation includes the requirements and specifications, technical descriptions of software developed, and the rationale for all major design decisions. For example, the overall design was undocumented. Requirements were not developed and recorded until fairly well into the project. Software documentation was sketchy and incomplete. Weak documentation meant that much time was spent reconstructing what had come before in order to effect repairs and modifications. It also meant that many design decisions were left until late in the project and tied to particular courses or course elements. This situation made it very difficult to achieve economies-of-scale by aggregating the needs of several courses. Clearly, this led to increased cost and schedule risk. Unfortunately, such experience is not atypical in the industry. Despite significant research into the process of information technology development, major corporations and government agencies often fall into similar traps when developing information systems.

In summary, the CLASS Project broke new technical and educational ground. Outstanding people worked long hours to develop 53 online high school courses. New technologies for user tracking and content delivery were invented and successfully tested. Given budget and schedule pressures, this was no small feat. While all involved can take pride in what was accomplished and discovered, flawed technical and managerial processes hampered the project and unnecessarily stressed the personnel involved.

LESSONS LEARNED AND RECOMMENDATIONS

As today's educators create content to be delivered via the Web or CD-ROM, they are becoming technical developers and managers. This section is therefore intended to provide educators with a brief introduction to common technical management methods and, in light of our experience in CLASS, recommendations based on those methods. The recommendations offered here are intended to help modern educators avoid the pitfalls commonly suffered by so many information technology–based projects.

There is a common perception that writing Web pages is not the same as writing programs in a programming language such as C, C++, or Pascal. The resulting effect is that Web pages are frequently written without even a modicum of the discipline that should be used for software development. The complexity of Web pages, however, is not unlike the complexity of small programs developed in C or C++. For the purposes of this chapter, the definition of software includes the classical languages such as C, C++, Java, and Pascal, as well as languages and procedures such as Javascript, HTML, XML, and "macros." Each of these latter examples suffers from the same foibles and difficulties as classically defined "software." The following discussion applies, therefore, to "just" writing Web pages as well as to large software development projects.

Given today's more mature software tools, development of online courses may be accomplished in a production environment with very little technical research and development. In such a setting, the process of creating online courses may be relatively straightforward. While the effort obviously does not require the same engineering rigor and oversight as developing a spacecraft or a weapons system, following a set of design principles, nonetheless, will help mitigate cost and schedule risk. If the project is, on the other hand, truly in a research and development phase involving uncertain technologies and methods, then strict timelines and budgets will be hard to follow. Even then limits should be set and used to stay within the committed budget and schedule. The principles covered in this section apply whether the project is being performed entirely by an individual or by a group of people. However, the principles become more important as the number of individuals involved increases simply because of the increasing need for a common set of operating principles and coordination. The following principles are presented as an overview for consideration by educators developing computer-based courses or course elements.

Management

First, strong and effective management is at the core of all successful projects. It is the responsibility of management to define the project and to document that definition. This is typically done in the form of a written description and a set of requirements. The description is an overview of what is to be developed, the limitations of time and budget, and any general process or management issues that apply to the development organization. The set of requirements should capture the needs to be satisfied by the software under development. Furthermore, the set should include both functional and performance requirements. For example, a functional requirement might be stated as, "The software will assess the ability of a student to perform second-year algebra manipulations and email the results to both the student and the teacher." Performance requirements, on the other hand, might indicate, for example, that the software will respond to any student input within 5 seconds. Based on such requirements, project managers should develop a project plan that includes the project organization, timelines, project budget, and identification of areas of risk and uncertainty. The project plan should also describe how time and funding margins or contingencies would be developed to mitigate risk and uncertainty. This is especially important given that it is not unusual for a software project based on uncertain requirements and immature technology to overrun 50% or much more in time and budget.

It is also important to note that software must be maintained even after it is determined complete. A long-standing rule of thumb in the software industry is that three to five times more will be spent on software after development than was spent on its creation (Burch & Hsiang-Jui, 1997; Herrin, 1985; Lientz, Swanson, & Tompkins, 1978). This cost results from the discovery and correction of bugs, the insertion of new features, and the accommodation of changes in technology and user need. This is not unlike the challenge faced by CLASS courses every time Netscape or Microsoft released a new version of their software. When the courses stopped working, engineers were taken off new development to fix problems in the completed courses. Be prepared for these problems by reserving "contingency" resources in funds and time.

Throughout the lifetime of the project, managers must control the budget and schedule by (1) guarding against changes in requirements (i.e., feature creep), (2) recognizing symptoms of increasing cost and slipping schedules with little or no development progress, and (3) using contingency resources in a frugal manner to avoid untoward reduction of time and resource margin. To accomplish this, milestones (or, in some cases, inch-pebbles) based on critical accomplishments should be identified and used to measure progress. At each milestone date, true progress and cost are compared against the predicted timeline and budget. Any variation must be addressed quickly. The impact of corrective actions must be closely monitored.

Engineering

Because developing computer-based systems is challenging and complex, strong engineering process discipline is needed to minimize the chance for cost and schedule overruns and to ensure that the completed system functions as expected. The steps to be taken include (1) defining the system based on the requirements that need to be satisfied, (2) developing prototype software to facilitate early review and criticism, (3) developing a system to catalog and track all versions of software and multimedia assets, (4) documenting the system and its elements, and (5) testing the system with real users in the expected operating environment.

First, it is important to create a good definition of the system or product to be developed. Requirements developed at the beginning of the project are converted into specifications for each of the required elements. For example, a requirement to assess the ability of the student to manipulate algebraic equations drives a specification stating that the software will provide four variables randomly in a polynomial format that can be reduced within five steps by a student. Similar specifications are written for graphic elements, videos, text, and so on, required to create the needed module. Concomitant to the creation of specifications, it is appropriate to identify how the software will be tested against those specifications. In some cases, engineering tests will be used. In others, a subset of users will be needed to exercise the software's functionality. The specifications then are used to identify the specific software that must be purchased or developed. If research and testing are required, they must be scheduled so that the findings are available in time to avoid delaying the application dependent upon them. If there is a significant uncertainty in when the research and development will be completed, then time contingency must also be included in the schedule.

A second requirement of good engineering process discipline is to develop prototypes of the course and to subject those prototypes to student and faculty review and criticism. Clearly, it is better to find problems early in the effort. It is easier to make changes near the beginning than near the end of the project. The author, for example, required that user manuals be developed first on several software projects. The manuals provided a mechanism for discussion and discovery, facilitating communication between engineers and customers.

The third step in the engineering process involves the development of the software, graphics, videos, text, and other media. As these items are developed, they should be cataloged and made available for future use. Nothing minimizes cost more than being able to use an intermediate product multiple times. However, such intermediate products are normally modified and updated as they are reused, resulting in multiple versions of a particular item. Analogously, it is likely that many versions of software elements will be developed as testing reveals errors that must be corrected, and as better understanding of specifications drives changes in the program. Corrections and changes result in new versions of the code. The process of ensuring that the latest or the most appropriate version of code or media asset is used in building the product is referred to as *configuration management*. While the need to catalogue and to utilize catalogue management practices may sound trivial, it is extremely important. In the press of completion, it is very possible to inadvertently insert an earlier version of software or asset, resulting in the reappearance of previously "solved" problems. Much time can be wasted in resolving this type of difficulty.

Fourth, as part of good management and engineering discipline, documentation plays a key role in minimizing the cost of debugging and maintaining software. Documentation of a project starts from the earliest description and ends when use of the project's products ceases. Documents should be created from the viewpoint of one needing to modify or correct elements of the product. Without good documentation, the individual performing maintenance must reconstruct why design decisions were made, the meaning of particular variables and commands, and the impact of specific software elements before he or she can make any changes. With good documentation, the "relearn" time is minimized and the chance for successful maintenance increased.

Finally, an online course and its elements must be functionally tested prior to application in the classroom. Some of the testing will be technical and will be performed in the development environment. Real students in a simulated course environment can test the educational functionality of the course. Identifying bugs, errors, and misunderstandings early in the project will help mitigate cost and delays. Repairs that result from realistic testing must again be subjected to testing to ensure that new errors have not been created.

LAST THOUGHTS

The CLASS Project successfully produced 53 online high school courses. This is a tribute to the talent and determination of those involved. The development process was not an easy one, however. It was marked by schedule slips, significant technical challenges, and unexpected course costs. The project was heavily dependent on research and development activities. Such activities, by their nature, have uncertainties in cost and schedule that mitigate against strong engineering and management controls. This conflicted with course production expectations—especially after the CLASS.COM™ marketing arm was established. The result was constant tension between the need to perform research and the pressure to produce courses. While this is not an atypical experience in the information systems industry, it contributed to the challenges faced by those involved.

Today's educators are spending an increasing portion of their time crafting computer-based courses and course elements, yet very few educators have had the opportunity to train in the formal processes of software engineering. As the complexity of their efforts increase, they are almost certain to fall into the same traps as those encountered by the CLASS developers. These can be avoided by techniques such as process documentation, requirements documentation, formal timeline development, user testing, configuration control, and schedule and cost risk management. Much written in this chapter is common sense, and managing information technology development is still much more an art than a science. Nonetheless, with care and forethought, many surprises can be avoided and the cost and schedule of the endeavor can be made reasonably predicable.

REFERENCES

Brooks, F. P., Jr. (1987, April). No silver bullet: Essence and accidents of software engineering. *Computer, 20*(4), 10–19.

Burch, E., & Hsiang-Jui, K. (1997). Modeling software maintenance requests: A case study. In M. J. Harrold & G. Visaggio (Eds.), *Proceedings of the International Conference on Software Maintenance* (pp. 40–47). Bari, Italy: IEEE Computer Society.

Herrin, W. R. (1985, March). Software maintenance costs: A quantitative evaluation. *ACM SIGCSE Bulletin, 17*(1), 233–237.

Lientz, B. P., Swanson, E. B., & Tompkins, G. E. (1978, June). Characteristics of application software maintenance. *Communications of ACM, 21*(6), 466–471.

AUTHOR NOTE

This work was made possible by a grant from the U.S. Department of Education to the CLASS Project, University of Nebraska–Lincoln. Opinions expressed are those of the author and not necessarily those of the funders. The author wishes to acknowledge Jill Hochstein, Gary Praeuner, and Mark Weakly of Nebraska Educational Telecommunications, Christy Horn of the Center for Instructional Innovation, and Char Hazzard of the National Center for Information Technology in Education for their review of this chapter and their many helpful suggestions. Each of these individuals also deserves credit for the hard work and long hours they spent as part of the CLASS Project.

Correspondence concerning this chapter should be addressed to Arthur I. Zygielbaum, 269 Mabel Lee Hall, University of Nebraska–Lincoln, Lincoln, NE, 68588-0230. Email: aiz@unl.edu

CHAPTER 9

THE PEDAGOGICAL IMPACT OF COURSE MANAGEMENT SYSTEMS ON FACULTY, STUDENTS, AND INSTITUTION

Charles J. Ansorge
Oksana Bendus
National Center for Information Technology in Education,
University of Nebraska–Lincoln

ABSTRACT

Course management systems (CMSs) such as Blackboard and WebCT are becoming increasingly important in supporting both distance education and on-campus courses. To obtain a comprehensive picture of CMS influence on teaching, learning, and assessment, evaluation of these systems is necessary. Faculty members ($n = 590$), administrators ($n = 115$), and students ($n = 401$) from the University of Nebraska–Lincoln (UNL) responded to the questions about the educational impact of these systems on the UNL campus. Results revealed that all the students in the sample had used a CMS, and approximately half of administrators and faculty members employed course management software in their teaching. The majority of the respondents across all of

Web-Based Learning: What Do We Know? Where Do We Go?, pages 169–190

the groups utilized Blackboard as their major CMS. The main objective in CMS usage was to post, review, or print the documents for traditional classroom courses. Despite the overall satisfaction with course management systems across the groups, the major obstacles for faculty in using CMSs were (1) lack of faculty interest, (2) lack of recognition for teaching via CMS, (3) difficulty finding the time to prepare for courses, and (4) difficulty finding the time to learn about CMS tools.

Course management systems (CMSs) have been utilized by many colleges and universities for several years now. Their purpose is to provide a teaching and learning environment that includes tools for retrieval of educational content, synchronous and asynchronous communication, administrative functions, and assessment (Ellis, 2001; Landon, 2002; Malloy, Jensen, & Reddick, 2001; Nichani, 2001; Smith, Murphy, & Teng, 2001). The first CMSs appeared in the period between 1995 and 1997 to manage the delivery of online courses and to facilitate the transition from traditional classroom instruction to Web-based instruction. Seven years ago there were only a few colleges and universities that utilized these systems' capabilities; today, however, the number is astonishing. For example, according to Blackboard, Inc. (2002), there are 2,400 institutions that use their product. WebCT, Inc. (2002), reports that 2,600 institutions in 84 countries are licensed to use WebCT. Moreover, the number of institutions that recognize the importance of CMSs in distance education and on-campus teaching is increasing. For example, according to the Campus Computing Survey, which included 590 institutions across the United States (Greene, 2001), a growing number of universities and colleges identify CMSs as "very important" in their institutional informational technology planning. Moreover, roughly three-fourths (73.2%) of the institutions participating in the survey have already established a "single product" standard for course management software, up from 57.8% in 2000; and approximately one-fifth (20.6%) of all college courses now use course management tools, up from 14.7% in 2000.

Implementation of such CMSs requires not only careful review of products before acquisition, but also a careful and thorough evaluation of the product after its selection and use. Therefore, the purpose of this chapter is to describe one such evaluation attempt conducted in spring 2002 by the National Center of Information Technology in Education (NCITE) with funding from the CLASS (Communications, Learning, and Assessment in a Student-Centered System) Project. The current study used survey methodology to address the educational aspects of the CMSs at the University Nebraska–Lincoln (UNL), including the efficacy of the current CMS technology in learning, teaching, and assessment. A second study, reported elsewhere (see Samal & Gopal, Chapter 10, this volume), used technological indicators to address issues relating to the CMS efficiency in course production, reuse of content, and course delivery. This chapter is organized into three broad sections: (1) the historical background of CMSs at UNL, (2) a detailed description of the current study, and (3) conclusions and implications for future projects. A discussion of these topics follows.

HISTORICAL PERSPECTIVE REGARDING COURSE MANAGEMENT SYSTEMS AT UNL

In the late 1990s, the number of CMSs available for use on college and university campuses increased dramatically. Because so many systems were available and because no single product emerged as a clear leader, it was not surprising that various colleges and even departments within the colleges acquired and tested systems to determine their effectiveness and to learn if they might have a favorable impact on students' learning. One of the earliest systems that was reviewed and later acquired by UNL was Lotus Notes. As early as 1993 it was adopted for use by the Educational Leadership and Higher Education (ELHE) program of the Department of Educational Administration to support 15 online courses. Since its inception, the ELHE program has been utilizing a collaborative-active learning philosophy, with both students and instructors engaged in constant learning interaction. The Lotus Notes software system effectively supported this learning model by including essential collaborative-process features such as email and a discussion board, and by emphasizing replication of the documents posted between client and server. Therefore, Lotus Notes seemed to be a good fit for the program's needs. Because evaluation of the students' work was done through written assignments, interaction among students, and a course project, Lotus Notes was also well-suited for assessment purposes. By fall 1996, there were at least three other systems in addition to Lotus Notes available on the UNL campus: TopClass (WBT Systems, Inc., n.d.), WebCT, and FirstClass (Centrinity, Inc., n.d.). TopClass had been acquired by Information Services, the campus Information Technology department, and was made available to university faculty. WebCT was an acquisition by Communications and Information Technology (CIT), and FirstClass was purchased and used in the College of Human Resources and Family Sciences. In the following two years, use of these systems was not extensive due to the lack of "user-friendly" system features, low processing speed of computers, and limited access to the Internet.

The event that triggered the growth of the use of CMSs on the UNL campus was the introduction of *Blackboard CourseInfo*™ at a faculty workshop event in January 1998. During the previous year Information Services had supported TopClass, but had learned that the cost for licensing the product for a year would be more than double the original price. This prompted a review of then-available CMSs to determine if more cost-effective and better products were available. This review included discussions with a number of vendors that were in attendance at the 1997 EDUCAUSE annual conference. The result of these discussions was an agreement between UNL and Blackboard to try their product for one year.

The 1998 faculty workshop event was attended by approximately 30 faculty and support staff and proved to be the kick-off for what has turned out to be an impressive growth spurt in the use of CMSs on the UNL campus. Once faculty learned that the skill set necessary to create Web-based courses did not require extensive training, the Blackboard CMS became widely accepted and its use grew at a pace far exceeding what many expected. Faculty learned that one of the additional benefits of the system was that it accommodated students at a distance as easily as students on campus. As a consequence, it is not surprising that the number of distance learning classes utilizing this software increased rapidly.

The fast growth in the use of *Blackboard CourseInfo*™ was not without problems. Although the system was and still is user-friendly, when it was first introduced, someone had to create every individual course. Likewise, rosters of students had to be created for every class. Both of these tasks required extra human resources. Early in the growth cycle of the CMS, the time requirements to complete these tasks were not excessive, but as the numbers of classes increased and the rosters of students increased, it became clear that there would be a need to find a more efficient way to "scale" the system. A solution was found in the form of a new version of Blackboard, *Blackboard Learning System*™ (Release 5), level three version (hereafter, Blackboard 5). The UNL campus acquired this product and installed it prior to the start of classes in fall 2000. Moving to Blackboard 5 represented a significant step for the campus because it was a much more expensive version of the CMS than that acquired in 1998. The licensing fee in 1998 was approximately $5,000 per year. The licensing fee of the new version was approximately $50,000. Other associated expenses, including extra hardware and support, required an additional investment of more than $250,000.

Nonetheless, Blackboard 5 included numerous benefits:

- It was scalable to thousands of courses and tens of thousands of students.
- It was possible to integrate it with UNL's existing administrative systems. For example, if a student added or dropped a course through Registration and Records, the change would be reflected in the Blackboard 5 rosters within one business day.
- Because Blackboard 5 was not course-centric, material could easily be reused and/or shared from one course to another and among multiple instructors.

- Existing course materials developed in Blackboard CourseInfo could be easily migrated into Blackboard 5.
- The architecture of Blackboard 5 was flexible enough to accommodate future Web-based teaching efforts at UNL. Blackboard, Inc., was committed to following standards for course materials that would allow materials to be easily moved between CMSs.

DESCRIPTION OF THE CURRENT STUDY

Purpose of Study

The purpose of this study was to evaluate the educational impact of CMSs used at UNL. Of particular interest was learning (1) how CMSs were used by faculty and students, (2) whether or not current CMS technology influenced the teaching approach of faculty, and (3) whether or not CMS usage facilitated students' learning. Additionally, there was interest in ascertaining whether the presence of certain factors or "obstacles" prevented faculty from using these systems or utilizing them more efficiently. Finally, data were collected to determine if the administrators and faculty members perceived the same factors as obstacles, and how their perceptions differed. Table 9.1 lists examples of the survey questions posed to each group of respondents.

Methods and Procedures

Data were collected from all subjects using a split methodology and survey instruments that were created with the assistance of the local division of The Gallup Organization (in Princeton, New Jersey). Approximately 1,800 faculty members and university administrators received an invitation to complete a Web survey, and 401 students were randomly selected for a telephone survey.

Web-based survey

Two hundred thirty-five administrators and approximately 1,600 faculty members were asked to participate in the survey by an email invitation with a hyperlink directed to a personalized survey site hosted by Gallup Organization. A list with participants' email addresses was obtained from UNL and was sent to Gallup Organization so they could invite the participation of eligible applicants. The qualified administrators were vice chancellors, deans, directors, department heads, and chairs; the eligible faculty members included instructors, lecturers, professors, and extension educators.

Table 9.1. Examples of Questions Posed to Faculty, Administrators, and Students

	Respondent groups	
Faculty	*Administrators*	*Students*
1. Identify the CMS you are currently using or have previously used. (Click all that apply.)	1. Do you use the CMS with any of the classes you teach?	1. Do you use any of the following course management systems?
2. Do you evaluate students' learning via the CMS?		2. Have you taken any exams, quizzes, etc., via the CMS?
3. Does the CMS allow you to use a full range of assessment tools?		
4. How would you describe the reactions of the students to your online efforts?	2. The university has clear guidelines regarding ownership of course materials.	3. How adequately does your instructor utilize the CMS?
5. Compared to traditional exams and quizzes, what is the level of difficulty of exams and quizzes used via the CMS?	3. How should faculty, who create Web-based material for their teaching, be compensated? a) stipends; b) course royalties; c) recognition; d) release time to prepare; e) no additional compensation is needed.	4. Compared to paper-and-pencil exams and quizzes, please rate the difficulty of the exams and quizzes via CMS using a 5-point scale.
6. Compared to traditional courses, how much time do you spend preparing for the courses using the CMS?	4. Web-based materials created by faculty for use in their classes are the property of UNL, not the instructor.	5. Compared to paper-and-pencil exams or quizzes, how much time does it take for you to complete the exams or quizzes via the CMS?
7. What feature of your preferred CMS do you find the most useful?	5. The acquisition of the Blackboard has been a good investment for the UNL campus.	6. How do you PRIMARILY use the CMS?

Table 9.1. Examples of Questions Posed to Faculty, Administrators, and Students (Cont.)

	Respondent groups	
Faculty	Administrators	Students
8. Which of the following statements best describes how your preferred CMS has or will change your approach to teaching?	6. Listed below are various forms of support that may be needed to increase faculty and student use of the CMS in classes at UNL. Indicate the extent to which you agree or disagree with these statements:	7. How would you rate the overall helpfulness of the CMS in your learning experience?
a) I can't teach as well as I rely even in part on the system	a) additional support is not needed;	
b) Minimal potential for change	b) tenure/salary recognition;	
c) My basic approach for teaching is unlikely to change but this helps me to do certain things better	c) additional instructional designers are needed.	
d) My basic approach to teaching seems to be changing, in part because of opportunities created by this kind of technology		
9. Listed below are potential obstacles for faculty in using course management software in their teaching. Indicate the extent to which you agree or disagree that these are obstacles:		
a) Finding time to learn about using the necessary tools		
b) Availability of satisfactory training workshops		
c) Lack of sufficient computer hardware		
d) Access to multimedia in a classroom		
e) Time for course preparation		
f) Lack of faculty interest		
g) Lack of technical support		
h) Lack of tenure/salary recognition (Note: not used in administrator's survey)		

Note. The total number of items included on the faculty survey was 47, on administrators', 23, on students', 22. Questions reflected pedagogical as well as technical aspects of evaluation.

Telephone survey

Undergraduate and graduate students who were registered for classes at the time and who were 19 years of age or older were contacted via telephone by Gallup Organization interviewers in late April 2002. Up to three calls (an initial call and two follow-up calls) were placed to each respondent in order to avoid a bias toward respondents easy to reach by telephone. A list of student participants, their telephone numbers, and current college standings was obtained from UNL's Office of Registration and Records.

RESULTS

Faculty Survey Results

Of the approximately 1,600 faculty members who were sent invitations to complete the online survey, 590 (39.3%) chose to respond. The respondents included professors (32%), associate professors (25%), assistant professors (20%), lecturers (11%), and extension educators (12%). A total of 55% of the respondents were tenured, while nontenure leading-track (hereafter nontenured) and tenure-track faculty represented 30% and 15% of the group, respectively. The largest percentage of respondents had 20 years or more of teaching experience (41%), with 30% having between 10 and up to 20 years of experience in higher education. While faculty from all colleges were represented in the study, faculty from Agricultural Sciences and Natural Resources represented the largest group (27%), followed by Arts and Sciences (25%) and Teachers College (9%).

The number of the respondents who answered the items related to the topic of pedagogy was substantially less than the number of faculty responding to the survey. This was due to the use of two screening items that identified and retained only those faculty members who were currently using a CMS in the teaching of their classes. The first key screening question was "Have you ever considered using a CMS in any courses you teach?" Surprisingly, more than half of the faculty said that they never considered using a CMS in their teaching, and only 27% of them stated that they had recently used CMSs. The remaining 18% of the group had discontinued using a CMS due to a variety of reasons. The most common reason mentioned was the finding of other, more efficient means to teach Web-supported classes, or spending too much time on the development of CMS-mediated courses. Moreover, the majority of respondents who were nonusers were either nontenured faculty members who had taught for less than a year (65.3 %), or tenured faculty who had taught for more than 10 years (52.9%).

The second screening item was "Do you currently use a course management system in the teaching of classes or have you used one since January 2000?" Of the 258 respondents who answered this question, 74% said "yes." Those most familiar with CMSs were tenure-track faculty who taught between 1 and 2 years (63.2 %), as compared to tenured or nontenured faculty whose teaching experience was less than a year or more than 2 years. Moreover, the most preferred CMS was Blackboard (79%), followed by www-class.unl.edu[1] (6%) and Lotus Notes (3%). The remaining respondents (12%) preferred other CMSs such as EDU Campus (Brownstone Research Group), eGrade (Wiley eGrade), and WebCT.

We turn next to a detailed explanation of the results pertaining to those survey items answered only by faculty members who had some experience using CMSs. When appropriate, we compare faculty responses to student and administrator responses to similar survey questions.

Most useful features of CMSs

The largest percentage of faculty respondents (69% of 192) reported the "posting of electronic documents" to be the most useful feature of CMSs. The second most preferred feature was the "discussion board," selected by 17% of the respondents. Smaller percentages of faculty selected the "assessment tool" (8%), the "chat feature" (1%), and "other tools" (5%). The ordering of these choices was consistent across the respondents regardless of their gender, academic rank, and tenure status. However, it differed for participants depending upon their teaching experience. Specifically, the discussion board was considered the second most important feature by faculty members who taught for 5 years or more, but not by those who taught for less than 5 years. It might be expected that faculty who were teaching at the graduate level would utilize the discussion board feature considerably more than faculty who primarily teach undergraduates, but this was not the case. Of the faculty principally involved with undergraduate teaching responsibilities, 14% preferred this feature. Meanwhile, only slightly more (19%) of the faculty who primarily taught graduate courses preferred this feature. It should also be noted that the distribution of faculty responses to this question was similar to the distribution of the students' responses to a question about primary use of CMSs (see Table 9.2), demonstrating converging evidence that CMSs at UNL were mainly used for posting, reviewing, or printing electronic documents.

Evaluating students' learning via CMS

Faculty respondents were asked whether or not they evaluated students' learning via the CMS. The available systems permit faculty to create a variety of different kinds of exams, including true–false, multiple-choice, matching, multiple response, and short answer. For most forms of assess-

**Table 9.2.   Distribution of Faculty and Student Responses to a
Question about Patterns of CMS Usage**

Respondents			
Faculty		*Students*	
What feature of your preferred CMS do you find the most useful?		How do you primarily use the course management system?	
Posting electronic documents	69%	To review or print course documents	77%
Discussion board	17%	To participate in the discussion board	8%
Assessment tool	8%	To participate in chat activities	1%
Chat	1%	To send emails	4%
Other	5%	To complete exams and quizzes	9%
		Don't know	1%
Total	100%	Total	100%

ment, the system can score the exams and automatically provide student feedback. Of the 191 faculty who used a CMS in teaching their classes, nearly two-thirds (65%) reported that they did not conduct any kind of assessment with the system. However, faculty with the rank of professor and faculty who had 10 or more years of experience indicated they used the CMS to collect assessment information more than other groups that were examined, with 43% and 40%, respectively, answering "yes" to this question. Moreover, approximately the same percentage of students (37%) stated that they took quizzes and exams via the CMS. Those faculty members who reported using the CMS to collect assessment data from their students were asked to indicate whether they were able to use a full range of assessment tools with the system. Slightly more than 60% of those responding answered "yes" to the question. Even though this represented a majority of the respondents, the fact remained that almost 40% found the assessment tools to be inadequate or at least limiting.

Level of difficulty of CMS quizzes and exams

Respondents were asked to rate the difficulty of the exams and quizzes they constructed when using the CMS. Only 58 of the approximately 190 faculty who reported using a CMS responded to this question. The majority of these respondents (75%) reported there was no difference in the difficulty of Web-based exams and quizzes versus traditional exams and quizzes. Meanwhile, 16% reported that Web-based exams and quizzes were more difficult, and 9% said they were easier. The results from the students' survey were in close agreement with faculty results, with the majority of students stating that the difficulty level of CMS quizzes and the exams was the same as of traditional assessment tools. However, the students' pattern of responses was more skewed to the "easy" side of the scale (average difficulty rating = 2.72, where 5 was "extremely difficult" and 1 was "less difficult"), demonstrating that students, to a greater degree than faculty, viewed CMS assessment as easier than traditional paper-and-pencil assessment.

Perception of students' proficiency in using CMS

CMSs continue to be relatively new innovations on college and university campuses. Although *Blackboard CourseInfo™* was introduced in 1998 and Lotus Notes has been around for longer than that, it has been only in the last two years that the systems have been used to a much wider extent due to the increased processing speed of computers and better and faster access to the Internet. How have the students been able to adapt to the changing technology now being made available to them? Faculty members were asked to report how proficient they thought their students were in using the CMS. Of the 189 faculty who responded to this question, 60% reported their students to be either "very proficient" or "proficient." Only 5% of the faculty thought their students had no proficiency in using the CMS. It would certainly appear that student proficiency in using the CMS is not a limitation for the campus. This notion was supported by students' own evaluation of their comfort level with using CMS. The average student rating was 4.25 (where 5 was "very comfortable" and 1 was "not comfortable at all"), suggesting that students rated their own abilities even higher than did the instructors.

Student reaction to instructors' online efforts

There were 182 faculty respondents who described the reactions of their students to their online effort. Nearly 80% indicated that their students had a positive reaction to their use of the CMS. Only 8 of the 182 faculty responding to this item reported a negative reaction on the part of their students. The rest of the faculty (18%) reported that the students were indifferent to their online efforts.

Perceived effect of CMS on current/future approach to teaching

CMSs provide a course environment that has the potential of influencing the way instructors teach. Indeed, 41% of the UNL faculty respondents reported that their basic approach to teaching seemed to be changing, in part because of the opportunities created by this kind of technology. Such a judgment made by such a high proportion of respondents reveals the potentially powerful effect of CMSs. Meanwhile, 5% of the respondents thought their use of the CMS either limited their teaching effectiveness or was likely to have a minimal influence regarding the way they approach the teaching of their classes. The largest percentage of the respondents (54%) indicated that their basic approach to teaching probably would not be significantly affected because of the CMS they used, but that they were now able to do some things better in their teaching because of CMS tools that provided students access to materials 24 hours a day and 7 days a week. There was little variability in the responses to this item by academic rank and level of courses taught. Responses to this question varied by the gender and tenure status of the respondents, however. With respect to the answer choice indicating a change in their teaching, 45% of the males (n = 56) and 34% of the females (n = 22) chose this option. Moreover, tenured faculty comprised the group with the largest percentage (50%) indicating such change, while the group with the smallest percentage (28%) was tenure-track faculty who were not yet tenured. It may be that the members of this latter group were focusing on other parts of their development as a faculty member.

CMS preparation time as a primary obstacle to CMS use

Of the 180 faculty who provided information about the impact of CMSs on time spent for course preparation, 75% of the respondents indicated more time was required for course preparation when a CMS was used, while only 6% of the respondents reported taking less time. The issue of having to spend a lot of time on preparation for CMS courses emerged as the biggest potential obstacle for faculty in using CMSs in their teaching. As shown in Table 9.3, of the 188 faculty respondents, 67% agreed that finding time for course preparation was an obstacle for CMS use, while 17% disagreed and 16% remained neutral. It is noteworthy that the majority of administrators (62%) also agreed that finding time for course preparation was an obstacle to faculty use of a CMS. However, a slightly larger percentage of administrators (25%) remained neutral in answering this question. Perhaps because not all administrators participating in the study taught classes via CMS, they could not give an accurate estimate of time required for preparing courses via CMS.

Lack of tenure/salary recognition as an obstacle to using a CMS

Nontenured faculty members often have the perception that spending too much time on their teaching at the expense of their research agenda may result in an unfavorable tenure review. Likewise, spending time preparing materials that related to their teaching may take time away from a possible publication that would more likely influence a salary increase. Thus, we included an item on the UNL survey to determine if tenure/salary recognition might be regarded as an obstacle for faculty members in using course management software. We were not surprised to learn that 57% of the respondents agreed or strongly agreed that these two factors

Table 9.3.   Distribution of Faculty and Administrator Responses to Questions about Potential Obstacles for Teaching via CMS

Obstacles [a]	Respondents	
	Faculty	Administrators
Time for course preparation	($n = 188$)	($n = 91$)
Strongly agree/agree	67%	62%
Neutral	16%	25%
Disagree/strongly disagree	17%	12%
Lack of tenure/salary recognition	($n = 159$)	(n = 88)
Strongly agree/agree	57%	52%
Neutral	13%	14%
Disagree/strongly disagree	30%	34%
Lack of faculty interest	($n = 171$)	($n = 91$)
Strongly agree/agree	49%	33%
Neutral	29%	23%
Disagree/strongly disagree	22%	44%
Lack of training workshops	($n = 168$)	($n = 86$)
Strongly agree/agree	27%	32%
Neutral	26%	26%
Disagree/strongly disagree	47%	42%

[a] *Note.* The exact wording of the question was: "Listed below are potential obstacles in faculty's teaching of courses via CMS. Indicate the extent to which you agree or disagree that these are the obstacles."

were potential obstacles, compared to only 30% who disagreed or strongly disagreed. Once again, the majority of administrators supported the faculty view on this question. A total of 52% of the administrators agreed and only 34% disagreed that lack of tenure or salary recognition for creating courses via CMS could prevent faculty from using CMS in their teaching.

The pattern of faculty responses remained consistent for this item regardless of participants' gender, academic rank, tenure status, years of experience, and level of courses taught. This finding was somewhat surprising because one might think that faculty not yet tenured but on a tenure-leading line would be more likely to report their tenure recognition as a potential obstacle. Such was not the case. It might be argued, however, that the faculty who answered this question may not have accurately reflected the entire population of university faculty members due to the fact that all respondents were users of a CMS.

Lack of faculty interest as an obstacle to CMS use

Of 171 faculty respondents, nearly 50% either agreed or strongly agreed that lack of faculty interest would likely be an obstacle to CMS use, while only 22% disagreed. The perceptions of the faculty and administrators were rather different regarding this item; only 33% of administrators agreed or strongly agreed that lack of faculty interest was an obstacle to faculty use of a CMS. It is interesting to note, however, that the perceptions of those administrators currently involved in teaching a class and who had used course management were much closer to the faculty. Apparently experience with a CMS offers some insights that affect the perception of this potential obstacle.

Availability of satisfactory training workshops as an obstacle to CMS use

Use of new technologies such as CMSs may require faculty development opportunities such as scheduled workshops. Lack of such training workshops might lead to frustration on the part of faculty and a lack of interest in developing course content. This was the thinking that led to our including a question about whether the "lack of training workshops" was a potential obstacle to CMS use. Only 27% of the faculty and 32% of administrators agreed with this premise, while 47% of faculty and 42% of administrators disagreed. These findings may suggest either that faculty did not require these workshops, or that there were already a sufficient number of workshops available to meet faculty needs.

Faculty survey summary

Faculty survey results demonstrated that the most useful feature of CMSs was posting of electronic documents and that the majority of faculty continued to assess students with paper-and-pencil measures rather than utilizing CMS assessment tools. In addition, the CMS exams and quizzes were considered equal to traditional exams and quizzes. The majority of faculty also thought their students were very proficient or proficient in the use of CMS, with faculty indicating that their online efforts were met positively by the students. The most significant obstacle in preventing faculty for using CMS in teaching was finding time for CMS course preparation, with the least significant being availability of training workshops. Perhaps most importantly, the results of this survey showed that the number of UNL faculty who thought that their basic approach to teaching would not be affected by CMS was almost equal to the number of those who thought that their teaching techniques were changing due to CMS technologies.

Administrator Survey Results

We next discuss additional results of the administrator survey not yet addressed above. All campus administrators at UNL were invited to participate, including personnel in the Office for the Senior Vice Chancellor for Academic Affairs, as well as deans, directors, and department chairs. Of the 115 administrators who responded, 7 (6%) were at the level of the vice chancellor, 53 (46%) were deans or directors, 39 (34%) were department chairs, and the remaining 16 (14%) were either associate deans or directors or classified as "other." When the administrators were asked to indicate whether they taught classes or not, of the 114 who answered the question, 49 (43%) indicated they did. Of these 49 administrators, 24 (49%) reported they used a CMS in their teaching. The CMS of choice for 96% of these administrators was Blackboard.

As already reviewed in the previous section (see Table 9.3), the administrators were asked to evaluate potential obstacles for faculty using course management software in their teaching. In addition, administrators responded to a number of items related to ownership of materials created via CMS and acquisition of Blackboard by UNL (see Table 9.4).

Table 9.4.   Distribution of Administrator Responses to Survey Items Related to Ownership of CMS Materials and Acquisition of Blackboard

Survey Item	Strongly agree	Agree	Undecided	Disagree	Strongly disagree
The university has clear guidelines regarding ownership of course materials ($n = 70$)	3%	24%	30%	37%	6%
Web-based materials created by faculty for use in their classes are the property of UNL, not the instructor ($n = 104$)	13%	25%	21%	24%	17%
The acquisition of Blackboard has been a good investment for the UNL campus ($n = 79$)	33%	48%	14%	1%	4%

Guidelines regarding ownership of course materials
    In recent years, many efforts have been underway to establish guidelines regarding ownership of course materials that have been created by faculty for the courses they teach using CMSs. Despite such efforts, there still seems to be ambiguity regarding the ownership of CMS course materials (see Odabasi, Chapter 11, this volume). Only a little more than one-fourth of 70 administrator respondents agreed or strongly agreed that "the university has clear guidelines regarding ownership of course materials," while

42% disagreed or strongly disagreed. The fact that 30% of the administrators were undecided suggests that the campus needs to continue in its efforts to clarify this issue. Administrators also were asked whether Web-based materials created by the faculty for use in their courses were the property of the institution or the faculty. Again, a total of 38% of administrators agreed or strongly agreed that ownership resided with the institution, while 41% disagreed or strongly disagreed.

This pattern of responses suggests that having a clear policy regarding the ownership of course materials may be an important issue to faculty. Faculty may be reluctant to invest time in the creation of course materials if they believe this course content is either not their property or they do not have rights to it beyond the classroom. University policies related to publishing a book or obtaining a patent for some invention may be clearer than those involving Web materials. However, it is possible such ownership issues may be less important in the future, because some campuses, such as Massachusetts Institute of Technology (MIT) are making all Web-based course content that is Web-based freely available to anyone to access. Their view is that content is less important than are those who are responsible for delivering it.

View on the acquisition of Blackboard

The 1998 introduction of *Blackboard CourseInfo*™ began a 4-year investment for the UNL community. In the beginning, the funding required was relatively insignificant. As previously noted, however, the amount of the investment increased significantly in the fall of 2000 with the introduction of *Blackboard Learning System*™ (Release 5), level 3. How has this increased investment been viewed by those individuals who were chiefly responsible for finding the necessary funding? Over 80% of the administrators agreed or strongly agreed that the acquisition of the Blackboard CMS has been a good investment. It is unusual to find such a high level of agreement for the acquisition of any teaching and learning software for a university campus, and the fact that only 5% of the administrators disagreed or strongly disagreed with the statement is evidence of strong support for Blackboard on the UNL campus.

View on faculty compensation

Faculty responses indicated that creating Web-based materials for courses requires a significant amount of time. Thus, administrators were asked to respond to the following question: "How should faculty who create Web-based material for their teaching, using systems like Blackboard or Lotus Notes, be compensated?" They were also prompted to offer various alternatives if they believed a form of compensation was reasonable. Nearly 80% of the administrators who responded thought there should be some form of compensation to the faculty for their efforts to make Web-based materials available to their students (see Table 9.5). It is interesting to note, however, that of the 110 administrators who responded to the question, 24 of them (22%) thought that faculty members did not require any additional time to create these materials. Other administrators, however, supported release time (39%), some form of recognition (15%), stipends (6%), or course royalties (5%) as possible compensation incentives to get faculty to commit time to the development of Web-based course content.

Table 9.5. Distribution of Administrator Responses to the Question Regarding Compensation of Faculty Members for Creation of Web Materials

Response options	Percent
How should faculty who create Web-based material for their teaching, using systems like Blackboard or Lotus Notes, be compensated?	
Release time to prepare	39%
No additional time is needed	22%
Recognition	15%
Stipends	6%
Course royalties	5%
Other	13%
Total	100%

Administrator survey summary

In summary, the results of our administrator survey demonstrated that, when they were functioning as faculty members, the administrators considered finding time for CMS course preparation to be the most substantial obstacle for faculty in using CMSs in teaching, and availability of training workshops as the least significant barrier. However, the faculty and administrators' opinions differed on whether or not lack of faculty interest was an obstacle, with more faculty members agreeing with this statement and more administrators feeling that it was not an issue. Moreover, the results revealed that UNL administrators were in some disagreement about the ownership of the materials created via CMS, supporting the idea that UNL did not have clear guidelines on this issue. Despite this contradiction in opinions, however, the majority of the administrators considered the acquisition of Blackboard as a good investment for UNL.

Student Survey Results

Finally, we discuss additional results from the student survey, not yet addressed above. The respondents to our telephone survey included 401 students 19 years and older, almost equally representing males and females. Of these students, 29% were seniors, 22% were juniors, 17% were sophomores, 14% were freshmen, and 17% were graduate students. In terms of their major, the majority of the students were affiliated with the College of Art and Sciences (26%) and the smallest groups were associated with the College of Architecture, General Studies, and Human Resources and Family Sciences (3% each). The participants used computers approximately 28% of their "working" time. When asked about how much time per week they spent using a computer, the average number was around 15 hours.

Use of CMS

Surprisingly, all students participating in the survey were familiar with some kind of CMS and, as previously noted, felt comfortable using them. When asked about their primary use of CMS, 77% of students chose printing and reviewing the documents and 8% chose participating in the discussion board and taking exams and quizzes (see Table 9.2 for a complete list of response choices). A plurality of students (48%) accessed the courses several times a week, while 32% visited the CMS only before major assignments, and 14% accessed the CMS every day. Only a small number of respondents (5%) visited their course site after each lecture. These last results may reflect the study habits of the students, suggesting that the majority of students studied either several times a week or only before exams and major assignments, with only a small number of participants reviewing learned material each day. Interestingly, further analysis of CMS access by year in school revealed that study habits depended on student maturity level. Specifically, 51% of freshmen accessed CMS only before major assignments and tests and none accessed them after each lecture, whereas 10% of graduate students visited their course site after each lecture, demonstrating usage of a more efficient studying methodology.

Evaluating the importance of the discussion board

The discussion board tool is thought to be beneficial to both students and instructors because it (1) does not require a physical presence of either party, (2) allows submitting the messages anonymously, and (3) permits posting the information to a group instead of sending it to each one individually. Moreover, by monitoring the discussion board activity, the instructor may readily detect common trends in students' thinking. However, did the discussion board play an important role in students' learning process? As previously noted, only 8% of the respondents said that their primary CMS use involved the discussion board. Further inquiries revealed that the majority of students (78%) never posted messages on the discussion board, 14% posted them once a week, 6% submitted them two to four times per week, and 1% posted the messages more than five times per week. Nonetheless, those students who did utilize the discussion board rated it as "somewhat important," with an average response of 3.18 on a 5-point scale, where 5 was "very important." Why, then, wasn't the discussion board used by a larger percentage of students? It is possible that the nature of the assignments or topics studied did not require discussion or perhaps that the students did not feel comfortable discussing their ideas "in front" of an audience, even with an option for anonymous postings.

Overall impressions

Overall, the students' perceptions of CMSs were positive. Of the respondents, 83% said that they had not experienced any problems with CMS within the last six months. Moreover, the majority of students rated their preferred CMS as user-friendly, where the average was 4.06 on a 5-point scale, with 1 being "very difficult to use" and 5 being "very easy to use." Finally, when asked about helpfulness of the CMS in their learning experience, the majority of students evaluated the systems as "helpful," giving the item an average rating of 3.57, where 1 was "not at all helpful" and 5 was "very helpful."

Summary of student survey results

The students' responses suggested a link between faculty members' primary use of CMSs for posting electronic documents, and students' primary use of CMSs for printing or reviewing these materials. Moreover, the results showed that the students considered the discussion board as somewhat important and CMS exams and quizzes to be slightly easier than traditional exams and quizzes. Most importantly, the majority of students evaluated CMSs as user-friendly and helpful in their learning experience.

CONCLUSION

In this chapter, we have discussed an attempt to evaluate the efficacy of the CMSs employed at UNL in terms of their perceived contribution to teaching, learning, and assessment. Overall, all three groups of respondents—students, faculty, and administrators—viewed CMSs as providing a positive contribution to teaching and learning at UNL. Students perceived CMSs as helpful in their learning experience, and the majority of faculty stated that they were now able to do some things better in their teaching because of the tools they had at their command. Administrators viewed acquisition of the major CMS, Blackboard, as a good investment. It was also found that the majority of classes utilizing CMSs at UNL were classroom-based courses and not distance-education classes, thus demonstrating that the main utilization of CMSs was to support traditional learning environments. Combining benefits of classroom methodologies with the unique features of Web technologies allows CMSs to connect directed-learning and open-ended learning at the same time (Hannafin, Hall, Land, & Hill, 1994), affording students the opportunity to become active decision makers in determining what they should learn and what steps they should take to enhance learning.

In spite of the positive overall perception of CMSs, not all available features were used with the same interest. In the course of the study, we discovered that respondents mainly used CMSs for posting documents, thus underutilizing such potentially useful features as the discussion board and assessment tools. This fact might be due to the nonintuitiveness of the software or to the lack of a strong need to use these features on the Web. For example, it might be that discussions taking place in the classrooms were more enriching and informative than discussions posted via the CMS. Meanwhile, the major reason for not utilizing CMS assessments more often could involve instructors' concern about the required effort. Faculty may not be aware of the fact that the majority of quizzes and exams can be created now with minimal effort using generic software programs and adapting them to meet the needs of a specific discipline. Almost certainly, however, the utilization of these features and CMS usage in general will be more widespread as faculty members already familiar with this technology and its tools share their experiences with their novice colleagues through workshops or simply by word of mouth.

The results of our study show that faculty members' and, correspondingly, students' involvement with CMSs was limited by lack of faculty interest, time for course preparation, and compensation that would have encouraged the faculty to develop Web courses. To increase faculty involvement with CMSs, we need to increase faculty interest in CMSs. This may be achieved—not only by creating compensation in a form of grants, salaries, and recognition—but also by publicizing system benefits such as reuse of content, convenient access to course material, ease of grading, and so on.

The current study by no means covers all the issues pertaining to the efficacy of CMSs in teaching and learning. Data like these can be linked profitably with data directly reflecting student and faculty CMS use (see Samal & Gopal, this volume). Future work in this area is needed to compare the perception and performance of CMSs at UNL to other institutions in the country. Moreover, understanding of both the positive and negative aspects of CMS usage could be enhanced by looking at case studies involving individuals from faculty, administrator, and student groups. Finally, yearly assessment of CMSs at UNL and other campuses in the form of a brief survey would provide a comprehensive picture of the influence of technology on education and track changes associated with such influence.

REFERENCES

Blackboard, Inc. (2002, May 13). *Blackboard announces revenue of $14.7 million for first quarter* [Online]. Retrieved July11, 2002, from http://company.blackboard.com/press/ viewrelease.cgi?tid=207

Brownstone Research Group. (2002). *EDU campus overview.* Retrieved September 12, 2002, from http://www.brownstone.net/products/edu/edu_campus _overview.asp

Centrinity, Inc. (n.d.). FirstClass 7.0: *Feature-rich, affordable, secure* [Online]. Retrieved September 12, 2002, from http://www.centrinity.com

Ellis, R. K. (2001, August). LCMS roundup. *Learning Circuits* [Online]. Retrieved April 20, 2002, from http://www.learningcircuits.org/2001/aug2001/ ttools.html

Greene, K. (2001). Ecommerce comes slowly to the campus. *The 2001 Campus Computing Survey* [Online]. Retrieved September 12, 2002, from http://www.campuscomputing.net

Hannafin, M. J., Hall, C., Land, S., & Hill, J. (1994). Learning in open-ended environments: Assumptions, methods, and implications. *Educational Technology, 34*(8), 48–55.

Landon, B. (2002). Retrieved July 12, 2002 from http://www.edutools.info/ course/productinfo/index.jsp

Malloy, T. E., Jensen, G. C., & Reddick, M. (2001). *Open courseware and shared knowledge in online education: The Utah open-source, Java-based learning management system* [Online]. Retrieved July 11, 2002, from http://www.psych.utah.edu/ learn/olms/OLMS-01-11-07.pdf

Nichani, M. (2001). LCMS = LMS + CMS (RLOs). *Elearningpost* [Online]. Retrieved April 20, 2002, from http://www.elearningpost.com/features/archives/ 001022.asp

Smith, C., Murphy, T., & Teng, T. (2001). *The perfect fit: Selecting the online environment of tomorrow today* [Online]. Retrieved June 27, 2002, from http://cite .telecampus.com/LMS/index.html

WBT Systems, Inc. (n.d.). *TopClass LMS* [Online]. Retrieved September 12, 2002, from http://www .wbtsystems.com/products/lms

WebCT, Inc. (2002). *Who uses WebCT?* [Online]. Retrieved July 11, 2002, from http:// www.webct .com/products/viewpage?name=products_webct_customers

Wiley eGrade [Online]. (n.d.). Retrieved September 12, 2002, from http://jwsedcv .wiley.com/college/egrade/0,10492,,00.html

AUTHOR NOTE

This research was made possible by a grant from the U.S. Department of Education to the CLASS Project, University of Nebraska–Lincoln. Opinions expressed are those of the authors and not necessarily those of the funders.

Correspondence concerning this chapter should be addressed to Charles J. Ansorge at MABL 245, Teachers College, University of Nebraska–Lincoln, Lincoln, NE 68588-0229. Email: cansorge@unl.edu

NOTE

1. Essentially, www-class.unl.edu is an instructional server created by Information Technology services at UNL to host Web pages individually created by instructors for their courses. The look and content of these Web pages is dictated by the level of instructor's sophistication with Web technologies. Moreover, access to these courses depends on the access limitations set up by the instructor. Some of the courses require no password to view the materials, whereas others ask for a valid student ID and password verification.

CHAPTER 10

TECHNOLOGICAL INDICATORS OF IMPACT OF COURSE MANAGEMENT SYSTEMS

Ashok Samal
Bhuvaneswari Gopal
National Center for Information Technology in Education,
University of Nebraska–Lincoln

ABSTRACT

Over the last decade, many course and learning management systems have been developed and deployed in educational environments. Many more new paradigms for learning will become available as further progress is made in the underlying technologies. Therefore, it is important to develop an evaluation strategy to measure the effectiveness of such systems with regard to delivery, learning, and assessment. The goal of this study was to provide the first step in developing such a strategy. A set of technological indicators was developed to determine how and when the Blackboard learning management system was used in a university environment. The pattern of use of the system was derived by examining a set of logs generated by the Web server, the

Web-Based Learning: What Do We Know? Where Do We Go?, pages 191–207

Blackboard system, and the operating system. Our results indicated that during the course of a semester almost 70% of the students and 20% of the instructors used the system. While a significant amount of course material was made available by the instructors, the system seemed to be used primarily as a publishing environment. With these results as background information, we suggest that researchers next investigate the interesting questions of how well the system works for learning and assessment.

One of the fastest-growing areas in technology-mediated education is the use of the Internet by colleges and universities both to supplement face-to-face courses with online components and sometimes to deliver courses completely online. Because the use of online course technology is a relatively new phenomenon, however, little is known about the extent to which and specific ways in which that technology is being used. Online technologies often provide records (system logs) that could be used as technological indicators of such activities; but, to date, instructional researchers have not widely capitalized on those indicators. In this chapter, we first provide some general background on Web course development tools and some specific information about the *Blackboard Learning System*™ (Blackboard, Inc.), a widely used learning management system (LMS) and one currently used at the University of Nebraska–Lincoln (UNL). Second, we present research illustrating how certain technological indicators may be derived from Blackboard and other system logs and used to answer potentially important questions regarding the use of online course technologies.

BACKGROUND

Until recently, many academic administrators had cost minimization as a primary concern in online instruction. In line with that concern, most vendors promoted their products as a way to lower costs. In practice, however, technology-mediated courses are quite costly, both initially and later, as Web-based content and delivery systems need to be continually updated (see Zygielbaum, Chapter 8, this volume). Over time it has become increasingly clear that the payoff from online course delivery comes not in cost savings but in improved quality of existing courses and, for online courses, increases in the size and diversity of learner populations that can be served. Thus, more administrators today are acknowledging that a significant investment in online education can yield long-term benefits that are well worth the cost. Increased functionality of current Web course development tools such as Blackboard and WebCT (WebCT, Inc.) are allowing more and more academic decision makers to justify technology-mediated learning initiatives, resulting in a growing demand for access to technology-mediated or "online" learning.

Web course development tools potentially provide two important advantages: (1) support for the collaborative and dynamic nature of learning, and (2) standards for locating and operating interactive platform-independent materials. They accomplish this by creating the potential for a collaborative environment and a standard interface for developing and distributing content. Designing courses using the integrated features of Web course development tools offers a single authentication scheme, directory structure, consistent interface, and a simple way to publish and update content. In contrast, HTML (1999) layout editors that were initially used to create course content produced static materials that were rigid and nonconforming to different learning environments. Individualization of online materials for specific courses therefore required significant amounts of technological experience, time, and constant attention to the requirements of rapidly changing technologies. The new generation of Web course development tools, however, has begun to provide features that let instructors easily adapt components according to learning outcomes of the course. We next discuss some of those general features and their relationships to teaching and learning, followed by a description of a specific learning management system, Blackboard.

Online Teaching and Learning

A *learning management system* (LMS) (sometimes also called a *course management system*, or CMS) is a Web course development tool designed to facilitate the creation of Web-based learning environments. It is a software application or Web-based technology used to plan, implement, and assess a specific learning process. Depending on its utilization, an LMS can promote collaborative learning, enhance critical thinking skills, and give every student an equal opportunity to participate in classroom discussions. It can create significant learning benefits provided it is based on sound pedagogical design, and can support a wide variety of course goals and teaching styles and philosophies.

LMSs such as the *Blackboard Learning System*™ can facilitate three basic types of interactions: (a) student with course content, (b) student with instructor, and (c) student with other students. In more traditional objectivist learning models, the instructor controls the material and the pace of learning and the emphasis is on knowledge transfer from teacher to student (relating to interaction types (a) and (b) above). This learning model is supported by LMS features that allow instructors to create and easily manage objective assessments and course content. In contrast, more modern constructivist learning models, which cast the instructor as a learning facilitator and emphasize learning as a dynamic process emerging out of social interaction with others (e.g., Jonassen, 1996; Vygotsky, 1986), are supported by LMS features accommodating online discussions, group projects, and individual exploration of content. Many LMSs provide students with the ability to use interactive features such as threaded discussions, video conferencing, and discussion forums, as well as the ability to share course content, asynchronous and synchronous communication tools, calendar tools, and online quizzes and grade books—all in a Web-based environment. LMSs also have the potential to engage students in the learning process by allowing them to control the pace of learning.

The Blackboard Learning System™

The present study focused specifically on the use of the *Blackboard Learning System™* (Release 5) at the University of Nebraska–Lincoln (UNL) during spring 2002. Blackboard, like other LMSs, provides an instructor with a way to create and deliver content, monitor student participation, and assess student performance. Blackboard, founded in 1997, is currently being used at more than 3,000 institutions in the United States and in more than 70 countries.

Blackboard was built on the belief that course management tools could play an integral role in online education (Yaskin & Gilfus, 2001). Blackboard offers a suite of enterprise software products and services that support what is described as an "e-Education infrastructure" for schools, colleges, universities, and other educational providers. The *Blackboard Learning System™* (Release 5 was in use at the time of our study) offers a course management system, customizable institution-wide portals, online communities, and an architecture that allows for Web-based integration of multiple administrative systems. Three different levels of the *Blackboard Learning System™* are available with their course cartridges and are briefly described below.

Level 1

The first level allows faculty from any discipline to create "CourseSites" by incorporating a variety of Web site applications that include multimedia tools for audio and video streaming, communication and collaboration tools (e-mail, discussion boards, and real-time chats), and online tests and quizzes. Faculty need not have any knowledge of HTML or other programming languages to use Blackboard Level 1 Course Manager.

Level 2

Blackboard Level 2 includes support for enterprise-grade relational databases such as *Microsoft SQL Server* and *Oracle8i*. These relational databases provide greater performance and scalability than other products using a flat file system. This adds flexible portal modules that provide features such as a personalized gateway to the Internet, online campus communities, and enhanced capabilities for tailored institutional branding, along with enterprise database support and customizable portal modules and information services. A Web-based email system is also included. This level is designed to provide support for users across an entire institution, manage users and course data, and manage large volumes of transactions.

Level 3

At Level 3, the *Advanced Course and Portal Manager* adds advanced integration and domain management capabilities for those institutions seeking a fully online campus. Level 3 additional features include a snapshot user management API (Application Program Interface), an event-driven (real-time) user management API, an end-user authentication (security) API, and a network protocol for passing user authentication data. In addition to enhancing Blackboard platform performance and scalability, the Level 3 system contains several additional features within the teaching and learning environment and the portal environment, as well as advanced system integration capabilities. These platform innovations include grade book and assessment enhancements, Blackboard Learning Units, aimed release of content, and enterprise data management and integration enhancements for Level 3 clients.

User view

A Blackboard course consists of a navigation path, a button bar, and content frames. Faculty type or upload their course materials into Blackboard. Blackboard can accommodate text, graphic, and audio mediums. Course materials do not have to be HTML documents; instructors can load Word documents or even PowerPoint presentations. The navigation path allows users to return to any page accessed between the main course page and the current pages. The button bar links users to the available content areas and tools. The content frame displays Web pages accessed through the button or navigation path. Typical assessment methods used in determining learning outcomes include tests made up of short answer, multiple-choice, or true/false items or combinations of all three.

Upon entering Blackboard, a user (instructor/student) views the main *Welcome* page, which provides links to all the other features on Blackboard. Its primary use is to provide links to other functions. The *Community* feature contains a catalog of interdisciplinary, departmental, and student organizations and keeps track of those of which the instructor or student is a part. The discussion boards available for participation are also listed here. In the version we studied, various links to various *Services* were grouped together, including links to UNL directories, online help resources, UNL student information, and the official UNL Web site. There also was a separate link connecting directly to the UNL library.

The most important link provides the users access to their courses. The main page of each course consists of features with titles such as *Announcements, Syllabus, Staff, Information, Course Documents, Assignments, Communication* (which provides facilities for sending individual/group emails, a discussion board, a virtual classroom, and roster and group pages), *Groups, External Links,* and *Tools,* along with links to *Resources* and the *Course Map* and the *Control Panel.* The main difference between the instructor view and the student view of the Blackboard system is that the former has the permissions needed to manage the course by adding content, setting up assessments, and providing resources to the students. For obvious reasons students do not have access to this facility.

The course management functions are provided to the instructors via a *Control Panel* feature on the main course page. Through the control panel the instructor can manipulate content areas (announcements, assignments, syllabus, staff information, external links), course tools (course calendar, tasks, send email, discussion board, virtual classroom, digital drop box), and course options (course settings, course images, course utilities, resources). In addition, the instructor can manage users (add users, remove users, list/modify users, manage groups), set up and manage assessments (using the assessment manager, pool manager, online grade book, and course statistics), and find technical assistance in the online manual or by contacting the system administrator.

Actual Use and Impact of LMSs

The descriptions above suggest that LMSs in general and Blackboard in particular have the potential to affect teaching and learning in a variety of ways. It is not enough, however, that Web course development tools offer the features and capabilities just detailed. Teachers must *use* the tools before they can impact learning. The Web is a different medium than the classroom, and instructors must learn to accommodate to a new pedagogy that uses technology as an integral component in teaching. Many faculty who have not used technology in the past to accomplish course objectives now have to learn to teach with technology. In addition, faculty often need to include components in the course that provide information to students about the technology itself.

Beaudoin (1998) states that, in this era of rapidly increasing technological resources for teaching and learning, the role of professorate is undergoing profound changes. Indeed, faculty pioneers already offer online courses that simulate traditional classroom environments by incorporating syllabi, schedules, course notes, assignments, and discussion rooms. In addition, students often are provided with the opportunity to communicate with instructors or other students through the use of e-mail, bulletin boards, and live chat rooms. In these situations, capabilities such as online assessment, simulations, multimedia, course delivery, and access to external resources provide potential advantages over lecture-only classes.

Not all instructors, however, have embraced the idea of online course delivery. Faculty resistance has likely resulted from the intimidating yet probably incorrect perception that using rapidly changing, newer technologies will result in a need to constantly keep up and update skills, and subsequent loss of control over the teaching process. Faculty may also have concerns about dealing with copyright issues that arise in making materials available for open access. Thus, although current technologies facilitating online course delivery have the *potential* to change approaches to teaching and learning, the extent to which that potential is being realized at most institutions is currently unknown.

The Current Study

As further progress is made in the underlying technologies, it is almost certain that many more new paradigms for learning will become available. It is important, therefore, to develop an evaluation strategy to measure the effectiveness of such systems with regard to delivery, learning, and assessment. The primary motivation for this study was to use technological indicators provided by various online technologies in order to study the impact that the Blackboard system has had at the University of Nebraska–Lincoln (UNL) as a tool to aid instruction. This was one of two related studies supported by the CLASS (Communications, Learning, and Assessment in a Student-Centered System) Project focusing on the utilization and impact of the Blackboard system. The first of these (see Ansorge & Bendus, Chapter 9, this volume) was an extensive survey conducted to examine the perceptions of students, instructors, and university administrators. The second study, which is presented in this chapter, focused on usage patterns within Blackboard as revealed by various technological indicators. Specifically, in this chapter we examined technological indicators to see what they revealed about how and when the instructors and students used Blackboard and about the types of materials being disseminated. The approach taken here was to examine the various log files generated by a variety of participating entities, both software and hardware, to determine the extent and pattern of the use of Blackboard. The results reported here are based on data for one semester of study in spring 2002.

It should be noted that this study was not designed to directly answer questions related to pedagogy and learning. Instead, the results of the study provide a basis for subsequently formulating appropriate pedagogical questions. In other words, this study used data that sheds light on how and when the students and instructors used the Blackboard system, not why. Furthermore, because such studies have not been done extensively in the past, there are no well-established technological indicators. In this research, we have developed such a set and have demonstrated their use.

MATERIALS AND METHODS

Our goal was to use technological data to derive a better understanding of how the Blackboard LMS was being used. Several approaches can be used to accomplish this goal. One approach is to define the indicators to be measured and then instrument the Blackboard system to compute them. This, however, would have required modification of the Blackboard system and was not feasible in this project. Fortunately, several alternative tools were available to measure many useful indicators.

The computing environment for Blackboard is organized as an application server and a database server. The students and instructors interact only with the application server, which also stores all the instructional materials. At UNL, the application server at the time of this study was a Sun E450 with four 400Mhz CPUs, 3GB of RAM, and over 70GB of mirrored disk storage. Much of the bookkeeping information was organized and stored in a relational (Oracle) database. Such information included course registration data, student and instructor information, and Blackboard access and activity logs. The database server consisted of a Sun Sunfire 3800 with four 750Mhz CPUs, 4GB of RAM, and over 18GB of mirrored disk space. Both servers were running the UNIX operating system and were connected to a 100MB Ethernet.

System Activity Logs

The UNIX operating system provides several utilities to monitor system activities. These tools are designed to allow a system administrator to view the performance of the system and identify bottlenecks. CPU utilization, I/O load, system idle time, and memory utilization are among a long list of activities that can be monitored. Selected activities are measured periodically and stored in log files. The logs generated by these utilities can also provide clues of importance for LMS managers. For example, peak CPU utilization at a certain time also indicates high usage of the LMS. For the purpose of the study, we had access to activity log files that recorded the CPU utilization, I/O load, and the system idle time at 1-hour intervals for a period of 3 weeks.

Web Server Logs

Students and instructors access the Blackboard system via a Web interface. The Web server process in the host machine monitors and records a number of activities in order to identify problems. The Apache server can generate a log of a long list of system activities. Every request received by the server is recorded in the log. Aggregate summaries of various types can be useful in understanding the usage of Blackboard. Such measures include the number of requests as a function of time, the requested file types (e.g., as identified by file extensions such as pdf, doc, ppt, etc.), and the distribution of hosts from which the server receives requests. The log files tend to get very large quickly and have to be cleared frequently. For this study we analyzed the log file over a period of 17 days.

Course Files

Instructors post their course content as files of various kinds to the Blackboard LMS. We studied the properties of these files to get an understanding of instructor activities. It should be noted that we did not look at the content of these files; we only examined general properties such as size, type, posted date, and so on. For this study we analyzed the Blackboard course contents for the spring 2002 semester.

Blackboard Logs

During the course of its operation the Blackboard LMS maintains a log of its activities in a database. All accesses by students, instructors, and administrators are recorded. Each entry in the database records a user identification variable, the course number, date and time of access, the module accessed, and other information. These entries give a direct view of how the Blackboard LMS is being used by the students and instructors.

Final Notes

All logs used in this study were for the spring 2002 semester of study at UNL. Note that system logs and Web server logs were available for only short intervals during this period. Furthermore, system logs gave only a very high-level usage summary and were not configured to give more detailed information that might also be of interest in this context. A more complete study would configure the environment to record all of these for longer durations of time. Finally, note that some technical aspects of Blackboard use could not be ascertained using the above approaches. For example, it is not possible to know what tools the instructors were using to develop their course content. Answers to some of these questions were obtained in a survey conducted by Gallup and are reported in Ansorge and Bendus (this volume).

RESULTS AND DISCUSSION

In this section we present the analysis of the log files described earlier. By giving indications of how and when the system was being used, the log files provided indirect evidence of Blackboard's effectiveness. We organized our results to answer the following four basic questions about the Blackboard LMS system:

1. What was the extent to which the Blackboard LMS was used?
2. How was it used by the instructors and students?
3. When was it used by the instructors and students?
4. What types of course content were presented via Blackboard?

Extent of Blackboard Use

We studied the overall usage of Blackboard on the UNL campus by analyzing the Web server and Blackboard's own system logs, examining the logs from April 7, 2002, to April 24, 2002. Prior to our efforts, there was no systematic study to measure the degree of use of Blackboard use at UNL. Both the Web server logs and the logs maintained by Blackboard clearly showed that the system was being used quite heavily by the students and instructors. The number of successful requests to the Web server exceeded half a million per day. The server provided access to nearly 180,000 pages per day with an average data transfer rate of nearly 2GB per day. During this period nearly 17,000 distinct files were accessed. The Blackboard logs also showed a high volume of use. It should be noted that the granularity of logs in the Web server and the Blackboard systems are different. The Blackboard logs showed over 6.3 million entries with an average of about 50,000 actions per day. About 90% of the entries in Blackboard resulted from student activities and the rest from the instructors. The number of students who used Blackboard was 14,643, which was about 69% of the total student enrollment at UNL for that semester. Close to 500 instructors had some level of activity recorded in Blackboard. Analysis of system logs showed that the Blackboard server environment was well-equipped to serve the needs of the users that semester. Even during the highest load on the system, the percentage of time the system spent on user tasks did not exceed 30%.

Almost 50% of the activities resulted from students enrolled in first- and second-year courses, and undergraduate courses accounted for 90% of the activities in Blackboard. These numbers closely reflected enrollment figures. The distribution of access among different colleges in the university showed that the College of Arts and Sciences, UNL's largest college, had the largest number of students using Blackboard. Interestingly, the College of Business Administration and Teacher's College also had very high percentages of accesses, though their total enrollments were about a fourth of Arts and Sciences.

During the 17-day period covered by the system logs, the Web server served a total of 9,535 distinct hosts. Many of the accesses came over high-speed connections, and over 60% came from various campus locations (e.g., public access computer rooms, laboratories, dormitories, and so on). Off-campus, RoadRunner, which offers broadband access, was the leading provider of Internet access.

Mode of Use

Much of the information about how the Blackboard system was used was derived from the logs created by Blackboard. Log records of each user's activity included user identificaton, a date and time stamp, course number, and the access area. The access area field gave us an indication of the type of activity the user was engaged in. For our analyses, we grouped the access types as follows:

1. *Contents:* Activities related to accessing the course material in Blackboard.

2. *Communications:* E-mail, chat room activities, and virtual classroom activities.

3. *Assessment:* Various activities related to course assessment.

4. *General:* Activities such as viewing announcements, class rosters, course calendars, editing personal information, and others.

5. *Administrative:* Operations related to the management of the courses.

6. *Web-related:* Visits to external links.

7. *Others:* All activities not falling into one of the above were listed in this category.

Figure 10.1 shows the distribution of the activities for the instructors and students. As shown, both students and instructors spent the most amount of time in Blackboard content areas, and also spent a considerable amount of time engaged in communication and general activities. Instructors, however, spent considerably more time engaged in assessment and administration than the students.

Figure 10.2 shows the frequency of use for the different colleges. Arts and Sciences (ASCI), Business Administration (CBA), Teacher's College (TEAC), and Agricultural Sciences and Natural Resources (ASNR) were the dominant users both among students and instructors. It is interesting to note that students from ASCI used the system more than TEAC, but the frequencies of use by the instructors from these two colleges were reversed. This would indicate significant commitment by the instructors in Teacher's College to LMSs such as Blackboard. Among all the departments in the university, the Department of Curriculum and Instruction led the way in the frequency of use by the instructors. The total accesses by students and

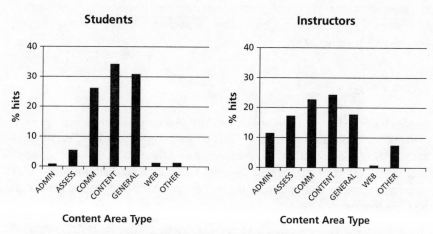

Figure 10.1.   Frequency of Blackboard use by students and instructors as a function of content types. Content types are described in text. Abbreviations for content types are as follows: Administrative (ADMIN), assessment (ASSESS), communications (COMM), contents (CONTENT), general (GENERAL), Web-related (WEB), and other (OTHER).

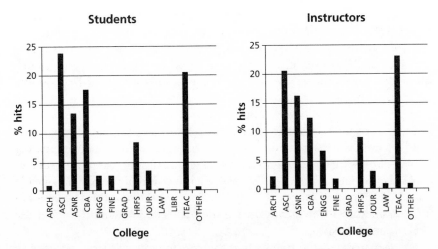

Figure 10.2.   Access pattern of instructors and students as a function of college. Abbreviations for colleges are as follows: Architecture (ARCH), Arts and Sciences (ASCI), Agricultural Sciences and Natural Resources (ASNR), Business Administration (CBA), Engineering and Technology (ENGG), Fine and Performing Arts (FINE), Graduate Studies (GRAD), Human Resources and Family Sciences (HRFS), Journalism and Mass Communication (JOUR), Law (LAW), and Teacher's College (TEAC).

instructors for the different course levels were comparable. However, because the number of students in lower levels is higher, it is evident that the students at higher levels used the system more frequently.

One final observation about the way the system is used is interesting to note. From the Web server logs, it appeared that a significant amount of material (about a third) was repeatedly accessed over short periods of time. This indicates that there was a high degree of clustering in the access pattern of course content pages. This clustering may result in more efficient access. For example, such activity may occur right before/after a lecture/test when many students are trying to access the same content from the course pages. When the same page is used repeatedly, the Web server caches the page in memory and can then provide the page immediately to a subsequent user requesting the page, instead of copying from the disk. This allows the server to provide faster service for the users.

Time of Use

The goal of this aspect of our analysis was to examine the temporal dimension in Blackboard usage. We analyzed the overall use of Blackboard as a function of days of the week from different views, with data derived from a variety of sources, including student and instructor frequencies of use from the Blackboard logs, page access frequencies from the Web server logs, and the load from the system logs. All of these indicators consistently showed that the greatest use of the system was on Mondays, with use gradually decreasing as the week progressed. System use was the least on Saturdays and picked up a little on Sundays.

Analysis of the use of the system during hours of the day showed little activity from 2:00 A.M. to about 7:00 A.M., but with use gradually increasing until peaking shortly before noon. It then gradually decreased with smaller peaks around 2:00, 4:00, and 10:00 P.M. Examination of the pattern outside our 17-day period of intensive study revealed that the monthly frequency of use remained relatively steady during the semester, with slightly higher use in February and April.

We also analyzed the times when the course materials were inserted to the system. It was interesting to note that almost 90% of the files were added during the months of January and April. This would imply that instructors had a significant amount of their course materials developed before the semester began. Examination of the activities in the month of January shows that about 60% of the files were added on or before the first day of class.

Course Content

We indirectly analyzed course contents by examining the external features (e.g., size and type) of files added to the system by the instructors during the semester; we did not actually examine the contents of the files that were inserted. In all, about 90,000 files with a total size of 10.5GB were added to the system during the spring 2002 semester. Out of more than 3,800 courses offered at UNL that semester, 726 (19%) had some content in the Blackboard.

The number of files added by the instructors from various departments was evenly distributed with the exception of one course that had a significantly larger number of files than all others. Biological Systems Engineering, Agricultural Economics, Computer Science and Engineering, Family and Consumer Sciences, and Educational Psychology were the largest contributors in terms of the number of files. However, examination of the total *size* of the files added to the system revealed that Biometry, Marketing, Civil Engineering, and Educational Psychology were the leading users of system disk space. Instructors in Biometry added a total of 2.5GB of material, almost 25% of all materials included in the Blackboard system.

Distribution of files and sizes showed, as expected, that the larger colleges (e.g., Arts and Sciences, Engineering, Teacher's College, Agricultural Sciences and Natural Resources, and Business) were the biggest contributors both in terms of number of files and amount of material. Upon analyzing the number of files and total file size for the different levels of courses, it was found that while the 400-level courses had significantly larger numbers of files, the total amount of material (in terms of computer storage space) was greatest for 100-level courses.

Based on their properties, we grouped the files into different categories such as content, assessment, administration, and so on. Almost 90% of the files added to the system could be classified as "content" files, with Web server logs showing that over 75% of the accesses in Blackboard were related to the "courses" directory that stores course-related information.

SUMMARY AND FUTURE WORK

The goal of our study was to examine the use of Blackboard at UNL, using a variety of technology-based indicators in a variety of system logs. These logs nonetheless allowed us a clear view of how and when the system was used. Our analyses also were able to provide a clear view of system use and performance that could aid in identifying bottlenecks.

Overall, our study showed that Blackboard was being very widely used on the UNL campus, with almost 70% of the students using the system in some way. On the other hand, only about 20% of the instructors were using it. As discussed elsewhere (see Ansorge & Bendus, this volume), reasons for these patterns are diverse. Two reasons for widespread use by students likely are that (a) the computing environment is excellent and bottlenecks are uncommon, and (b) broadband access to the Internet is widely available in many public laboratories on campus and dormitories. These findings matched the expectations of the study team. Perhaps the most important observation from our study, however, is that the system appears to be used primarily as a publishing environment, with the instructors posting their material on the system and students accessing it as needed. Very few interactive discussions and assessment activities were recorded in the system logs. This finding is in direct contrast with suggestions by some (Jonasson, 1996) that online learning should be closely related to the constructivist approach to learning.

This study could be extended in many different directions. For example, the present study provided a composite view, but significant benefits could be obtained by examining the usage patterns of individual students and instructors. Examination of the activities of individual students could provide further clues about how students are using the system, including the actual time spent by the students within the Blackboard system as well as their access patterns. Such data could be related to measures of learning and motivation. In addition, our study focused on the system during only a single academic semester, but user behavior could be more completely understood by analyzing the various entities for longer durations. Finally, the systems could be automated to gather the Web server and system logs that are descriptive in a continuous manner and tools could be developed to generate summaries of Blackboard use that would be useful to students, instructors and administrators.

REFERENCES

Beaudoin, M. F. (1998). A new professoriate for the new millennium. *Distance Learning Online, 8*(5) [Online]. Retrieved from http://www.music.ecu.edu/ DistEd/ Beaudoin.html

Bloom, B. S. (1981). *All our children learning.* New York: McGraw-Hill.

Cuban, L. (1993). *How teachers taught* (2nd ed.). New York: Teachers College Press.

Hofstetter, F. (1998). *Cognitive versus behavioral psychology* [Online]. Retrieved from http://www.udel.edu/fth/pbs/webmodel.htm

HTML. (1999, December 24). *4.01 Specification- W3C Recommendation* [Online]. Retrieved from http://www.w3.org/TR/html401/

Jonassen, D. H. (1996). *Computers in the classroom: Mindtools for critical thinking.* Englewood Cliffs, NJ: Merrill Prentice Hall.

Neal, E. (1998, June). *Does using technology in instruction enhance learning?* [Online]. Retrieved from http://horizon.unc.edu/TS/commentary/1998-06.asp

Vygotsky, L. (1986). *Thought and language.* Cambridge, MA: MIT Press.

AUTHOR NOTE

This work was made possible by a grant from the U.S. Department of Education to the CLASS Project, University of Nebraska–Lincoln. Opinions expressed are those of the authors and not necessarily those of the funders. We thank Art Zygielbaum and the National Center for Instructional Technology in Education (NCITE) for their leadership in bringing an interdisciplinary group of researchers to focus on a wide variety of problem-related instructional technology. We thank Sandy Gahn for providing us with invaluable technical and editorial assistance throughout this effort. Other members of the team, Charles Ansorge and Oksana Bendus, provided invaluable support for this work. Paul Erickson at Information Services helped us in obtaining and parsing the many different logs used for this research. Rippy Singh and Catherine Gray at Blackboard helped us get a better understanding of the logs generated by Blackboard. We also profoundly thank Roger Bruning, the co-director for NCITE, for his patience and comments in preparation of this manuscript.

Correspondence concerning this chapter should be addressed to Ashok Samal at 115 Ferguson Hall, Department of Computer Science and Engineering, University of Nebraska–Lincoln, Lincoln, NE 68588-0115. Email: samal@cse.unl.edu

CHAPTER 11

INTELLECTUAL PROPERTY CONSIDERATIONS FOR ONLINE EDUCATIONAL MULTIMEDIA PROJECTS

What You Don't Know Could Byte You

Turan P. Odabasi
University of Nebraska–Lincoln

ABSTRACT

Intellectual property issues are a primary consideration in the development of online educational multimedia projects. This chapter discusses the basic principles of copyright, patent, trademark, trade secret, and Internet or "cyber" law (with an emphasis on copyright), and how these principles relate to the development and delivery of online educational multimedia projects.

Over the past decade, virtually every institution of higher education has developed online educational material of some type. The vast array of materials available in the digital universe provides educators with unique

Web-Based Learning: What Do We Know? Where Do We Go?, pages 209–230
Copyright © 2003 by Information Age Publishing
All rights of reproduction in any form reserved.

209

opportunities to incorporate pictures, sound, video, and text into effective, tailored, educational works. Many educational institutions have begun to market their online courses and multimedia tools. As the use of the Internet and digital technology as an educational medium has increased, so has the attention of authors and owners of copyrighted works seeking to protect their intellectual property rights. Legal issues involving intellectual property are a primary consideration in any venture into the creation of online educational multimedia works. Claims of intellectual property infringement by third parties can threaten the ability of an institution to use the educational multimedia works they have developed. Accordingly, the developers of these works need to be acquainted with the basic principles of intellectual property law. This chapter is intended to provide background on these basic principles as well as some discussion about handling typical situations that may arise in this area.

It's best to start with the most basic of questions: What is "intellectual property"? This term is commonly used to refer to the legal fields of copyright, patent, trademark, trade secret, and Internet or "cyber" law. The following sections discuss the particulars of each of these fields and how they relate to the creation and delivery of educational online multimedia materials.

COPYRIGHT

Most intellectual property issues encountered in the development of educational multimedia works involve principles of copyright law, particularly those pertaining to the ownership and use of copyrighted works.

What Is Copyright?

The genesis of copyright law is found in the United States Constitution. Article I, section 8, clause 8 of the Constitution grants Congress the authority to establish a system of copyrights "by securing for limited Times to Authors and Inventors the exclusive Right to their respective Writings and Discoveries" as a means to "promote the Progress of Science and the useful Arts." As defined in 17 U.S.C. §102(a), copyright serves to protect the rights of creators and/or owners of "original works of authorship fixed in any tangible medium of expression."

In order to be considered an "original work of authorship," two tests set forth in 17 U.S.C. §101 must be met: (1) The author must have expended a modicum of intellectual effort in the creation of the work, and (2) the work must be original, not copied entirely from another. A work is "fixed in a tangible medium of expression" when its embodiment in a copy or phonorecord[1] is "sufficiently permanent or stable to permit it to be perceived, reproduced, or otherwise communicated for a period of more than a transitory duration."

Copyright generally serves to protect the particular *expression* of a thought or idea, but not the idea itself. For example, an author can obtain copyright protection for a book that describes a scientific process. However, copyright protection will only apply to the unique expression or description embodied in the book, not to the process described. Once the author has revealed the work to the public, he or she places the underlying abstract idea into the public domain and may only prevent others from copying the *form* in which the concept was expressed. The public is free to utilize the ideas set forth in the book without infringing the author's copyright in the work.

Works of authorship capable of copyright protection are listed in 17 U.S.C. §102 and include literary works; musical works (including words or lyrics); dramatic works (including music); pantomimes and choreographic works; sound recordings; motion pictures and other audiovisual works; multimedia works; architectural works created after December 1, 1990; and pictorial, graphic, and sculptural works.

Ownership and Rights of Owners

Ownership of copyright in a work initially vests in the author or authors of the work. In the case of a joint or collective work prepared by two or more authors and intended to be inseparable parts of a complete work, the authors are co-owners of copyright in the work (see 17 U.S.C. §201). The rights of copyright owners are set forth in 17 U.S.C. §106. The owner of a copyright has the "exclusive right to reproduce the copyrighted work, to prepare derivative works[2] based on the copyrighted work, to distribute copies to the public by sale, rental or lease, the right to perform the work in public and the right to display the work in public." In addition, the owner of a copyrighted work can use the work without having to account for the rights of third parties in the work.

Although copyright ownership initially vests in the author or authors of a work, ownership of copyright in a work can be transferred to individuals or entities other than the author. The most common situation in which this occurs is known as a *work made for hire*. In the case of a work made for hire, ownership of the work is retained by the employer or other person for whom the work was prepared. There are two types of works made for hire defined in 17 U.S.C.§101: (1) a work prepared by an employee within the scope of his or her employment; and (2) a work prepared by an independent contractor, *but only if* the parties have signed a written agreement specifically stating that the work is to be considered a work made for hire *and* the work itself falls within one of the following nine categories of works:

- a contribution to a "collective work,"
- a part of a "motion picture" or other "audiovisual work,"
- a translation
- a "supplementary work,"
- a "compilation,"
- an "instructional text,"
- a test,
- answer material for a test, or
- an atlas.

It is particularly important to understand the work-made-for-hire doctrine if your institution hires independent contractors to develop educational multimedia works or other copyrightable works. Furthermore, the work-made-for-hire doctrine can affect the ownership of works created by employees whose job duties do not include the development of educational multimedia works.

The work-made-for-hire doctrine is frequently misunderstood. It is often assumed that if an author is retained as an independent contractor, the hiring party automatically owns the copyright to any works created by the author during their period of employment. However, unless both of the requirements set forth above are met—that a written agreement is made between the parties specifically stating that the subject work is to be a work made for hire, *and* the work falls within one of the nine categories specified in 17 U.S.C. §101—the work cannot be considered a work made for hire and the copyright in the work will belong to the author. Another common misunderstanding of the work-made-for-hire doctrine involves works created by employees within the scope of their employment. Not every work created by an employee is automatically owned by their employer. The work must be created *within the scope of employment;* an employer cannot claim copyright to works created by an employee if those works were created outside the scope of the employee's job duties.

Determining if a work was created within the scope of employment involves an examination of three court-established standards, each of which must be met. These standards are that the work (1) is the kind of work the employee is employed to perform, (2) was created substantially within authorized work hours and space, and (3) is actuated (or motivated), at least in part, by a purpose to serve the employer (*City of Newark v. Beasley*, 1995). For instance, if a University requested one of its biology professors, employed solely to teach classes and conduct research, to create an online course in genetics, the work created by this professor may fall outside of the scope of his job duties and may possibly not be considered a work made for hire. On the other hand, if an employee whose job is to develop educational multimedia content developed such a course, the work would most likely be deemed to have been performed within the scope of employment, thus qualifying as a work made for hire.

Having employees and independent contractors retain ownership of the works they create can lead to many problems. For instance, if an employee creates a work that is not considered a work made for hire, the employee retains *all* rights to that work and the employer cannot use the work in any manner without the permission of the employee. This can mean that the employer will have to pay the employee a fee for permission to use the work in addition to the salary the employee originally received to create the work.

As shown in the examples above, it is not sufficient to rely solely on the work-made-for-hire doctrine to ensure that your organization will retain the right to use works created by employees and contractors. As a practical matter, it is highly advisable to always have a signed agreement in place with any author, employee, or contractor not directly employed to create such works. Such an agreement should include an assignment clause similar to the following:

> *To the extent that any work created by Author is not deemed to be a work made for hire, Author hereby assigns and transfers to Institution all right, title, and interest in the work and agrees to execute any additional documents deemed necessary by Institution to evidence such assignment.*

An assignment clause such as this will transfer ownership of any work created by an employee or contractor during the course of their employment to their employer. A standard "work made for hire" agreement including an assignment clause is included in Appendix A.

Institutional policies may also transfer rights to certain works to an employer while allowing the employee to retain the rights to other works. For example, under the Policies of the Board of Regents of the University of Nebraska (2002, p. 94), ownership of "Traditional Works of Scholarship" (i.e. works resulting from purely scholarly endeavors such as journal articles, research bulletins, textbooks, and instructional materials) is retained by the author. Also, title to works created by students who are not employees of a university almost always remains with them, although the policies of different universities vary.

Term of Copyright Protection

Copyrights provide protection to their owners for "limited times." The period of time during which an author or owner can enforce rights in a work depends on the date the work was created and, in certain circumstances, whether the author or owner initially published the work with proper copyright notice and renewed their copyright registration.[3] In October 1998, Congress passed the Sony Bono Copyright Term Extension Act, which served to extend the term of U.S. copyright protection by 20 years. Currently, an author or owner of a work created after January 1, 1978, can enforce their rights under copyright law as soon as a work is recorded in some concrete fashion (i.e., fixed in a tangible medium of expression). Protection for a work created under the current law (and for all works created after January 1, 1978) begins at its creation and lasts for the life of the author plus 70 years. For works made for hire, the term of copyright protection is now 95 years from the date the work was published or 120 years from the date the work was created, whichever expires first.

The 20-year extension also applies to works created prior to January 1, 1978, if the work was still protected by copyright as of October 27, 1998, the effective date of the new law. Thus, works published with notice from January 1, 1923, to December 31, 1977, now have a 95-year term if the copyright in the works was properly renewed. Works published without proper notice from 1923 to 1977 are in the public domain, as are works published during this period for which copyright was not properly renewed. Any work published prior to 1923 is in the public domain.

These terms, however, may be affected in the near future by the outcome of *Eldred v. Ashcroft* (2001), currently on appeal to the U.S. Supreme Court. In that case, the Sony Bono Copyright Term Extension Act was challenged as unconstitutional based on the constitutional mandate that Congressional authority to provide copyright protection is proscribed to "limited times." At issue is whether the repeated extension of the term of copyright protection by Congress circumvents this constitutional mandate.

While current law does not require registration or notice to claim or protect copyright in a work, registering a work with the U.S. Copyright Office is a straightforward, inexpensive process that should be considered. Registering a copyright involves filing a copy of the work, a registration form, and a fee with the Copyright Office. The appropriate forms can be downloaded from the Copyright Office's Web site, *www.loc.gov/copyright*. Registration provides the owner with the ability to enforce his or her rights in federal court and to claim statutory and treble damages and attorneys fees in copyright enforcement actions.

Public Domain

Determining the life span of a copyright is especially helpful in determining whether a work can be considered to be in the public domain. Public domain status fundamentally means that no one can enforce copyright in the work. As a result, works in the public domain are free to be used by the public.

There are several ways a work may end up in the public domain. First, any work for which copyright protection has expired is in the public domain. Second, authors may place their works in the public domain. Finally, the U.S. government cannot claim or enforce copyright in its own works (see 17 U.S.C. §105), so these works are in the public domain. However, the U.S. government can and does hold title to and enforce copyright in the works of others that have been assigned or bequeathed to the government, so it is a misconception that *any* work controlled by the U.S. government is in the public domain.

The development of the Internet has complicated public domain issues. The contents of Web sites are not necessarily in the public domain and should not be copied at will. This also applies to Web sites owned by the U.S. government, for the reasons set forth above. Most (if not all) Web sites may be protected without copyright notice. Also, because many Web sites contain pirated works, it is not wise to assume that the author of the Web site owns or has permission to use all of the work displayed on the Web site. It is advisable to look for copyright restrictions or notices on the Web site or to simply contact the author for further information if necessary.

Finally, derivative works based on a work in the public domain may be protected by copyright. For instance, although the *Mona Lisa* was originally painted in 1506, the image of the *Mona Lisa* has been used in scores of caricatures, parodies, and modified illustrations, many of which were created after 1923 and are capable of copyright protection. Do not assume that such modified works are automatically in the public domain.

Fair Use

One of the most contentious areas of copyright law is the doctrine of "fair use." The rise of the digital age and the creation and explosion of the Internet, specifically file-sharing Web sites such as Napster, has precipitated a spirited debate between content owners and fair use advocates.

The doctrine of *fair use* is often defined as "the privilege in others than the owner to use the copyrighted material in a reasonable manner, without consent, notwithstanding the monopoly granted the owner" (*Rosemont Enterprises v. Random House, Inc.*, 1966). The doctrine acts as an affirmative defense to a claim of copyright infringement. In other words, the nonconsensual use of copyrighted work may not always trigger liability for infringement *if* the underlying use of the work can be considered a "fair use." The fair use doctrine seeks to balance the exclusive rights of copyright owners with the public interest in disseminating the material, thus improving society by increasing its base of knowledge. This balance also extends to the public's First Amendment rights. Fair use serves to protect the use of copyrighted works for purposes such as criticism, commentary, open discussion, news reporting, teaching, scholarship, and research.

Unfortunately, there is no bright-line test to determine whether or not the use of a copyrighted work for educational purposes without the consent of the owner will be considered a fair use. In considering cases involving fair use, courts must follow the language of 17 U.S.C. §107. This statute provides the court with four factors to balance in determining whether or not the nonconsensual use of a work can be considered a fair use: (1) the purpose and character of the use (e.g., nonprofit/educational use vs. commercial use), (2) the nature of the copyrighted work (e.g., a factual work of little creativity vs. an imaginative or creative work), (3) the amount and substantiality of the portion of the work used in relation to the copyrighted work as a whole (e.g., copying a small portion of the work vs. copying the entire work), and (4) the effect of the use on the potential market for the copyrighted work.

The doctrine of fair use has been complicated even further with the passage of the Digital Millennium Copyright Act (DMCA) of 1998. The DMCA essentially did away with the defense of fair use for digitized, encrypted media. Under the DMCA, most circumventions of an encryption or protection of a digitized work are considered violations of the DMCA, regardless of whether the use of the work would ultimately be considered a fair use. Most importantly, violations of the DMCA carry both civil and criminal penalties. For example, if a course designer wanted to use an encrypted or copy protected image found on a Web site, bypassing the encryption or copy protection to download the image would be an automatic violation of the DMCA regardless of whether the underlying use of the image could be considered a fair use. This violation could subject the designer to large financial liability and potential criminal prosecution.

The passage of the DMCA removed an entire category of works from protection under the doctrine of fair use and caused understandable distress within the educational community. Recognizing the problems the DMCA created for the educational community, Congress recently passed the Technology, Education and Copyright Harmonization Act of 2001 (the TEACH Act).[4] The TEACH Act does not address the use of multimedia works under the doctrine of fair use, but instead expressly provides for the use of multimedia works for certain nonprofit educational purposes. The TEACH Act allows educators at nonprofit educational institutions to transmit portions of *legally acquired* multimedia works over distance learning networks without having to first obtain permission from the owner of the work, so long as the following conditions are met:

1. The use of the work is at the direction of or under the actual supervision of an instructor "as an integral part of a class session."
2. The work is transmitted to students "officially enrolled in the course" through the use of security measures that prohibit public access to the work, to the extent that such measures are technologically feasible.
3. The institution only retains transient copies of the work for the amount of time "reasonably necessary to complete the transmission."
4. The institution applies technological measures to "reasonably prevent unauthorized access to and dissemination of the work."
5. The institution must "institute policies regarding copyright" and must educate its faculty members about copyright law.

The permission of the owner is still required to transmit works that were created "primarily for instructional use." In addition, the TEACH Act requires the U.S. Copyright Office to convene a conference of interested parties within two years to develop guidelines for the use of copyrighted works for distance education under the fair use doctrine and sections 110(1) and 110(2) of the Copyright Act.

It is highly advisable *not* to rely solely upon fair use as a justification for the use of third-party works simply because the use is for an educational, noncommercial purpose. When dealing with issues regarding fair use, it is wise to consult and follow certain guidelines. There are many sources for guidelines on educational fair use available on the Internet.[5] Although these guidelines are not law, operating within these guidelines increases the likelihood that your institution's use will be a fair use. In general, two guidelines for copying material from books and periodicals should be observed: First, a brevity restriction applies, so restrict your copying to as brief a portion of the work as possible. Second, a spontaneity restriction applies, so your decision to use the work must be so close in time to the use that it would be unreasonable to expect a timely reply to a permission request. Regarding educational multimedia and distance learning projects, copying portions of a work is generally allowed for up to two years if the project is password protected, or 15 days if the project is unprotected. However, it is still highly advisable to obtain the owner's permission to use the work, if possible.

Obtaining Necessary Permissions and Potential Liability

Unless the use of a copyrighted work is allowed by law, the permission of the owner must be obtained in order to use the work. The failure to obtain proper permission can potentially lead to a claim of willful copyright infringement by the owner of the copied work. A copyright infringer is liable for any profits made off of the work in addition to the copyright owner's actual damages. At the option of the copyright owner, statutory damages may be awarded instead of actual damages and profits. Statutory damage awards ordinarily must be between $500 and $20,000, but can be lessened to a minimum of $200 in cases involving "innocent infringement" or increased to $100,000 for cases of "willful infringement." In addition to these damages, the infringer can be made to pay all attorneys fees in any court actions related to the infringement.

The main principle to be followed in obtaining permissions is to avoid any potential liability for a claim of willful copyright infringement by making a good faith effort to obtain the permission of the owner. Document and maintain records of all attempts to locate the owner of the work. Often, the owner of the work will be evident from any copyright notice attached to the work. However, because notice is no longer required to claim copyright in a work, many works often lack notice or include the name of someone who is not the actual or current copyright owner. If no notice is provided, it is a good idea to contact the publisher and search the Internet for information. If all else fails, consider hiring a professional search firm or contact the U.S. Copyright Office to conduct a search. The Copyright Office charges hourly fees to search copyright information, but these searches are usually very cost efficient.

Once you have found contact information for the owner, at least two permission requests should be sent, the last one via certified mail. Again, document and maintain records of your institution's attempt to contact the owner. Owners have wide discretion when responding to permission requests. The request may be granted or denied, and sometimes may only be granted in return for the payment of a fee, which can be exorbitant. However, for most uses of works for nonprofit educational purposes, you will often find that copyright owners are quite understanding and cooperative.

Always remember to request permission for all the rights you need for your project. Be up front and as specific as possible with the owner regarding the nature of your project and the use of their work in it. If there is any possibility that the work will be used in a for-profit manner, the owner must be informed of this. If permission to use a work is originally requested for nonprofit uses, the new work may not be licensed to a commercial entity or used in a for-profit manner without obtaining a new for-profit permission. The owner of the work should be informed of the following:

- how long the work will be used (e.g., for a specific term of months or years, for the life of the project, or only once),
- whether the work will be used as-is or modified (e.g., whether the work will be translated into Spanish),

- how the work will be distributed (e.g., in print, over the Internet without password protection, or on a secure server with password access), and
- how many users will have access to the work (e.g., how many students are enrolled in the course in which the work will be used).

The easiest way to request permission from an owner is to send the relevant information in a letter such as the sample permission request letter included in Appendix B. If it is appropriate for your project, consider using a large commercial vendor of copyrighted works, such as Corbis™ or Photodisc™. These commercial vendors can grant rights to works in a very straightforward manner, usually for a reasonable fee, and often for all purposes including for-profit use.

Summary

Although the preceding considerations may seem daunting, copyright considerations for the development of online educational multimedia projects really boil down to a few main points. The following outline can be used as a checklist for your project:

I) What work developed during the project does my institution own?

   A) Keep "work made for hire" considerations in mind:

   1) Have all institutional employees on the project acted within the scope of their job duties? If so, ownership will be retained by the institution. If not, ownership may be retained by the employee(s) and their permission may be necessary to use the work.

   2) Have all independent contractors performed work subject to a written agreement designating that their work is a work made for hire and does their work fall within one of the nine categories defined in 17 U.S.C. §101? Or...

   3) Have all independent contractors signed an agreement containing an assignment clause transferring ownership of their work to your institution?

   B) What are the policies of my institution regarding copyright ownership? Do these policies address the ownership of the project?

II) Am I using any third-party works in my project, and if so, do I have the right to use these works without the permission of the owner?

   A) Are the works in the public domain? If so, you may use the work at your discretion.

B) Does my use of these works constitute a "fair use?" If so, you may use the work within the boundaries of the "fair use" doctrine.

   1) Is the work digitized and encrypted or copy protected? If so, the fair use doctrine does not apply and the work cannot be used without the permission of the owner.

III) I need to obtain the permission of the owner to use the work.

   A) Does the author also own the work?

   B) If the owner is not readily known, consider hiring a professional search firm or the U.S. Copyright Office to search for information about the owner.

   C) Send a permission request letter informing the owner of all possible uses of their work in your project.

   D) Document all attempts to request permission from the owner.

PATENTS

The law of patents also emanates from Article I, section 8, clause 8 of the Constitution. Patents may be obtained for "new and useful processes, machines, compositions of matter, or any new and useful improvement thereof." Patents cannot be obtained for principles of science and laws of nature. There are three types of patents, each of which covers a different type of invention. *Design patents* serve to protect the ornamental design of an object. *Plant patents* serve to protect asexually reproduced plant lines. *Utility patents* serve to protect processes, machines, articles of manufacture, compositions of matter, and methods of doing business. A patent grants to its owner the right to prohibit others from making, using, selling, offering for sale, or importing any product, process, or method covered by the patent, or an equivalent thereof, for a period of 20 years from the date the patent application is filed.

To be patentable, an invention must be (1) novel, (2) useful, and (3) unobvious to one of ordinary skill in the art. To be considered novel, an invention cannot have been conceived of and reduced to practice (i.e., fabricated or produced) by another prior to the conception and reduction to practice by the prospective patent applicant. In order to be considered useful, an invention must be shown to provide some benefit to the public. The obviousness standard involves a determination of whether the invention would have been obvious to one of ordinary skill in the art based upon the technology known to the public at the time the invention was made, without the benefit of hindsight.

```
                              BOOK ORDER
                ST. MARTIN'S COLLEGE              9363.005-02


    Supplier:      Dawson UK Ltd.       Reference:
    Order date:    29/06/05             Order number: SM04006415
    Quantity:      1                    ISBN:         1593110022
    Unit price:    21.95 GBP            Format:       Paperback
    Instructions: Carlisle


    Author:    Nebraska Symposium on Informaion
               Technology (1st (2002  Lincoln, Neb
    Title:     Web-based learning  what do we know where do we go / edited
               by Roger H. B
    Publisher: Information Age

    Site:      CAR
    Budget:    CARICT
    Stock Cat: 7 day
    Quantity:  1

                                        Dawson ref: 949958-021
```

Patent considerations are particularly important to online multimedia projects, in that patents can be obtained for computer software as a method of doing business (*State Street Bank & Trust Co. v. Signature Financial Group*, 1998). In the past five years, patents claiming software have been filed at a breakneck pace. Many patents have been filed on methods of delivering online courses. This creates potential patent infringement liability for any institution that creates its own software for use with its courses (in particular for delivering online educational materials) and, as with copyright, claims of willful patent infringement could result in tremendous financial liability or expensive legal defense costs for your institution.

In deciding whether patent considerations are necessary in a given project, you must determine whether any materials other than course content were developed during the project. For example, was any software developed for any facet of either the delivery or enhancement of the educational content? Was any software developed to test students or track their progress? Was any server-related software developed (e.g., firewall software or server access or interfacing software)? Was any graphic interface developed through which students or users interact with the educational content?

If the answer to any of the above questions is yes, then it is highly advisable to contact a patent attorney to help with some potentially complicated issues that can arise in the context of software patents. A patent attorney can perform a patent search to find out if anyone else has patented software covering the same functionality as your software and whether or not such patents limit your "freedom to operate," or your ability to use your software without triggering infringement liability to a third party.[6] If the software will be licensed to a commercial entity, it may be advisable to obtain an "opinion of counsel" in which the attorney will provide a written opinion as to whether the software infringes the rights of any third party. An opinion of counsel provides a patentee with a defense to a finding of willful patent infringement. Also, you may want to consider pursuing a patent on your software if you feel it is an appropriate investment. Costs to obtain a patent are significantly higher than copyright or trademark registration, frequently totaling several thousand dollars in filing fees and attorneys fees.

Under the Bayh-Dole Act, title to intellectual property resulting from research funded by the federal government may be retained by the institution performing the research (see 35 U.S.C. §200-212). However, patents or inventions that result from work performed pursuant to a grant from the federal government are subject to federal disclosure and licensing requirements (see 37 C.F.R. §401). These requirements vary from agency to agency, and it is advisable to check the Code of Federal Regulations to determine what disclosure and/or licensing rights a particular agency requires. With regard to licensing requirements, most often federal agencies will require either the grant of a nonexclusive license to the invention to the federal government, or the agency will retain what is known as a "march-in right," allowing the federal government to take over commercialization of a technology in the event the owner fails to do so. Failure to disclose and provide the required licensing rights to the federal government can result in a loss of title to inventions. Make sure all disclosures are made and all license requirements are met, and keep good records of your compliance with these requirements.

TRADEMARKS

A trademark is a word, slogan, symbol, name, device, or combination thereof adapted by a manufacturer or merchant that is used to identify the origin or source of its goods and/or services and to distinguish its goods and/or services from those of others (see 15 U.S.C. §1121). Some examples of famous trademarks include Coca Cola, Xerox, McDonald's, and Microsoft. Trademarks can be used to protect words, designs, sounds, and even colors, so long as those devices are used in a trademark context. However, words that are merely descriptive or considered generic are incapable of trademark protection. Trademarks can be registered with the federal government and with state governments, but, as with copyrights, they do not need to be registered to be enforceable. Trademark rights arise from the *use* of the mark on goods or in connection with the provision of services, so simply using a trademark can provide legal rights to the owner.

In the context of online multimedia projects, trademark issues frequently center around any names used in conjunction with the project and the registration and use of domain names for any Web sites utilized in the project. Be sure to search any names that are not completely descriptive or generic that you are using in relation to your project.[7] As discussed later in this chapter, domain names can infringe trademarks, so it is wise to search these as well before registration and use. As with copyright and patent, claims of willful trademark infringement can carry tremendous financial liability and legal defense costs for your institution.

TRADE SECRETS

A trade secret is confidential information generally not known by the public and valuable to a business. Trade secrets typically include information used in the course of business that provides a competitive advantage and is not generally known within the trade or industry. For example, trade secrets can be used to protect items such as a formula for a chemical compound, a process for manufacturing or treating materials, research and development information, customer lists, methods of bookkeeping, business plans or designs, and computer programs. Unlike the other forms of intellectual property protection that have a federal basis (e.g., patents), trade secrets are only protected under state law. In order to claim trade secret protection, the information or subject of the trade secret must, obviously, be kept secret or confidential. Trade secrets are therefore protected through contractual measures such as the use of confidentiality agreements and secrecy clauses in employment agreements. Trade secrets may become a concern in online multimedia projects if outside personnel, either from another university or the private sector, are brought in to help on a project. These individuals should be required, as a condition of their employment, to keep confidential any trade secret information they may be provided as a result of their work. Otherwise, they may be free to use this information at their discretion.

INTERNET LAW OR "CYBERLAW"

The law of the Internet, obviously, is a fairly new creation. Legal principles have still not been developed in many areas related to the Internet. However, there are several legal issues to be aware of relative to the development and delivery of online educational material.

Internet law often overlaps with the area of copyright. This is particularly true with the practice of linking to third-party Web sites. There is currently no definitive legal precedent in this area, but the case of *Kelly v. Arriba Soft Corp* (2002) may provide a roadmap to future legal doctrine. The plaintiff in this case was employed as a photographer and had developed a Web site on which he displayed copies of his photographs. The defendant owns and runs the Internet search engine Ditto.com. When used to search images, Ditto.com would present the user with reduced-size or "thumbnail" images from third-party Web sites. By clicking on these images, the user could pull up a full-size version of the image from the third-party Web site within a new frame on the Ditto.com Web site, a practice known as in-line linking. The court found that the thumbnail images could be shown on the Ditto.com Web site, but that the in-line links could not be used to display full-size images within the Ditto.com Web site without the permission of the owner.

This case helps clarify the circumstances under which permission is necessary to link from one Web site to another. Basically, providing a hypertext link on a Web site is still permissible without the consent of the owner of the linked site. However, in the event that the owner of a Web site wants to provide an in-line link or a deep-link (when a page from another Web site is opened within the same frame of another Web site), permission must be obtained from the owner of the linked site. In addition, caching a Web site, or saving the contents of a third-party Web site on a server under the control of another party, is essentially copying the contents of that site and, as such, also requires the permission of the owner.

As briefly discussed earlier, Internet law also overlaps with the area of trademark law, particularly when the trademarks of others are used in domain names and on Web sites. Domain names can infringe the rights of trademark owners, particularly when the domain name incorporates a famous trademark (*Panavision International, L.P. v. Toppen*, 1998). The practice of registering domain names incorporating the trademarks of others was the motivation behind the passage of the Anti-Cybersquatting Consumer Protection Act of 1999. Under this act, the bad faith practice of registering a domain name that incorporates the trademark of another in an attempt to profit off of the fame of the trademark is actionable in federal court, carrying both civil and criminal penalties.

Finally, if you are delivering content via a Web site, be sensitive to the use of trademarks in any metatags on the Web site. Metatags are lines of HTML code embedded into Web pages that are used by search engines to store information about a Web site. They frequently contain keywords, descriptions, site author information, and copyright information. The use of the trademarks of others in metatags on Web sites has been found to constitute trademark infringement (*Eli Lilly & Co. v. Natural Answers, Inc.*, 2000).

FINAL THOUGHTS

Obviously, the primary consideration in the development of online multimedia educational works is producing the best quality work possible to enhance the student's learning experience. In the process of developing these works, it is easy to place intellectual property concerns behind many other considerations. But, unlike most other considerations, failure to properly understand and address intellectual property issues can lead to tremendous financial liability and can render entire projects useless. Rather than waiting until the end of the project and fixing problems retroactively, planning ahead and considering intellectual property issues at the start of a project makes it much easier and cheaper to deal with problems as they arise. With appropriate preparation and a sharp eye for potential issues, negotiating the tricky waters of intellectual property rights can be a straightforward process.

REFERENCES

Anti-Cybersquatting Consumer Protection Act of 1999, Pub. L. No. 106-113 (November 29, 1999) (codified at 15 U.S.C. §1125(d)).

Bayh-Dole Act, 35 U.S.C. §200-212 (1980).

City of Newark v. Beasley, 883 F. Supp. 3, 7 (D.N.J. 1995) *quoting* Restatement (Second) of Agency § 228 (1958).

Digital Millennium Copyright Act [DMCA], Pub. L. No. 105-304, 112 Stat. 2860 (October 28, 1998) (codified at 17 U.S.C. §1201 *et seq*).

Eldred v. Ashcroft, 239 F.3d 372 (D.C. Cir. 2001).

Eli Lilly & Co. v. Natural Answers, Inc., 86 F. Supp. 2d 834 (S.D. Ind. 2000), *aff'd,* 233 F.3d 456 (7th Cir. 2000).

Kelly v. Arriba Soft Corp, 280 F.3d 934 (9th Cir. 2002).

Panavision International, L.P. v. Toppen, 945 F. Supp. 1296 (C.D. Cal. 1996), *aff'd,* 141 F. 3d 1316 (9th Cir. 1998).

Policies of the Board of Regents of the University of Nebraska [Online]. (2002). Retrieved from http:// www.nebraska.edu/board/board_policies.shtm.

Rosemont Enterprises v. Random House, Inc., 366 F.2d 303, 306 (2d Cir. 1966).

Sony Bono Copyright Term Extension Act , Pub. L. No. 105-298, 111 Stat. 2827 (October 27, 1998) (codified at 17 U.S.C. § 301 *et seq*).

State Street Bank & Trust Co. v. Signature Financial Group, 149 F.3d 1368 (Fed. Cir. 1998).

APPENDIX A: WORK-MADE-FOR-HIRE AGREEMENT

This Agreement is entered into as of the _____ day of_____, 200_, between [Name], located at [Address], a corporation duly organized and existing under and by virtue of the laws of the State of _____ (hereinafter referred to as "University"); and [Name] of [Address], (hereinafter referred to as "Writer").

1. SERVICES

University hereby engages Writer, and Writer agrees to be engaged, subject to the terms and conditions of this Agreement, to write [description of the work] (hereinafter referred to as the "Work").

2. DELIVERY

Writer shall deliver to University on or before [Date] a complete and final version of the Work in content and form satisfactory to University. Writer shall make any additions to, deletions from, alterations of, or revisions in the Work that University in its sole judgment determines are necessary.

3. COMPENSATION

In full consideration for all services rendered by Writer and for all rights granted or relinquished by Writer under this Agreement, University shall pay Writer the sum of $_____, as follows:

$_____ upon execution of this Agreement, and

$_____ upon written notification from University to Writer that University has accepted the Work as satisfactory.

4. OWNERSHIP

4.1 The Work shall be a work made for hire and the property of University.

4.2 University shall have the right to secure copyright protection for the Work.

4.3 In the event that the Work is not copyrightable subject matter, or for any reason cannot legally be a work-made-for-hire, then, and in such event, Writer hereby assigns all right, title, and interest to said Work to University and agrees to execute all documents required to evidence such assignment.

4.4 Without limiting the foregoing, Writer gives and grants to University the sole and exclusive right throughout the world in all languages and in perpetuity to use all work prepared by Writer pursuant to this Agreement.

4.5 University's rights shall be exclusive and Writer will not use, license, or permit the use of the Work for any other purpose.

4.6 Without limiting the foregoing, Writer hereby waives any and all claims that Writer may now or hereafter have in any jurisdiction to so-called "moral rights" or rights of "droit moral" with respect to the results and proceeds of Writer's Work and services hereunder.

5. NATURE OF EMPLOYMENT

Writer is an independent contractor and shall be solely responsible for any unemployment or disability insurance payments, or any social security, income tax or ether withholdings, deductions, or payments that may be required by federal, state, or local law with respect to any sums paid Writer hereunder. Writer shall not be entitled to any University employee benefits of any nature whatsoever.

6. AGENCY

Writer is not University's agent or representative and has no authority to bind or commit University to any agreements or other obligations.

7. TERMINATION

7.1 University may terminate this Agreement if Writer fails to deliver the Work by the time specified in Section 2 hereof (except where such delay is caused by circumstances beyond Writer's control and Writer has promptly notified University of such delaying circumstances) or if University determines, in its judgment, that the Work is not satisfactory. If University terminates this Agreement because of Writer's failure to deliver the Work on time, Writer shall immediately repay to University all sums theretofore paid Writer under this Agreement. If University terminates this Agreement because it determines that the Work is unsatisfactory, Writer shall retain all sums theretofore paid Writer as full satisfaction and discharge of all of University's obligations and liabilities under this Agreement.

7.2 Notwithstanding termination of this Agreement, University shall have the right, without further obligation to Writer, to use the Work in any manner it deems appropriate, including, without limitation, editing, altering, and revising the Work, except that if University subsequently uses the Work in substantially the form submitted by Writer, University shall pay Writer the amount that would otherwise have been due Writer on acceptance of the Work under Section 3 hereof.

8. REPRESENTATIONS AND WARRANTIES

8.1   Writer represents that no third party has any rights in, to, or arising out of, the Work supplied.

8.2   Writer agrees to hold University and its respective assigns and licensees, harmless from any loss, damage, or expense, including court costs and reasonable attorneys' fees, that University and its assigns and licensees may suffer as a result of a breach or alleged breach of the foregoing warranties or as a result of claims or actions of any kind or nature resulting from the use in any way of the Work.

9. WRITER'S REMEDY

Writer's remedy, if any, for any breach of this Agreement shall be solely in damages and Writer shall look solely to University for recovery of such damages. Writer waives and relinquishes any right Writer might otherwise have (a) to obtain injunctive or equitable relief for any reason, and (b) to proceed against any dispute arising under this Agreement.

10. ENTIRE AGREEMENT

This Agreement sets forth the entire agreement between University and Writer and supersedes any prior Agreements or understandings, whether oral or written.

11. GOVERNING LAW

This Agreement shall be governed by and construed under the laws of the State of
_____.

IN WITNESS WHEREOF, the parties hereto have executed this Agreement through duly authorized representatives as of the date set forth.

WRITER

Signature:_____

Date:_____

UNIVERSITY

Signature:_____

Name:_____

Title:_____

Date:_____

APPENDIX B

(DATE)

(NAME)

(ADDRESS)

(CITY, STATE, ZIP)

Re: Copyright Permission

Dear (NAME):

I am contacting you on behalf of the Curriculum Development Unit of the University of Nebraska–Lincoln to obtain permission to reproduce (DESCRIBE WORK) for our course entitled (NAME OF COURSE OR DETAILED DESCRIPTION OF PROJECT).

(PROVIDE BIBLIOGRAPHICAL INFORMATION OR CITATION TO THE ORIGINAL WORK OR ATTACH A COPY OF THE WORK, IF AVAILABLE)

The Curriculum Development Unit is a not-for-profit division of the University of Nebraska–Lincoln that creates educational courses. The Curriculum Development Unit incorporates numerous (SELECT ONE: QUOTES, IMAGES, ETC.) within its courses to improve the student's overall experience with the courses and enhance their learning experience. As your work will be used for non-profit, educational purposes, I respectfully request this permission be granted at no cost, although we are able to pay a reasonable fee if it is within our means. We foresee the (NAME OF COURSE) course having a life expectancy of approximately ___ to ___ years, with an expected enrollment of approximately ___ students per year.

I would appreciate your signing the enclosed form allowing us permission to use your work and also suggesting an appropriate credit line to be used in combination with your work. Your signing this letter will also confirm that you own (OR YOUR COMPANY OWNS) the copyright to use the above described material. Also, please let us know if you will require a fee for use.

We look forward to hearing from you.

Very Truly Yours,

NAME

Copyright Coordinator

University of Nebraska Curriculum Development Unit

ADDRESS

PHONE

FAX

E-MAIL

Course/Project: (INSERT TITLE OF COURSE OR PROJECT)

Title of Work: (INSERT TITLE OF WORK)

PERMISSION GRANTED FOR THE USE REQUESTED ABOVE:

By:_____

Title: _____
(IF CONTACTING A COMPANY)

Date: _____

PERMISSION CREDIT LINE:

_____

_____

_____

_____

_____

AUTHOR NOTE

Correspondence concerning this chapter should be addressed to Turan Odabasi, 239 Varner Hall, University of Nebraska–Lincoln, Lincoln, NE 68583-0745. E-mail: todabasi1@unl.edu.

NOTES

1. Phonorecords are defined as "material objects in which sounds, other than those accompanying a motion picture or other audiovisual work, are fixed by any method now known or later developed, and from which the sounds can be perceived, reproduced, or otherwise communicated, either directly or with the aid of a machine or device. The term "phonorecords" includes the material object in which the sounds are first fixed." See 17 U.S.C. §101.

2. A derivative work is defined as "a work based upon one or more preexisting works, such as translation, musical arrangement, dramatization, fictitionalization, motion picture version, sound recording, art reproduction, abridgement, condensation, or any other form in which a work may be recast, transformed or adapted. A work consisting of editorial revisions, annotations, elaborations or other modifications which as a whole represent an original work of authorship is a derivative work." See 17 U.S.C. §101.

3. Copyright notice is most often accomplished through the use of the symbol © or the abbreviation Copr., followed by the year of publication and the name of the owner (e.g., © 2002, The Board of Regents of the University of Nebraska).

4. The TEACH Act, S. 487, was signed by President Bush on November 2, 2002. A copy of the act can be obtained at *http://www.ala.org/washoff/teach.pdf.*

5. Two excellent sites that discuss the doctrine of fair use and provide guidelines for the use of certain works can be found at *http://www.utsystem.edu/ogc/intellectualproperty/copypol2.htm* and *http://www.cetus.org/fairindex.html.*

6. If you would like to perform your own patent search, the United States Patent and Trademark Office Web site, *http://www.uspto.gov*, contains a keyword search engine and provides access to all patents issued since 1790.

7. As with patents, federally registered trademarks can also be searched at *http://www.uspto.gov*. An Internet search with a search engine such as Google or AltaVista is also helpful in finding any unregistered or "common law" trademarks.

CHAPTER 12

LESSONS LEARNED ON THE LINE

Working with Web-Based Courses

Patricia B. Campbell
Lesley K. Perlman
Campbell-Kibler Associates, Inc.

Earl N. Hadley

ABSTRACT

Based on their work as the primary evaluators of CLASS courses, as well as the work of others in the field, Campbell-Kibler Associates, Inc. (C-KA), developed a series of brochures to help different populations make more effective decisions about Web-based learning. Brochures were developed for policymakers (*Dealing with Educational Inequities: Are Web-Based Courses an Answer?*), teachers and school administrators (*Going Web-Based? Helping School Administrators Make Informed Choices about Web-Based Courses*), and parents and students (*Are Web-Based Courses Right For My Child?*). The brochures were reformatted for publication in this volume. The original brochures can be downloaded from *http://www.campbell-kibler.com*.

Web-Based Learning: What Do We Know? Where Do We Go?, pages 231–252
Copyright © 2003 by Information Age Publishing
All rights of reproduction in any form reserved.

In addition, through interviews and surveys, information was collected from teachers and administrators using CLASS courses and from a sample of students who successfully completed two or more CLASS courses. A summary of their perceptions of what helps students succeed in online courses (*Teachers, Students and CLASS: Some Voices from the Field*) was developed and is included in this chapter. It can also be downloaded from *http://www.campbell-kibler.com*.

DEALING WITH EDUCATIONAL INEQUITIES: ARE WEB-BASED COURSES AN ANSWER?

An Overview of Web-Based Courses

There is increasing interest in using the Web to deliver courses. Web-based courses are a form of education called distance learning, which also includes courses by mail, videotape, CD, DVD, television, satellite broadcast, and video conferencing. In distance learning there is either no instructor or one who can be reached by mail or electronically.

Some distance learning is done in "real time," called *synchronous*. Students and an instructor, who are connected by Web, satellite, or video conferencing, simultaneously participate in the same or similar activities. Other distance learning is *asynchronous*, where students progress through courses at their own pace. In asynchronous distance learning, there may be e-mail or snail mail contact with an instructor or the feedback may be totally computer generated.

The Web is the primary source of information, activities, and interaction for Web-based courses. Web-based courses can also have e-teachers who interact with students electronically, onsite teachers, and supplemental materials such as textbooks and CDs.

Over the past few years there has been great interest in Web-based courses at the high school level. Currently, Web-based courses are offered at every skill level from Basic Math to Advanced Placement Calculus and for subjects from Personal Finance to Advanced Japanese.

Web-based courses can meet a number of school and student needs, including:

- increasing the variety of courses available to students
- increasing school scheduling options
- providing alternatives for home-schooled students
- providing an alternative way for students to retake failed courses.

As more attention is being paid to educational inequalities, Web-based courses are also being explored as a way of dealing with inequities in course access and student achievement.

Access to Web-based courses is provided through:

- *Virtual schools* where students enroll on a per-course basis and pay tuition, which costs around $300 per course. Examples include Virtual Greenbush (*http://www.virtualgreenbush.org/*) and CompuHigh (*http://www.compuhigh.com*).
- *Statewide schools* where state residents can enroll in courses for free or at a nominal cost. Examples include Florida Virtual School (*http://www.flvs.net*) and Kentucky Virtual High School (*http://www.kvhs.org/*).
- *Cross state consortiums* where partner schools develop courses for their students and others. An example is the Virtual High School (*http://www.govhs.org/website.nsf*).
- *School- or district-wide contracts* where course providers such as Apex Learning (*http://apexlearning.com*) and class.com (*http://www.class.com/*) are contracted to deliver courses for students from that school or district.

Unequal Access to Advanced Courses

Having a high quality academic high school curriculum is one of the strongest predictors of college completion, especially for African American and Hispanic students. (Adelman, 1999)

High schools serving predominantly low income and minority students typically offer far fewer advanced, Honors and Advanced Placement (AP) courses than do other schools. (Oakes, Muir, & Joseph, 2000)

To deal with this inequity states like Michigan (*http://www.mivu.org/mivhs/Apex/Apexl.htm*) and California (*http://uccp.org/*) are providing their students access to Web-based advanced courses.

Using Web-based courses to fill curricular "holes" has a number of advantages, including:

- Making it cost effective to offer AP or other advanced courses to individuals or to small groups of students
- Allowing advanced courses to be offered in schools where there are no teachers qualified to teach the course
- Allowing students to take advanced courses at their high schools rather than at local colleges.

There can be some disadvantages as well, including:

- The need to provide students with computer access and broadband Web access before, during, and after school

- Little data on the relative effectiveness of Web-based AP and Honors courses compared to in-school courses
- Lower course completion rates.

Low Student Academic Performance

Having qualified teachers with strong content knowledge is related to higher student achievement; however, these teachers are less apt to be found in schools with larger numbers of poor and minority students. (Wenglinsky, 2000)

There is no substitute for qualified, available teachers. However, many schools don't have these qualified teachers, especially in mathematics and science. In these cases, the availability of remedial and basic-level Web-based courses and the ability of these courses to make use of graphics, audio, video, diagrams, and photographs have helped make Web-based courses an attractive way to improve student performance.

Supporting this belief, states such as Florida provide their students from low-performing schools with preferential free access to Web-based courses.

There are a number of possible advantages to using Web-based courses with low-performing students:

- Students progress at their own pace
- A variety of instructional modes can be used
- Tests and activities can be done more than once
- Students may feel more comfortable in an online environment.

The major disadvantage of using Web-based courses with low performing students is that studies have found that distance learning works better with students who are eager to learn than for those who may need motivation. It appears to be less suitable for lower performing students, particularly when remedial work is needed (Campbell & Storo, 1996; Campion, 1991).

However, teachers have suggested that Web-based courses can be effectively used with at-risk, low-literacy students if they are used in small groups with a good onsite facilitator.

What's Needed to Make Web-Based Courses Work?

Technical and financial resources are key. Schools need to have enough technology and Web access to make Web-based courses a viable alternative. They may also need money to pay not only for the courses but for student instructional materials, the necessary instructional and technical support, and even onsite teacher training.

In addition, the courses have to be good. Good Web-based courses have:

- Accurate content at the appropriate level of difficulty
- Activities and assessments that are accurate and tied to the content and the course goals
- Certified e-teachers who are qualified in the content area
- E-teacher and computer-generated feedback that is timely and helpful
- Met state and/or local standards
- The potential to keep students interested and motivated.

If schools choose to use Web-based courses, they need to be aware that:

- Students need out-of-class computer and Web access
- E-teacher response to student questions is not immediate and can take a day or more
- E-teachers tend to have more limited knowledge of students than onsite teachers
- Hands-on activities, especially science labs, can be difficult to do in Web-based courses
- Onsite instructional support may be needed, including:
  - Onsite teacher/facilitators with technical and subject area knowledge
  - Tutors
  - Books and other instructional materials

So Are Web-Based Courses an Answer?

First, several other questions need to be asked.

Do Web-based courses increase student achievement?

A meta analysis of studies of distance learning found few differences between the achievement of distance learning students and students in conventional classrooms (Cavanaugh, 1999). However, dropout rates can be a problem. More needs to be learned about completion rates and achievement test scores of students taking Web-based courses and comparable students in conventional classes.

Do Web-based courses decrease the digital divide?

While the in-school digital divide is closing, there are still major differences by race/ethnicity and socioeconomic status in the amount of computer and Web access students have outside of school. To decrease the divide, schools may need to provide students with before-school and after-school access to computers and the Web and not assume they can work on the courses at home.

Are Web-based courses cost effective?

If schools already have the hardware, software, and Web access needed for students to effectively use Web-based courses and to ensure the security of student data, courses can be cost effective, depending on the cost of the courses and of the offsite and onsite supports.

Are Web-based courses sustainable?

Web-based courses will need to reflect state and local standards and need to be tied to state testing and graduation requirements if they are to survive. In addition, students and schools need some insurance that courses will continue and will be maintained.

Resources

Distance Learning Resource Network: *http://www.dlrn.org/*

Virtual High Schools: State of the States (2000): *http://www.cait.org/shared_resource _docs/vhs_files/vhs_study.pdf*

A Review of Secondary Net-Courses and Virtual Schools (1997): *http://www.concord .org/pubs/review.html*

GOING WEB-BASED? HELPING SCHOOL ADMINISTRATORS MAKE INFORMED CHOICES ABOUT WEB-BASED COURSES

Why Web-Based Courses?

Web-based courses use the Web as the primary source of information, activities, and student interaction. Some courses have e-teachers (who interact with students electronically) and supplementary materials. Schools can use Web-based courses:

- *To increase the variety of courses open to students.* Currently, there are Web-based courses for every skill level from Basic Math to Advanced Placement Calculus and for subjects from Business to Japanese. Web-based courses can be used when there is no qualified subject area teacher.
- *To increase scheduling options.* Most Web-based courses can be taken at any time, offering flexibility in scheduling, providing options for stu-

dents needing specific courses and an alternative to too many senior study halls.

- *To serve out-of-school students.* Providing access to Web-based courses can be a relatively inexpensive way to support students who are unable to attend school.
- *To provide alternatives to summer school.* Students can use Web-based courses to retake failed subjects, reducing the need for summer school.
- *To expand educational options.* Web-based courses can provide an instructional alternative for home-schooled students or for those who are not doing well in conventional classes.

What Do Schools Need to Consider before Implementing Web-Based Courses?

Schools need a lot of up-front preparation before they can successfully use Web-based courses...including teacher preparation and technological preparation.... Schools need to know what their students will need to be successful in a Web-based course and how much mentoring they as the school are willing to do. (e-course company executive, 2001)

These questions may help with up-front preparation:

- *Content.* For what purpose do you want to offer the courses? In what content areas? For what grade levels?
- *Students.* About how many students will enroll? Will students need prerequisites in order to enroll? A specific GPA? Teacher recommendations?
- *Teachers.* Will e-teachers be used? Will there be additional onsite instructional support? What training will be provided to onsite teachers?
- *Technology.* What servers, computers, and broadband access are available? Will students be able to access courses out of school? Who will provide students with technical support?
- *Management.* Who will coordinate the overall effort? Are resources available to pay for the courses and other related costs?

Who Does Well in Web-Based Courses?

> The students who are the most successful are the ones who have learned on their own to be self-motivated and have some drive. (e-learning teacher, 2001)

Ideally, and in many marketing materials, the answer to who does well in Web-based courses is "everyone." The reality is much more complex. The typical distance learning student, which includes Web-based students, has been described as 16 years old with a GPA of at least 3.0 who plans to enroll in college upon graduation. This description reflects the wider view that "students must be mature, self-disciplined and motivated to use distance learning effectively" (Campbell & Storo, 1996). Teachers currently working with Web-based students are not sure that Web-based courses work for students who are already in trouble. Their concern reflects earlier work that found distance learning can actually exacerbate students' academic difficulties (Campbell & Storo, 1996).

Not surprisingly, Web-based courses don't work very well if students are unmotivated, especially if the students don't like the subject covered. In the words of one student: "If you don't like what you are studying, don't take it online" (Trotter, 2001).

Web-based courses can attract at-risk students who like the subject area or who are excited about the novelty of working on the Web. Their teachers feel at-risk students are most apt to be successful if the Web-based courses are:

- Well organized
- Easy to follow with clear instructions
- Written at an appropriate reading level
- Include an onsite educator to provide supervision and guidance.

What Helps Students Succeed in Web-Based Courses?

Teachers, working with e-students, rated the following factors as important to student success.

- *E-teacher student feedback.* Timely, informative feedback to students and, as necessary, to onsite supervisors is key. Unlike the classroom, where response to questions is immediate, Web-based students often wait a day or more for their answers.
- *Student academic ability.* Average and basic students can do well when Web-based courses are matched with students' ability levels and there is onsite support.

- *Student ability to keep to deadlines.* Providing students with deadlines for the completion of units, activities, tests, and the course as a whole can help students progress through courses.
- *Regularly scheduled times to work on courses.* Specific locations and times for students to work on their courses can be helpful.
- *Frequent access to computers.* More access can be provided by making school computers available before and after school, giving student passwords and/or course CDs so they can work on their Web-based courses out of school, giving them "loaner laptops" and letting them print course components so they can work on their courses offline.
- *Other sources of student support.* Supports can include onsite adults with technical and subject area knowledge, tutors, books and other instructional materials.

What Shall I Look for in Selecting a Web-Based Course Provider?

Once we worked out the bugs, it was good. We had a wonderful setup. (teacher, 2001)

We've had some unsuccessful experiences with (a company). There were additional materials that they failed to tell us we needed to purchase after we had paid our tuition. It was hard to get a hold of them, it took a long time to get the teacher feedback—students had to email quite a bit to get a response. And there was no one to call. (teacher, 2001 [This teacher's quote did not refer to CLASS but to a provider they previously used.]).

Some Web-based course providers will do a better job of meeting your needs than will others. The following criteria can be useful to keep in mind as you select a provider.

Course quality

Having teachers and students review courses is a good way to assess course quality. They can assess:

- Content level and accuracy
- Appropriateness of the activities and assessments
- The value of feedback given to students
- Course potential to keep students interested and motivated.

Accreditation

If accreditation is important to you, you should check if the course and/or program is accredited and if so, by whom.

State curriculum standards

Even if courses are described as "standards based," you may want to check which of your state or local standards are met by the courses and how that's determined.

Costs/licensing options

"How much?" and "What is and isn't included?" are bottom-line questions. It is useful to ask if the cost includes all student instructional materials, necessary instructional and technical support (including maintenance and upgrades), and onsite teacher professional development.

There are a variety of ways to "buy" Web-based courses including site licensing, where for one price there is no limit on the number of students or the number of courses they take; individual enrollments, where there is a fee for each student enrolled; and collaborations of districts who negotiate agreements with course providers.

E-teachers

Some course providers use e-teachers for instructional support. You may want to ask those who do about their e-teacher training and supervision; the quality, quantity, and timeliness of e-teacher communications; and what you can do if you are dissatisfied with an e-teacher. If you are using your own teachers, you may want to ask about professional development for onsite teachers.

Technical supports

It is important to know where students can go for help when they have technical problems, what support is available, and if it is available by phone as well as e-mail.

Evaluation

You may want to ask for evaluation information, including the numbers and percentage of students completing the courses and any information that ties course completion to increased standardized test scores. You may also want to know if they have provisions for students to drop a course with a full or partial refund and what percentage of students do this.

Some Sources of Courses

Remember, things on the Web change quickly. Some resources that are here today may not be tomorrow. The following URLs are listed as resources only; no endorsement is intended or given.

- *http://apexlearning.com*
  Apex Learning offers 30+ courses, including Advanced Placement courses. They provide schools and districts with instructional, administrative, and technical support services.
- *http://www.class.com*
  class.com offers 40 high school courses. It builds partnerships with districts, consortiums, and high schools providing the technical platform, courses, and support services.
- *http://www.jonesknowledge.com/*
  Jones Knowledge offers the Florida Virtual High School and Apex professional development courses. They have Web-based course management, a delivery platform, e-mail, and telephone technical support.
- *http://www.ncslearn.com/*
  NCS Learn offers courses for preschool through adult learners, including GED Preparation. They offer onsite support, telephone support, and software installation, as well as teacher professional development.
- *http://www.gofhs.org/website.nsf*
  Virtual High School is a collaboration of high schools that develops Web-based courses and offers them to students in member schools. It also offers teacher professional development.
- *http://www.dlrn.org/*
  Distance Learning Resource Network offers further information.

ARE WEB-BASED COURSES RIGHT FOR MY CHILD?

What Are Web-Based Courses?

Web-based courses are increasingly being considered, by families and others, as alternatives to traditional schooling. The U.S. Department of Education estimates that, during the 2001–2002 school year, 40,000–50,000 students will enroll in a Web-based high school course. Some students will take one or two courses, while others will earn their entire high school diploma online.

Web-based courses are a form of education called distance learning, which also includes courses by mail, videotape, CD, DVD, television, satellite broadcast, and video conferencing. In distance learning there is either no instructor or there is an instructor who can be reached by mail or electronically.

Web-based courses can be *asynchronous*, where students progress through courses at their own pace. Students may have e-mail or mail contact with an instructor, or the feedback they receive may be totally computer generated. Courses can also be *synchronous*, where students and an instructor are connected through the Web, satellite, or video conferencing and simultaneously participate in the same or similar activities.

Web-based courses may have instructors, called e-teachers, whose primary interaction with students is electronic. E-teachers correct papers, ask and answer questions, and generally provide students with support. Unlike the classroom, where students get immediate responses from their teachers, students in asynchronous courses usually have to wait a day or two for responses from their e-teachers.

Range and Types of Web-based Courses

A great variety of Web-based courses are offered at the high school level. Courses range in skill level from Basic Math to Advanced Placement Calculus and cover required and elective high school courses ranging from Personal Finance to Advanced Japanese. The following is a short introduction to two sample Web-based courses, which are part of the high school curriculum offered by class.com.

Algebra I. Using text, graphics, and audio you cover 69 different topics in six units. Within the course, you can try lots of problems: sample problems, practice sets, and summary practice sets. When you solve a problem online, the computer tells you if you're right or wrong and asks if you would like an explanation of the solution. Along with solving the problems, you take computer-scored quizzes, unit tests, and a final exam. There are three written assignments that the e-teacher grades and an online discussion group where you "talk" about algebra with other students.

U.S. History II covers the years 1865–1974 in four units, each of which includes five different views of history: political, cultural, minority, military, and economic. Each page has pictures, text, and links to Web sites with maps, quotes, timelines, and additional information related to the units. During the course you take computer-scored quizzes, write four short essays, and do a final project covering the history of the United States from 1974 to the present. The essays and the final project are e-mailed to the e-teacher for grading and feedback.

The best way to find out what Web-based courses are like is to try them. Most course providers have demos that allow you to do that.

Will My Child Do Well in Web-Based Courses?

> The students that are the most successful [in Web-based courses] are the
> ones that have learned on their own to be self-motivated and have some
> drive. (e-teacher, 2001)

There is general agreement that mature, self-disciplined, motivated students who are independent learners are most likely to be successful in Web-based courses (and in education in general). Not surprisingly, Web-based courses don't work very well if students are unmotivated and if they aren't interested in the subject. In the words of one student, "If you don't like what you are studying, don't take it online" (Trotter, 2001).

There is a lot of writing in Web-based courses. Writing e-mails, discussion group entries, and assignments are the primary ways you let people know what you are learning. Students who are unable or unwilling to write will most likely have difficulties completing Web-based courses.

Parents should know that the chances of average and basic-level students doing well in Web-based courses can be increased by matching the courses with students' ability levels and providing the following supports as needed:

- A quiet place and regularly scheduled times to work on the course
- Agreed-upon deadlines for the completion of units, activities, tests, and the course as a whole
- Adults with some technical and subject-area knowledge
- Tutors
- Related books and other instructional materials that can often be found at local libraries.

A variety of informal quizzes and tip sheets have been developed to help students decide if Web-based courses are for them. You can access a number of them at the Illinois Online Network (*http://www.ion.illinois.edu/ION resources/onlineLearning/*). The results of these quizzes are useful in parent/child discussions about what it takes to do well in Web-based courses.

Technology and Web-Based Courses

> We are so rural that the technical connections did not work for us. We were
> shut off so many times during the time he tried to work that he dropped the
> [Web-based] classes and did not finish either of them. He did enjoy them, however. He liked the graphics and the content. We had planned to take more
> until we developed the problems. (mother of a Web-based student, 2000)

No matter how good the course or the student, if the technical aspects of a Web-based course don't work, the student will not be successful. There are a number of technical questions you will need to answer:

Will the course run on your computer?

Before registering for a course, check to make sure the course will run on your existing hardware and software. If you are not sure, check with the course provider. Different courses have different requirements in such areas as processing speed, operating systems, storage space, CD readers, and speakers. Buying new hardware and/or software can add a lot to the cost of the course.

Do you have a fast, reliable Internet connection?

An unreliable Internet connection can lead to lost work, frustration, and, as indicated in the quote above, dropping courses. A slower phone connection can mean a wait of 30 minutes or more to get a 3–5 minute video. If the course has a lot of audio/visual, a lot of time will be spent waiting for things to download.

Is there technical support?

Most people will have technical problems at some point in the course. It is important to know where students can go for help when they have minor and major technical problems, what support is available, when it is available, and if the support is available by phone as well as e-mail.

How is student privacy assured?

Your child will be sending a lot of information, including applications and essays, over the Web to the course provider. You may want to check what happens to that data and who has access to it.

Selecting a Web-Based Course: Some Criteria to Consider

The first step in selecting a Web-based course is to be clear what your goals are. If, for example, you want the course to provide your child with opportunities to interact with other students online, your criteria may be quite different than if your goal is for your child to take advanced courses for possible college credit.

General criteria include:

- *Accreditation.* If your child is interested in taking a course for credit, it is important to know if the course is being offered by an accredited provider and if course credits will be accepted by high schools and recognized by colleges.

- *Course appropriateness.* Web-based courses can work for at-risk and low-literacy students who like the subject area and/or are excited about the novelty of working on the Web. These students, teachers say, will have a greater chance to be successful if the Web-based courses are well organized, easy to follow with clear instructions, written at an appropriate reading level, and able to keep students interested.
- *Student feedback.* Timely, informative feedback to students is a key to their success. Most students need more feedback than finding out whether an answer was right or wrong. They need to find out why a certain answer is wrong and where they made a mistake or what they misunderstood. Some of this feedback can be generated by computers; however, in many cases, teacher feedback is needed as well. In addition, some level of e-teacher and/or peer interaction may be needed to help students stay on track. You may want to find out about the amount and kinds of course feedback your child will receive as well as the qualifications of the people providing it.
- *Success.* Before your child takes a course, you may want to know how many others have taken the course, how many have completed the course, and if there are provisions for students to drop a course and receive a full or partial refund. Some parents may also want to know if there is information available that ties course completion to increased standardized test scores.
- *Costs.* "How much?" and "What is and what isn't included?" are bottom line questions. It is important to find out if the cost includes all student instructional materials, as well as any necessary instructional and technical support. Per course costs tend to be about $300, but many providers offer steep discounts to those taking an entire program of study online. Some states allow residents to take online courses for free or at a reduced cost. Your state department of education should be able to tell you if that is an option for your child. They can be found at *http://www.ed.gov/Programs/EROD/ERODmap.html*
- *Course format.* Web-based courses should make use of the Web's interactive and multimedia capacities. Text should be integrated as necessary, rather than being the primary way information is presented. If a course is going to be primarily the reading of text, it most likely should not be on the Web.
- *Additional criteria* to consider can be found at *http://www.dlrn.org/k12/criteria.html*

Sources of Courses for Individual Students

Remember, things on the Web change quickly; some URLs that are here today may not be tomorrow. The URLs listed below are intended as examples; no endorsement is intended or given.

- *http://apexlearning.com*
  Apex Learning offers more than 30 Advanced Placement (AP), foreign language, general studies, and technology courses.
- *http://www.babbagenetschool.com/index_home.html*
  Babbage Net School offers more than 50 high school and AP courses in English, math, science, social studies, foreign languages, music, and art.
- *http://www.clonlara.org/compuhigh.htm*
  Compuhigh offers more than 20 high school courses in social studies, language arts, science, math, computing, and career planning.
- *http://www.dennisononline.com/dolwelcome.shtml*
  Dennison Academy provides over 30 courses in humanities, science, mathematics, fine arts, and technology leading to a high school diploma.
- *http://www.flvs.net*
  Florida Virtual School serves Florida residents offering an entire high school curriculum of more than 60 courses.
- *http://www.iacademy.org*
  Internet Academy predominantly serves Washington State residents and offers a complete high school curriculum of over 35 courses.
- *http://www.laurelsprings.com*
  Laurel Springs has over 40 courses available for 9th through 12th graders including courses for special needs and honors students.
- *http://www.dlrn.org/k12/virtual_list.html#state*
  The Virtual School List has information on a wide variety of courses and schools.

TEACHERS, STUDENTS, AND CLASS: SOME VOICES FROM THE FIELD

We had one student [who] just bolted out of the gates and finished half the course by the first semester. By Christmas, he will finish the whole course. [He] wants to go to engineering school...didn't really have anyone pushing him, just himself. (CLASS course facilitator, 2001)

Thirteen facilitators of CLASS courses—including seven teachers, two principals, two counselors, one curriculum coordinator, and one director—from 11 secondary schools were interviewed at the end of 2001 to get their perspectives on what helps students to succeed in online courses. In addition, six students who successfully completed at least two CLASS courses and who were not affiliated with the 11 schools responded by mail to a survey questionnaire. It is important to note that this summary includes just a sample of schools and individual students that used CLASS courses and is not meant to be indicative of the experience of taking a Web-based course.

Facilitators noted the most common reasons for enrolling students in online courses are a lack of certified teachers (six schools)—most often in physics, mathematics, or Spanish—and the chance to offer a more extensive curriculum with greater choices (five schools). Schools also offered CLASS courses so students could retake courses they had failed (two schools) and to fill up students' free time when there were no regular classes scheduled (two schools). In addition, one school offered CLASS courses to provide students with an online learning experience.

Students at basic, average, and advanced/honors levels all enrolled in CLASS courses, although students from the 11 schools and the individual students were most apt to be classified or classify themselves as being at average ability levels. Six of the 11 schools had criteria students had to meet before they were allowed to take online courses. Two of the six schools added requirements after their students started using online courses. They felt, based on their experiences, that they needed some guidelines in selecting which students would be allowed to take online courses. Sample criteria included:

- teacher or counselor recommendations (three schools)
- student personality characteristics: self-motivated, independent learners (three schools)
- previous student academic success, including GPA and attendance records (three schools)
- student computer skills and computer access in their homes or time in the students' schedule to use the school's computer facilities (two schools)
- age (only upper-class students can take courses) (two schools)
- fulfillment of academic prerequisites, for example, for students taking Physics, most had already completed Algebra 2, Geometry, and Physical Science (one school).

All schools had students taking courses in school, either alone (nine) or as part of a group (seven). Seven schools allowed students to print out portions of the course or take the course CD with them to allow them to work on the course at home or elsewhere.

Students at 10 of the 11 schools used Macintosh, Pentium 2, or faster computers and had broadband access (cable, T1, or DSL lines). There were few technical problems other than occasional access problems due to Internet traffic and some reports of students saying they sent work to e-teachers but the e-teachers had not received it. However, one school noted problems with students getting "kicked out" when taking tests or quizzes because a computer froze or the Internet connection dropped, which caused lower grades because it looked as if the student had left questions unanswered.

Being Successful Online

The students that are the most successful are the ones that have learned on their own to be self-motivated and have some drive on their own. They have to know what it's like to go after something themselves. (CLASS course facilitator, 2001)

For students who don't do well on tests, it's not any better than a classroom experience. [I'm] not sure that this works for students who are already in trouble. (CLASS course facilitator, 2001)

I have one student who was doing Algebra I and Spanish I. She got to Spanish and finished that pretty quickly, with the map that you click around. When she got to the Algebra, she just couldn't stay motivated. If the math could have been made to hold her attention a bit better, that could have been more successful. (CLASS course facilitator, 2001)

Facilitators' discussions of factors related to student success often centered on motivation. Facilitators also often mentioned the need to impose some sort of pacing mechanism on students to push them toward completion. Some schools only allow students one semester to complete the class. They also noted that the "more often deadlines appear during a course, the better off the kids are." Others suggest adding in "small deadlines" within the course—such as dates when units have to be finished to help the students pace themselves. One teacher felt guidance on how long it usually takes to complete certain sections would be helpful.

Getting started was a problem for one facilitator who emphasized the necessity of getting the students to sign up immediately—because after they enroll, they have to wait a week or two before the materials arrive.

Three of the six individual students did not get or need help in technical areas, although the other three got help from CLASS/ISHS, from a family member or friend, and a teacher or adult in their school. Help for content-related areas came from a family member or friend and a teacher or adult in the student's school.

CLASS facilitators were asked to rate nine factors and individual students were asked to rate seven factors in terms of their importance to student success online. As can be seen from Table 12.1, facilitators feel that e-teacher feedback and being good at keeping to deadlines are very important to students successfully completing CLASS courses, although individual students didn't feel these factors are as important. Facilitators also note academic ability, having a regularly scheduled time to work, and having frequent access to computers are important to student success. Individual students feel that having frequent access to computers and having an interest in the subject area are most important to their success. Working with other students was seen as least important for both groups.

Table 12.1.   Factors Related to Student Online Success

	Facilitator mean rating	*Student mean rating*
E-teacher feedback	1.3	2.2
Being good at keeping to deadlines	1.3	2.0
Academic ability	1.5	Question not asked
A regularly scheduled time to work	1.5	2.0
Frequent access to computers	1.5	1.2
Familiarity with computers	2.0	Question not asked
Other teacher support	2.1	3.0
Support of family	2.3	Question not asked
Interest in the subject area	Question not asked	1.5
Working with other students	2.7	3.0

Note. Ratings ranged from 1 = very important, 5 = not important

E-Teachers

[Students] can't get their questions answered when they need it. They won't be answered that day. The feedback itself was good and explained well, but the timing messes things up, as they have to wait two days. (CLASS course facilitator, 2001)

All but one of the schools interviewed used the CLASS e-teacher. Overall, they felt e-teacher feedback was fairly helpful, rating it a 2.4 on a scale of 1 = very helpful to 5 = not at all helpful. The six students found the e-teacher feedback less helpful, rating it a 2.7; one student noted that the e-teachers differed too much to give one rating and another student gave one e-teacher a "1" and another a "4." While the facilitators thought the "interaction with online teachers and keeping up with email" helped the students to be successful, they were also concerned about the timing of the responses. Facilitators mentioned problems with the lack of immediacy that is intrinsic to asynchronous learning. Contrary to the anytime-any-where nature of the Internet and access to Web-based classes, there can be a time lag, typically one or two days, when students have questions and are unable to continue without an answer, and they have to wait for the e-teacher to respond. A facilitator noted instances when they tried to set up a time for the student and e-teacher to be online at the same time but felt that the e-teacher was "not very flexible" in setting up a time.

As can be seen in Table 12.2, facilitators indicated that most e-teachers would typically respond quickly to student emails in one to two days, although some e-teachers from other courses would take longer, up to three or four days. Students replied that e-teachers would typically respond within four days to student emails and grading of assignments, but different e-teachers varied greatly. There was less commonality when facilitators were asked about the length of time it took e-teachers to grade student tests and assignments.

Table 12.2. E-Teacher Average Response Times

	Facilitator response		Student response	
	Response to student email	Grading of tests and assignments	Response to student email	Grading of tests and assignments
1–2 days	8	4	2	3
3–4 days	4	6	3	3
5–6 days	0	3	0	0
7–10 days	0	1	0	0
10+ days	0	2	0	0
Teachers differed greatly	—	—	2	1

Note. The total number of responses is greater than the number of facilitators interviewed and students surveyed because many schools and students took more than one class and as a result, had different e-teachers who had different response rates.

Onsite Facilitators

Unless you have a really motivated kid, a teacher needs to be there to encourage, motivate, and help get things done. (CLASS course facilitator, 2001)

Nine schools had a classroom teacher available to provide additional support to students, either in the same classroom when the students were on the computers or accessible when the students had questions. Four facilitators reinforced how important it was to have someone there onsite.

In some schools, students have access to other classroom teachers, tutors, paraprofessionals, the librarian, other students, and even related textbooks to get help in the course and to answer their questions about the material.

Pedagogy

> The [courses] are not consistently developed. The audio portion for some of the classes like Spanish are close to impossible to get to work.... The test materials are radically different. The classes should look more alike and be more consistent so that students and teacher didn't have to learn a new way of doing it. (CLASS course facilitator, 2001)

Facilitators had a variety of concerns about course pedagogies. For example, individual facilitators felt in some courses there was too much text or they were at too high of a level and that having lower reading levels in beginning and intermediate courses would be more appropriate for lower-level students. However, as the above quote indicates, there is a great deal of differences in content, level, and testing.

Communication between course providers, e-teachers, and onsite facilitators has been important and productive. For example, after Physics students in one site decided to "beat the system" by giving answers to the tests and "sharing" their lab and written assignments with others, Greenbush and the school changed the procedures. The facilitator commented that while there are a lot more Cs and Ds, "students are learning now."

AUTHOR NOTE

Unless otherwise cited, information comes from Campbell-Kibler Associates, Inc., evaluations. © 2002 Campbell-Kibler Associates, Inc. All rights reserved.

Production of this material was made possible by a grant from the U.S. Department of Education to the CLASS Project, University of Nebraska–Lincoln. Opinions expressed are those of the authors and not necessarily those of the funders.

Correspondence concerning this chapter may be directed to Campbell-Kibler Associates, Inc., 80 Lakeside Dr., Groton, MA 01450. Email: *Campbell@campbell-kibler.com,* Web site: *www.campbell-kibler.com*

REFERENCES

Adelman, Clifford. (1999). *Answers in the toolbox? Academic intensity, attendance patterns, and bachelor degree attainment.* Jessup, MD: Education Publication Center.

Campbell, Patricia B., & Storo, Jennifer (1996). Reducing the distance: Equity issues in distance learning in public education. *Journal of Science Education and Technology, 5*(4), 285–295.

Campion, Michael G. (1991). Distance education: Access, equity and participation and/or efficiency and effectiveness. In J. Hardie (Ed.), *ASPESA papers: Number 10* (pp. 59–70). New South Wales, Australia: Australian & South Pacific External Studies Association. (ERIC Reproduction Service No. ED 338226)

Cavanaugh, Catherine S. (1999). *The effectiveness of interactive distance education technologies in K–12 Learning: A meta-analysis.* (ERIC Reproduction Service No. ED 430547)

Oakes, Jeanne, Muir, Kate, & Joseph, Rebecca (2000). *Course taking and achievement in mathematics and science: Inequalities that endure and change* [Online]. Retrieved from http://www.wcer.wisc.edu/nise/News_Activities/Forums/Oakespaper.htm

Trotter, Andrew (2001, January 24). Cyber learning at online high. *Education Week,* 28–33.

Wenglinsky, Harold (2000). *How teaching matters: Bringing the classroom back into discussions of teacher quality.* Princeton, NJ: Educational Testing Service.

ABOUT THE CONTRIBUTORS

Charles J. Ansorge
National Center for Information Technology in Education (NCITE),
University of Nebraska–Lincoln

Charles Ansorge is an NCITE Scholar and Professor in Teachers College at the University of Nebraska where he teaches undergraduate- and graduate-level introductory and advanced statistics to both campus and distance students in the Department of Educational Psychology. He is also the co-chair of the campus Teaching, Learning, and Technology Roundtable. Among the first faculty at UNL to explore the use of technologies such as email, gophers, Web sites, presentation software, and streaming video, Dr. Ansorge has supervised and taught numerous workshops and met one-on-one with faculty members to help them understand how it is possible to effectively use technology to promote student learning and teaching. In 2002, he was asked to lead a faculty mentoring program that is being sponsored by the Office of Extended Education and Outreach. In summer 2003 he will be teaching a summer institute for faculty to learn more about teaching online.

Oksana Bendus
National Center for Information Technology in Education (NCITE),
University of Nebraska–Lincoln

Oksana Bendus is a graduate student in Quantitative and Qualitative Methods in Education at the University of Nebraska–Lincoln. Her current research interests include measurement and scale validation, emotional

Web-Based Learning: What Do We Know? Where Do We Go?, pages 253–259
Copyright © 2003 by Information Age Publishing
All rights of reproduction in any form reserved.

intelligence, and the study of factors involved in girls' decisions to pursue careers in science and technology.

Roger Bruning
Center for Instructional Innovation, National Center for Information Technology in Education, University of Nebraska–Lincoln

Roger Bruning is Velma Warren Hodder Professor of Educational Psychology and co-director of the Center for Instructional Innovation and the National Center for Information Technology in Education at the University of Nebraska–Lincoln. His research interests focus on literacy, especially development of motivation to read and write, and on the role of technology in education. Dr. Bruning has taught courses in applied cognitive psychology and in educational measurement and research, written numerous articles, and served as a consultant and evaluator for many projects of the National Science Foundation, Agency for International Development, Environmental Protection Agency, Satellite Educational Resources Consortium, and U.S. Department of Education. In 1982–83 he was a Visiting Scientist at the Center for the Study of Reading at the University of Illinois and in 1988 and 1993 was a Visiting Scholar at Stanford University and the National Reading Research Center. From 1987 to 1991 Dr. Bruning served as Associate Dean of Graduate Studies at the University of Nebraska–Lincoln. He currently serves on the Editorial Boards of the *Journal of Educational Psychology*, *Educational Psychology Review*, and *Scientific Studies of Reading*, and is the coauthor of three textbooks.

Patricia B. Campbell
Campbell-Kibler Associates, Inc.

Patricia B. Campbell is the president of Campbell-Kibler Associates, Inc., and has been involved in educational research and evaluation with a focus on issues of gender, race, and disability in science and mathematics since the mid-1970s. Dr. Campbell, formerly a professor of research, measurement, and statistics at Georgia State University, headed the team doing the summative evaluation of CLASS (Communications, Learning, and Assessment in a Student-Centered System).

Richard E. Clark
Rossier School of Education, University of Southern California

Richard Clark is Professor of Educational Psychology and Technology at the Rossier School of Education at the University of Southern California, where he is Interim Chair of the Division of Learning and Instruction. His research interests include the design of research and evaluation studies on media and technology, and instructional design theories for the teaching of complex knowledge and motivation. Dr. Clark's most recent books include *Turning Research Into Results: A Guide to Selecting the Right Performance Solutions* (with Fred Estes; 2002, CEP Press), and *Learning from Media: Arguments, Analysis and Evidence* (2001, Information Age). In 2002 he was awarded the Thomas F. Gilbert Distinguished Professional Achievement Award by the International Society for Performance Improvement.

Bhuvaneswari Gopal
National Center for Information Technology in Education (NCITE),
University of Nebraska–Lincoln

Bhuvaneswari Gopal has been a Research Associate with NCITE and the Department of Computer Science and Engineering at the University of Nebraska–Lincoln since October 2001. She has worked on a state of the practice study about Learning Management Systems on the UNL campus. She earned her Bachelor's degree in Physics from Madras University, Chennai, India, in 1996, and her master's degree in Applied Physics from Anna University in Chennai, India, in 1998, both with distinction. Ms. Gopal's interest in and aptitude for computer science led her to obtain an advanced post-graduate diploma in e-commerce applications and eventually secured her a position as a lead developer in the Web applications development department of the Chennai branch of Transys Technologies, based in Princeton, New Jersey, from 1999–2001. Her current research interests are educational technology and software engineering.

Earl N. Hadley

Chief editor of *Gender Policy Review,* Earl Hadley is an independent gender consultant who has worked on projects for the World Bank and the European Parliament. He has also conducted gender-related research in Africa and in the United States as a Ford Foundation Fellow and Fellow of the Thomas J. Watson Foundation.

Christy A. Horn
Center for Instructional Innovation, University of Nebraska–Lincoln

Christy Horn is the Co-Director of the Center for Instructional Innovation and the founding Director of UNL's Accommodation Resource Center and the Great Plains Accommodation Technology Institute. She is internationally known for her work in assistive technology in higher education for accommodating students with disabilities. Dr. Horn's research interests include motivation, the impact of technology on learning, and compensating for disability using assistive technology.

Barbara Humes
Office of Educational Research and Improvement,
U.S. Department of Education

Barbara Humes is acknowledged as a contributor to this volume for her outstanding leadership and support of the Nebraska Symposium on Information Technology in Education. She received her Master of Library and Information Science from the University of Maryland and currently serves as an Education Program Specialist in the Office of Educational Research and Improvement at the U.S. Department of Education. With over a decade of experience in the public school and community college systems, Ms. Humes has coordinated programs of directed research studies pertaining to areas such as adult literacy, libraries, and community-based education. She currently serves on the Star Schools Program team as project officer for the federally funded CLASS Project and administers the Eisenhower Regional Mathematics and Science Education Consortia program.

L. Brent Igo
Center for Instructional Innovation, University of Nebraska–Lincoln

L. Brent Igo is a doctoral student in Educational Psychology at the University of Nebraska–Lincoln. A former public school teacher, his research interests include student motivation, construction of knowledge, and human information processing. His current publications address self-efficacy and attention.

Eric J. Jolly
Senior Scientist and Vice President, Education Development Center, Inc.

Eric Jolly is Vice President and Senior Scientist at the Education Development Center, a not-for-profit research and development think tank that operates projects in more than 40 countries and 500 communities within the United States. He is a senior fellow for the UCLA School of Public Policy and has also been a Kellogg National Leadership Fellow and an Osher Fellow for the Exploratorium of San Francisco. Dr. Jolly is the former Assistant to the Chancellor at the University of Nebraska–Lincoln, having previously served in leadership capacities at universities around the country, including posts of department chair, acting dean for education, and associate dean of arts and sciences.

Douglas F. Kauffman
Department of Educational Psychology, University of Oklahoma

Doug Kauffman is currently Assistant Professor of Educational Psychology at the University of Oklahoma. He obtained his PhD in Educational Psychology with a concentration in Learning, Cognition, and Development from the University of Nebraska–Lincoln in 2001. Dr. Kauffman's research interests include at-risk populations, motivation, and the development of self-regulated learning in Web-based environments.

Steve Lehman
Department of Psychology, Utah State University
Steve Lehman is working as Assistant Professor in the Department of Psychology at Utah State University. He obtained his PhD in Educational Psychology with a concentration in Learning, Cognition, and Development from the University of Nebraska–Lincoln in 2000. Dr. Lehman's research interests include relevance and coherence in text processing, situational interest, seductive details in text, increasing deeper processing in online environments, and cognitive load.

Richard E. Mayer
Department of Psychology, University of California, Santa Barbara
Richard E. Mayer is Professor of Psychology at the University of California, Santa Barbara (UCSB), where he has served since 1975. He received a PhD in Psychology from the University of Michigan in 1973, and served as a Visiting Assistant Professor of Psychology at Indiana University from 1973 to 1975. Dr. Mayer's research interests are in educational and cognitive psychology. His current research involves the intersection of cognition, instruction, and technology with a special focus on multimedia learning and problem solving. He is past president of the Division of Educational Psychology of the American Psychological Association, former editor of the *Educational Psychologist* and former co-editor of *Instructional Science*, former Chair of the UCSB Department of Psychology, and the year 2000 recipient of the E. L. Thorndike Award for career achievement in educational psychology. He is on the editorial boards of 10 journals, mainly in educational psychology. He is the author of 18 books and more than 250 articles and chapters, including *Learning and Instruction* (2003), *e-Learning and the Science of Instruction* (with R. Clark, 2003), and *Multimedia Learning* (2001).

Matthew McCrudden
Department of Educational Psychology, University of Nevada–Las Vegas
Matthew McCrudden is a doctoral student in the Learning and Technology program in the Department of Educational Psychology at the University of Nevada–Las Vegas. His research interests include cognitive load and text learning. Mr. McCrudden currently teaches undergraduate courses in educational psychology and is involved in developing online instructional materials.

Roxana Moreno
Educational Psychology Program, University of New Mexico
Roxana Moreno is Assistant Professor in Educational Psychology at the University of New Mexico. She obtained her doctoral degree in Psychology with an emphasis on Cognitive Science from the University of California,

Santa Barbara in 1999. Dr. Moreno's research is centered on testing cognitive theories within the domain of educational technology and examining individual differences in cognition. More specifically, her current research interests include the use of software agents, multimedia, and virtual reality to promote experiential and reflective cognition.

Turan P. Odabasi
Special Associate General Counsel for Intellectual Property,
University of Nebraska

Turan Odabasi is a patent attorney and intellectual property specialist with the Office of General Counsel at the University of Nebraska and the University of Nebraska–Lincoln Office of Technology Transfer. He represents the University in areas related to patents, copyrights, trademarks, Internet law, and licensing, and was involved in the development of intellectual property strategies for the University's CLASS Project and the University's license arrangement with Class.com, Inc.

Lesley K. Perlman
Campbell-Kibler Associates, Inc.

Lesley K. Perlman works at Campell-Kibler Associates in Massachusetts as a researcher on math, science, and technology education programs with an emphasis on issues of gender, ethnicity, and students with disabilities.

Lisa M. PytlikZillig
Center for Instructional Innovation, University of Nebraska–Lincoln

Lisa PytlikZillig is a Research Assistant Professor at the Center for Instructional Innovation at the University of Nebraska–Lincoln. Her research interests broadly include human motivation, emotion, and personality and she is currently involved in projects investigating student motivation, farmer motivation, strategies for negative mood regulation, and the relationships between personality traits and cognitive-emotional motivational states.

Ashok Samal
National Center for Information Technology in Education (NCITE),
University of Nebraska–Lincoln

Ashok Samal is Associate Professor in the Department of Computer Science and Engineering, University of Nebraska–Lincoln. His research interests include computer vision and image understanding, geospatial analysis, and computer-assisted learning.

Mary Jane White
Department of Educational Psychology, University of Minnesota,
Twin Cities
Mary Jane White is a doctoral student in Educational Psychology at the University of Minnesota. Her program of study is Psychological Foundations of Learning with an emphasis in Learning and Cognition. Her current research interests include text comprehension, beliefs, and applied educational statistics.

Arthur I. Zygielbaum
National Center for Information Technology in Education (NCITE),
University of Nebraska–Lincoln
Art Zygielbaum is the CLASS Project Principal Investigator and Co-Director of NCITE. He is a member of the UNL administrative faculty and Associate Professor (Courtesy) of Computer Science and Engineering. Mr. Zygielbaum is a member of the congressionally chartered NASA Aerospace Safety Advisory Panel. He joined UNL in January 1998 after nearly 30 years at the NASA Jet Propulsion Laboratory (JPL). At JPL he was a senior manager and engineer in information systems, Co-Principal Investigator for the Consortium for the Application of Space Data to Education, and creator of JPL's Minority Science and Engineering Initiatives Program. He has several patents and has received numerous NASA awards.

AUTHOR INDEX

A

Abrahamson, C. E., 5
Adelman, C., 233
Ajzen, I., 109
Alesandrini, K., 73
Anderson, J. R., 15, 62
Anderson, R. B., 39
Anderson, T., 73
Anderson, V., 73
Armbruster, B., 73
Arrison, S., 47
Atkinson, H., 146
Atkinson, R. K., 11, 12

B

Baddeley, A., 25
Bandura, A., 10, 145, 146
Barrett, K., 126, 152
Barron, B., 82
Battistich, V., 144
Baumeister, R. F., 145, 146
Beaudoin, M. F., 196
Becker, H., 51, 107, 119
Bereiter, C., 83, 101
Bimber, B., 51
Birch, S. H., 138
Birman, B., 107
Boire, M., 39
Bonk, C. J., 60, 101
Bransford, J., 15, 58, 80

Brooks, F. P. Jr., 160, 161
Brophy, S., 15
Brown, A. L., 58, 61, 80, 81, 83, 101
Brown, J. S., 81
Bruner, J., 110
Bruning, R., xi, xviii, xix, xxi, 57, 58,
    79, 80, 83, 109, 126, 129, 133,
    145, 148, 152, 156, 207
Burch, E., 164, 167

C

Campbell, D. T., 147
Campbell, P. B., xvii, xx, xxi, 231, 232,
    235, 238, 251
Campion, M. G., 235
Campione, J., 58, 81, 83, 101
Carmen, D., 51
Carr, S., 8
Carvin, A., 48
Cavanaugh, C. S., 236
Centrinity, Inc., 171
Cervone, D., 145, 146
Chall, J., 17
Chandler, P., 10, 14, 25, 33, 34
Chaplin, D., 47
Chi, M., 80, 81, 100
Chiu, M., 80
Christian, D., 60, 67
Chun, D. M., 41
Clark, C. C., xvii, 24, 42

Clark, R. E., xvii, 2, 3, 4, 6, 8, 15, 17, 18, 137, 144
Cobb, T., 5
Cocking, R. R., 80
Cognition and Technology Group at Vanderbilt, 82, 83
Cohen, J., 147
Cole, C. L., 13
Collins, A., 81, 83, 101
Cook, T. D., 147
Corneille, O., 14
Corno, L., 17
Craig, S. D., 11, 12
Craik, F. I. M., 70, 72, 73
Cronbach, L. J., 3, 13, 14, 16, 17, 112, 113
Cuban, L., 46
Cummings, J. A., 60

D

Daytner, G., 101
Daytner, K., 101
de Croock, M. B. M., 15
de Leeuw, N., 80
Dean, K., 111, 125
Deci, E. L., 100, 109, 146
Dennen, V., 101
Desmarais, S., 100
DiCintio, M. J., 109
Dick, W., 15
Dieter, M., 6
Dillon, A., 13, 14
Dreher, M. J., 58
Driscoll, M., 15
Dubois, N. F., 58, 60, 67
Dunwoody, S., 7, 8
Durán, R. P., 107, 108, 112, 116, 130, 144
Dweck, C. S., 145

E

Eccles, J. S., 9, 10, 144
Ellis, R. K., 170, 189
Enwefa, R. L., 106, 116
Enwefa, S. C., 106, 116

Eveland, W. P., 7
Everson, H. T., 17

F

Feldlaufer, H., 144
Ferrara, R., 58
Fong, A., 51, 54
Frankola, K., 9
Fredericksen, E., 9
Friend, C. L., 13

G

Gabbard, R., 13, 14
Gauvain, M., 82
Gee, S., 109, 112, 115
Gentile, L. M., 110
Gimino, A., 10
Gladieux, L. E., 144
Glass, G., 2
Glover, R. A., 58
Good, T. L., 60
Graesser, A. C., 42, 81, 100
Graziano, M., 58, 75
Greene, K., 170
Grice, H. P., 83, 93
Grzondziel, H., 41
Guthrie, J. T., 58

H

Hakkinen, P., 99
Hall, C., 188
Halpern, D. F., 81
Hannafin, M. J., 188
Hannafin, R. D., 13
Hegarty, M., 37
Heiser, J., 35, 38
Herrin, W. R., 164
Hewitt, J., 80, 82
Hidi, S., 73
Hill, J., 103, 188
Hiltz, S. R., 5, 8, 9
Hislop, G., 9
Hixson, J., 110
Hoffman, D. L., 51

Horn, C. A., xi, xviii, xix, xxi, 45, 79, 83, 103, 105, 108, 109, 126, 129, 130, 133, 145, 148, 152, 156, 168

J

Jarvela, S., 99
Jensen, G. C., 170
Jonassen, D. H., 13, 15, 194
Judd, C. M., 14
Just, M. A., 37

K

Kalra, M., 100
Karsenti, T., 6
Karweit, N. L., 110
Kauffman, D. F., xviii, xix, 57, 60, 67, 80, 83, 103, 109, 129, 145, 150, 152, 156
Kennedy, C., 9
Kiewra, K. A., 58, 60, 67
King, A., 58, 59, 72, 73
Kintsch, E., 72
Kirshstein, R., 107
Kitchen, D., 5
Knapp, M. S., 109, 116
Kozma, R. B., 3, 15
Kramer-Schlosser, L., 146
Kuhn, D., 81, 87

L

Ladd, G. W., 138
Land, S., 188
Landon, B., 170
Leary, M. R., 145, 146
Lebiere, C., 15
Lee, Y., 143, 151
Leggett, E. L., 145
Lehman, J., 143
Lehman, S., xviii, xix, 79, 83, 87, 109, 133, 145
Lenhart, A., 58, 75
Lester, J. C., 32
Leutner, D., 41
Levin, D., 107
Levin, H. M., 2, 5

Lewis, L., 7, 8
Lientz, B. P., 167
Lin, X., 15
Lipsey, M. W., 147
Lockhart, R. S., 70, 72, 73
Lonn, S., 35, 38
Loranger, A. L., 59
Lorch, R. F. Jr., 36
Low, R., 10, 32

M

Madden, N. A., 110
Malikowski, S., 101
Malloy, T. E., 170
Mathias, A., 34
Mautone, P. D., 36
Mayer, R. E., xviii, 11, 12, 13, 23, 24, 25, 32, 33, 34, 35, 36, 37, 38, 39, 40, 41, 42
McDougall, D., 5
McEwan, P. J., 2, 5
McMillan, M. M., 110
McShane, A., 60, 67
McWhirter, A. M., 143, 146
McWhirter, B. T., 143, 146
McWhirter, E. H., 143, 146
McWhirter, J. J., 143, 146
Means, B., 109, 112, 115, 116
Meister, G. R., 2
Mendrinos, R. B., 110
Merrill, D. M., 4, 15
Meyer, B. J. F., 36
Meyer, L., 108
Midgely, C., 144
Monaghan, J., 107
Moreno, R., xviii, 11, 23, 32, 35, 37, 38, 39
Mousavi, S., 10, 32
Mrtek, R., 6
Mullen, J., 50
Murphy, T., 170

N

Nassersharif, B., 50

National Center for Education Statistics (NCES), 51, 54, 107, 108
National Telecommunications and Information Administration (NTIA), 47, 49, 50
Newman, S. E., 81
Nichani, M., 170
Noddings, N., 146
Novak, T. P., 51

O

Oakes, J., 233

P

Paivio, A., 25
Pajares, F., 146
Pape, A. D., 47
Patterson, L. E., 146
Payne, B. D., 110
Payne, D. A., 110
Pierson, M. E., 107
Pieter, W., 9
Plake, B. S., 58
Plass, J. L., 41
Pollock, E., 34
Puma, M. J., 47

R

Rak, C. F., 146
Ravitz, J., 51, 55, 107
Reddick, M., 170
Reisetter, M., 133
Reynolds, M., 51
Richey, R., 15
Riding, R., 42
Riel, M., 107, 119
Riley, R. A., 50
Robinson, D. H., 60, 67
Rumberger, R. W., 110
Russell, T., 130, 131
Ryan, R. M., 100, 102, 109, 146

S

Sack, J. L., 111

Salomon, G., 3, 8, 10, 137, 144
Savenye, C., 143,
Scardamalia, M., 80, 82, 83, 101
Schallert, D., 143
Schaps, E., 144
Schnotz, W., 41
Schramm, W., 3
Schraw, G., 87
Schwartz, D., 15
Senyak J., 51
Shaw, G. P., 9
Shin, E., 143
Simon, M., 58, 75
Sims, S.,100
Sims, V. K., 39, 40
Singer, M., 81
Slavin, R. E., 110
Smith, C., 170
Snow, K.,17
Snow, R. E., 3, 13, 14, 16,17
Snowman, J., 73
Solomon, D., 144
Spires, H. A., 32
Stahl, G., 82
Staley, R. K., 60, 67
Stapleton, P., 87
Stephens, M., 107
Storo, J., 235, 238
Strover, S., 51
Sugrue, B., 4
Sullivan, H. J., 13, 14
Swail, W. S., 144
Sweller, J., 10, 14, 24, 25, 29, 32, 33, 34, 35, 38, 42
Symonds, W. C., 141

T

Teng, T., 170
The Children's Partnership, 51, 52, 53
Therriault, D., 6
Tobias, S., 17
Toulmin, S., 87
Trabasso, T., 81
Trotter, A., 238, 243

V

Vagge, S., 39
Valenta, A., 6
van Merrienboer, J. J. G., 14, 15, 18, 24,
Vygotsky, L., 194

W

Watson, M., 144
Weiner, B., 146
Wenglinsky, H., 108, 234
Werner, E. E.., 146

White, M. J., xix, 83, 103, 105, 109, 125,
    126, 130, 145, 151, 152
Wigfield, A., 9, 10
Wilhelm, T., 51
Willoughby, T., 100
Wittrock, M. C., 24, 25, 73
Wong, Y. T., 51, 107
Wood, E., 100

Y

Yang, Y. C., 6, 19

SUBJECT INDEX

A

academic risk factors (*see* students, at-risk)

access to instruction or information, ix, 2, 4, 6, 7, 8, 46, 54, 58, 111, 131, 156, 180, 184, 186, 188, 190, 192, 196, 197, 201, 203, 204, 206, 217, 219, 221, 233, 234, 237, 250
   barriers, 51, 58
   cultural barriers, 53
   language barriers, 53
   literacy barriers, 52, 53
   social barriers, 2

access to technology use, ix, xiv, xviii, 45–55, 109, 111, 119, 171, 179, 192, 201, 204–206, 234–239, 247–250
   barriers, 47, 51, 52, 109, 185
   by group, 50, 51, 52, 54, 108, 114, 201
   defined, 51
   technological indicators of (*see* course management systems, technological indicators)

accreditation, ix, xiv, 240, 245

achievement, 3, 8, 19, 51, 54, 55, 85, 106, 107, 108, 126, 131, 142, 233, 234, 236, 252

active choice, 8, 9

active learning (*see* learning)

active processing, 23, 25, 26, 28, 41

assumption, 23, 25, 26

aligning (*see* contiguity effects)

animation, 11, 12, 19, 24, 26, 29, 32–39, 41, 43, 44, 155
   animated agents, 11, 12, 19, 42, 44
   narrated, 24, 28, 32–41

application program interface (API), 195

assessment, ix, xiii, xiv, xv, xx, 2, 4, 18, 21, 55, 65, 68, 80, 85, 101–103, 108, 131, 153, 154, 159, 169–171, 177–179, 182, 186–192, 195–197, 201, 202, 205, 212, 221, 236, 239, 243, 248, 250
   graphical interactive, 155
   Nebraska Statewide Writing Assessment, 101
   norm-referenced testing, 79, 83–87, 90, 91, 99, 100
   online, ix, 3, 8, 91, 94, 135, 139, 155, 194, 197, 234, 236, 251
   specific types, 24, 44, 65–69, 73, 84, 85, 86, 90, 91, 94, 96, 97, 195, 241, 245
   (*see also* National Assessment of Educational Progress)

asynchronous (*see* interaction; learning; online communication; Web-based learning)

audiovisual, ix, 80, 101, 154–157, 159, 194, 195, 211, 212, 229, 234, 242, 244, 251

Web-Based Learning: What Do We Know? Where Do We Go?, pages 267–275
Copyright © 2003 by Information Age Publishing

auditory/verbal channel, xviii, 25, 26, 32, 33, 42
automated data gathering, 100, 206
autonomy, 6, 102, 109

B

belongingness (relatedness), x, 145

C

cache/caching, 157, 158, 159, 224
caring (*see* interaction)
CD-ROM/DVD, 51, 232, 242, 244, 248
CLASS (*see* Communications, Learning, and Assessment in a Student-Centered System)
CMF (*see* computer mediated functions)
CMS (*see* course management systems)
cognitive demand (*see* cognitive load)
cognitive load, xvii, xviii, 7, 14, 17, 21, 23–29, 33–44
    incidental, 37
    intrinsic, 33, 42
    types of cognitive demand, 28, 32, 33, 42
    (*see also* cognitive overload)
cognitive load theory (*see* cognitive theory and research)
cognitive overload, xviii, 13, 23–25, 28, 29, 32–42
cognitive processing, 3, 4, 10, 12, 18, 19, 23–40, 42, 75
    deep, 24, 86
    essential, 40
    incidental, xviii, 28, 29, 35–38, 42
    representational holding, xviii, 28, 29, 38–40
    (*see also* cognitive load)
cognitive restructuring and growth, 81, 82, 101
cognitive strategies, 16
cognitive styles, 16, 44
cognitive theory and research, xviii, xix, 1, 15, 21, 23, 25, 26, 28, 29, 35, 39–42, 80, 102

cognitive load theory, 22, 25, 43
cognitive theory of multimedia learning, xviii, 23, 26, 28, 29, 35, 39, 41
theory of working memory, 25
coherence effect, 35, 36, 44, 103
collaborative learning (*see* learning, collaborative)
communication, xiv, 2, 3, 18, 51, 83, 99, 130, 131, 138–140, 145–149, 166, 194, 197, 202
    chat, 143, 177, 197, 201
    nonverbal, 11, 99
    online (*see* online communication)
    (*see also* interaction)
Communications, Learning, and Assessment in a Student-Centered System (CLASS)
    project, ix–xxii, 80, 103, 126, 131–133, 138, 141, 150–170, 190, 197, 206, 231, 232, 239, 247–251
    www.class.com, 233, 241, 242
communities, xi, 7, 47–56, 102, 103, 112, 120, 126, 138, 140, 144, 195, 216
    low-income, 55
    minority, 50, 53, 55
    of learners, 80, 82, 102, 138–140, 144, 145, 150, 184, 216
    online, 83, 194, 195
    rural, 49–52, 111, 115, 126, 244
    technology-based, 83
    underserved, xi, 47, 49, 51, 52, 56
    (*see also* underrepresented populations)
complex knowledge (*see* knowledge)
complex learning (*see* learning)
complex thinking (*see* critical thinking)
computer mediated functions (CMFs), 105, 112–116, 121, 127
Computer Supported Intentional Learning Environments (CSILE), 83
computer-assisted instruction, 6, 7, 20, 21, 24, 44, 51, 59, 114, 115, 141, 164–167

(*see also* Web-based instruction;
Web-based learning)
computer-generated feedback (*see* feedback)
conceptual knowledge (*see* knowledge)
constructivism, xv, 20, 43, 55, 74, 107, 125, 126, 193, 205
constructivist design theory, 15, 20
contiguity effects, 12, 37, 39, 44
spatial, 37
temporal, 39
(*see also* screen design)
control, 13, 14, 19, 20, 61, 102, 167, 194, 196, 224, 226
instructional, 13, 70, 72, 75, 83, 100, 109, 193, 197
learner, 1, 13, 14, 19, 20, 34, 72, 151, 194
navigational, xiv, xvi, 13, 14, 17, 53, 92, 98, 101, 195
managerial, 162, 165, 167
copy and paste function, 58, 68–75
copyright (*see* intellectual property)
cost effectiveness, 2–7, 145, 150, 154, 162, 172, 192, 218, 234, 236
(*see also* engineering issues, cost management)
cost management, 236, 238, 240, 244, 245
(*see also* engineering issues, cost management)
cost-benefit analysis (*see* cost effectiveness)
course management systems (CMS), xx, 153, 154, 169–196, 241
Blackboard, xx, 169–173, 177, 179, 183–207
EDU campus, 189
efficacy of, 173
eGrade, 177, 189
extent and type of use, 172, 177, 187
FirstClass, 171, 189
Lotus Notes, 171, 177, 179, 184
obstacles for using, 180–185
technological indicators, 170, 191, 192, 197–200
TopClass, 171, 189

WebCT, 169, 170, 171, 177, 189, 192
course resource utility (CRU), 159, 160
critical thinking, 24, 26, 54, 73, 79–100, 103, 116, 193, 206, 224
CSILE (*see* Computer Supported Intentional Learning Environments)
cues (*see* note taking cues; signaling; communication)
cyber law (*see* intellectual property, Internet law)

D

decision making, 73, 74, 87, 125, 188, 192
about instructional technology, xv, 4, 59, 107, 192, 231, 232
declarative knowledge (*see* knowledge)
design experiment, 57, 61
design strategy, 2, 17
(*see also* instructional design)
digital divide, xvii, xviii, 45–48, 51, 54–56, 236
distance education, ix, xi, xvii, 2–9, 18–22, 83, 133, 170, 172, 188, 216, 217, 232, 234, 236, 238, 242, 252
asynchronous/synchronous (*see* learning; online communication; interaction; Web-based learning)
dual coding theory, 25, 43, 44
dual channel assumption, 23–26, 41, 42
dual task measures, 10

E

educational inequities, 231, 232, 234
(*see also* digital divide; underrepresented groups)
effort (*see* student effort)
electronic bulletin boards (*see* online communication)
electronic discussion boards (*see* online communication)

engagement/disengagement, xix, xxi,
  24, 33–39, 54, 68, 80, 87, 93, 116,
  125, 129–151, 194
  off-task behaviors, 64, 135, 143
engineering issues, 154
  configuration management, 166
  cost management, 161–167, 192
  development schedules, 161
evaluation, xiv, xvi, xvii, xx, 3, 80, 81,
  116, 142, 143, 154, 167–171, 179,
  191, 197, 241
expectations
  CLASS project members, xvi
  student, xv, xix, 8, 130, 137, 138,
    144, 150

F

feedback, xv, xxii, 6, 9, 11, 84, 87, 88,
  102, 130, 133, 138–149, 178, 232,
  239, 240–245, 249, 250
  computer-generated, 80, 150, 235,
    242, 243, 245
  (*see also* assessment; communica-
    tion)
field dependence/independence, 16,
  17
frustration with technology, 130, 131,
  135–138, 144, 149, 182, 244

I

individual differences and individualization, ix, xiv, 2, 16, 19, 40, 41,
  71, 105, 107, 111–113, 116, 123,
  130, 149
  (*see also* underrepresented groups)
InfoGather (*see* note taking)
information technology, x, 48, 107,
  155, 156, 163, 167
  (*see also* National Center for Infor-
    mation Technology in Educa-
    tion)
instructional design, ix, xiv–xvii, xxi,
  1–4, 14–22, 28, 40, 41, 100, 140,
  141, 149, 153–155, 162, 206, 216
  models, 1, 2, 4, 14, 15

Web-based, ix, xiii, xvii–xix, xxi, 2,
  7, 13
  (*see also* screen design; Web-based
    courses)
instructional methods, 3, 4, 15, 18, 19
instructional support, 2, 14–18, 59,
  139, 140, 169, 171, 172, 188, 193,
  194, 235–243, 251
  (*see also* technical support)
instructional system design (ISD)
  model, 14
intellectual property, xv, xvii, xx, 209,
  210, 221, 223, 224
  copyright, xv, xx, 197, 209–228
  fair use, xx, 215–217, 220, 229
  Internet law, 209, 210, 223, 224
  patent, 184, 209, 210, 220, 221, 222,
    230
  public domain, xx, 211, 214, 215,
    219
  trade secret, 209, 210, 222, 223
  trademark, 209, 210, 221, 222, 224
interaction, xix, 6, 81, 82, 93, 98, 99,
  101, 171, 193, 194
  asynchronous, 83, 170, 194
  caring, xxi, 130, 131, 145–150
  face-to-face, 9, 83, 93, 99, 101, 132,
    138, 139, 145, 192
  interactive technology and multime-
    dia content, xiv, 3, 24, 34, 84,
    99, 101, 130, 155, 156, 193,
    194, 221, 246
  student-student, xv, 43, 51, 82–85,
    88, 91–102, 109, 120, 121,
    123, 138–141, 146, 150, 171,
    197, 237, 245
  synchronous, 170, 194
  teacher-student, xix, 9, 10, 109, 120,
    131, 133, 138–148, 197, 240,
    242, 250
  Web-based, 43, 83–85, 88, 91–99,
    102, 233
    (*see also* interaction, student-stu-
      dent and teacher-student)
  with experts, 101
  (*see also* communication, feedback)

interest, x, 8, 9, 29, 75, 76, 82, 99, 100,
133, 137, 141, 170, 173, 182, 185,
188, 200, 213, 216, 217, 226, 232,
233, 235, 240, 243, 245, 249
Internet access (*see* access to technology)
Internet law (*see* intellectual property)
ISD (*see* instructional system design
model)

K

knowledge
basic, 86, 91, 94
complex, 1, 14, 15, 22, 44
conceptual, 14, 97
construction of, 80, 82, 83, 100, 103
content, 85, 97, 234, 235, 239, 243
declarative, 15
modes of, 26
prior, 13–17, 24, 26, 81, 151
procedural, 15, 18

L

learning
active, 26, 171
assumptions about, 1
asynchronous, 9, 20, 21, 232, 242,
250
collaborative, 6, 193
complex, 2, 14–18, 22, 51
conceptual, 74
contexts, 2
disabilities, xi, 106, 110, 111, 120,
121, 226
discovery, 13
distance (*see* distance education)
environments, 7, 9, 11, 20, 42, 102,
108, 130, 170, 193, 195
goals, 10, 12, 61
individualized (*see* individual differences and individualization)
meaningful, 23–25, 28, 35, 40, 41,
43
multimedia (*see* multimedia learning)

outcomes, 24, 130, 131, 193, 195
processes, 8, 60, 100, 109, 143, 149,
193, 194
relational, 64, 68, 71
standards, xiv
strategies, 14, 16, 17
styles, xvi, 1, 6, 16, 17, 22, 41
synchronous, 232
tasks, 3, 5, 7, 10, 14, 16, 28, 36, 54
transferable, xviii
Web-based (*see* Web-based learning)
learning management systems (LMS)
(*see* course management systems)
learning theory, 72, 74
generative, 25
social cognitive theory, xv, 80, 82,
151
(*see also* cognitive theory of multimedia learning)
limited capacity assumption, 23, 25, 26,
32, 35, 40, 41
(*see also* cognitive load)
LMS (*see* course management systems, learning management
systems)
local resource disk (LRD), 159, 162

M

media
attributes, 3
benefits of, 2–5
development, xvi, 166
encrypted, 216, 220
selection, 2, 4, 22
(*see also* multimedia)
memory
long-term, 26
overload (*see* cognitive, overload)
working, 10, 11, 21, 26, 28, 32, 34,
38–40, 43
mental effort (*see* student, effort)
mental models, 15, 24, 28, 34, 40, 80,
81, 102
metacognition, xix, 20, 81, 101

minorities (*see* underrepresented
    groups)
modality effect, 32
mood/emotionality, 10
motivation
    active choice, 8, 9
    and media, 1, 5–8, 11
    classroom, 79, 83, 93, 94, 97
    collaborative learning effects on, 6
    enhancement, 83
    enhancement/reduction, 88, 91,
        93, 96, 98, 100, 105, 109, 111,
        119–124, 133, 137, 141
    goals, 18
    intrinsic, 94
    motivating communication, 131,
        140, 145–150
    motivational outcomes, 80
    persistence, 5–10, 146
    processes, 131
    student, xix, 5, 79, 83, 93, 94, 97,
        116, 119, 141, 145, 146, 235,
        238, 243, 247, 248, 251
    teachers as motivators, 140, 141
    theory, 145, 146
    varieties, measures of, 8, 10, 17, 99,
        146, 206
multimedia assets, 155, 165, 194, 210
    intellectual property consider-
        ations (*see* intellectual prop-
        erty)
multimedia design, xiv, 40, 41
multimedia instruction, xvi, 24, 25, 32,
        34, 36–44, 51, 53, 108, 132, 136,
        137, 155, 197, 209, 219–223
    defined, 24
multimedia learning, xiii, xviii, 19,
        23–29, 41–44, 59
    defined, 24
    misconceptions about, xvii, 2, 3, 17
    theory of, 23, 41, 43

N

NAEP (*see* National Assessment of Edu-
    cational Progress)
narration, 5, 11, 12, 24, 28, 32–41

National Assessment of Educational
    Progress (NAEP), 108
National Center of Information Tech-
    nology in Education (NCITE),
    xxi, xxii, 170, 190, 206, 207
navigation
    of online instructional materials
        and tools, ix, 92, 101, 195
    of the Internet, 53
    rules, 17
    tools, xvi
    (*see also* control, navigational)
NCITE (*see* National Center of Infor-
    mation Technology in Educa-
    tion)
nonverbal communication (*see* com-
    munication)
norm-referenced testing (*see* assess-
    ment)
note taking
    cues, 62, 63, 64, 67, 68, 70, 75
    decisions, 58, 73, 74
    InfoGather, xviii, 57–75
    organizers, xviii, 58, 60–65, 68,
        70–75
    strategies, 58, 69, 70
    tools, xviii, 57, 59

O

off-loading, 29, 32
online collaboration, 5
online communication, 9, 51, 83, 93,
        98–101, 131, 132, 135, 138, 139,
        145, 148, 192, 194
    asynchronous, 139
    email, 81, 85, 103, 126, 132, 133,
        136, 138, 139, 147, 152, 164,
        171, 173, 194, 196, 197, 232,
        239, 240–244, 250
    (*see also* communication; interac-
        tion)
online instruction, xiv, xvi, xix–xxi,
        1–10, 14, 17, 42, 79, 80, 83,
        131–137, 140, 143–150, 153, 154,
        163, 166, 167, 170, 171, 192, 197,
        210, 212, 221, 232, 245, 247

(*see also* Web-based courses, assessment, Web-based learning)

P

patent (*see* intellectual property)
pedagogical agent (*see* animation)
persistence (*see* motivation)
problem solving, 15, 21, 24, 32–40, 76, 116
  problem-solving transfer, 24, 32–40
problem-based learning/instruction, xvii, 1, 13, 15, 42
production environment, 154, 163
production expectations, 156, 161, 167
programming languages
  C, C++, 163
  HTML/XML, 163, 193, 194, 195, 206, 224
  Java/Javascript, 163, 189
  Pascal, 163
propositions, 58, 62–67
public domain (*see* intellectual property)

R

recall, 7, 22, 24, 65, 71, 74, 76, 81, 118
  cued, 7, 65, 71, 73
  delayed, 7
  immediate, 7
redundancy effect, 12, 19, 37, 38, 44
rehearsal effects, 68, 71
relational learning (*see* learning)
representational holding, xviii, 28, 29, 38–40
research and development (R&D), xiii, xix, 15, 75, 154–156, 160–163, 167, 223
  contingencies, 162–166
  documentation, 162, 166, 167
  principles, 153, 154, 164
  schedule risk, 161–167
resilience, 150, 151
retention of students (*see* student dropout)
rubric-based scoring, 87, 91, 97

rural schools, 49, 50–52, 56, 111, 115, 126, 244
  (*see also* underrepresented populations)

S

scaffolding, 2, 14, 15, 101
screen design, 1, 2, 10–13, 17, 24, 29, 32, 37, 38, 62
  complex, 10
  for note taking (*see* note taking, tools)
  (*see also* contiguity effects, segmentation effects, signaling effects)
segmenting/segmentation effects, 32, 33, 34, 41
selecting-organizing-integrating (SOI) theory, 25
self-efficacy, 6, 10, 64, 80–100, 114, 121, 124, 127, 146, 148–151, 170, 187, 188
self-explanations, 80, 81, 98, 100, 102
self-motivation, 143, 238, 243, 247, 248
self-regulation, 13, 130, 143, 144, 149
short-term memory (*see* memory)
signaling/signaling effect, 36–38, 41, 43
  (*see also* screen design)
simulations, 108, 116
site licensing, 240
social cognitive theory (*see* learning theory)
social cues, 99
  (*see also* communication)
social distance, 99
software
  complex, 107
  course management (*see* course management systems)
  drill and practice, 54, 109, 121
  game, 51, 107
  Microsoft SQL Server, 194
  Oracle8i, 194
  tracking (*see* tracking students)
software design

accidental difficulties, 160, 161
essential difficulties, 160, 161, 162
software development, 161, 163, 166
configuration management, 160, 166, 167
documentation, 162, 166, 167
engineering issues, 153–167
feature creep, 162, 165
functional requirements, 164
specifications, 161, 162, 165, 166
SOI (*see* selecting-organizing-integrating theory)
spatial ability effect, 40
(*see also* cognitive overload)
split-attention effect, 29, 43
(*see also* cognitive overload)
standardized tests (*see* assessment)
strategies (*see* cognitive strategies, design strategy, learning strategies, teaching strategies, notetaking strategies)
student dropout/retention, 2, 7, 8, 9, 24, 234, 236, 241, 245
student efficacy (*see* self-efficacy)
student effort, 8–11, 20, 21, 40, 146–151, 179, 182
student persistence (*see* motivation)
students
at-risk, xix, 83, 103, 105–151, 238
general education, 106, 113–119
gifted, 106, 113–119
special education, 105, 111–119, 124

T

TEACH Act, 216, 217, 229
teacher roles in online courses, 139, 140
teaching strategies, 9, 10
technical problems, 136, 140, 144, 153, 154, 167, 240, 244, 248
technical support, 196, 235, 238, 240, 241, 244, 245
technology use
complex, xix, 121
in classrooms, 106, 107, 108, 111

simple (skill and drill), 109, 115, 119, 121, 141
with at-risk students, 105–116, 121, 124, 129, 130
technology-based learning (*see* multimedia learning, Web-based learning)
telecommunication, x, xi, xiv, 5, 47, 55, 154, 156, 168
temporal contiguity effect (*see* contiguity effects)
third party, 221, 227
works, 217, 219
tracking students, xiv, xvi, 92, 155–159, 162, 163
trade secret (*see* intellectual property)
trademark (*see* intellectual property)

U

underrepresented groups
African American, 49, 50, 53, 233
disabled, 49, 52, 70
Hispanic, 49, 50, 53, 233
Native American, 50, 55
rural, 49, 50–52, 111, 115, 126, 244
uniform resource locator (URL), 63, 68, 71, 143, 156, 241, 246

V

value
for learning goals, 10
of the course, 9, 10
visual information, xviii, 1, 10–12, 16, 17, 21, 25, 26, 29, 32, 33, 38–41, 44, 101, 108, 116, 127, 133
visual/pictorial channel, 25, 26, 32, 33, 38
voiceover narration (*see* narration)

W

Web links, ix, x, 80, 99, 187, 188, 196, 223, 224
Web server, 157, 159, 162, 191, 199, 200, 201, 203, 205
Web Server, 199

Web standards, 161
Web-based activity, xvi, xviii, 85
Web-based applications, xvi, 100
Web-based case studies, 9
Web-based courses (*see* Web-based
    instruction)
Web-based email, 195
Web-based environments, xviii, 60, 90
Web-based instruction, ix, x, xiii,
    xvii–xix, 1, 4–18, 61, 76, 80, 83,
    84, 90, 93, 96, 98–100, 131, 143,
    145, 170–173, 188, 232–246
    assessment of (*see* assessment)
    benefits, 2
    (*see also* access)
Web-based learning, ix, x, xiii, xvi, xvii,
    4, 7, 100, 193
    asynchronous, 9, 20, 21, 83, 194,
        232, 242, 250
    cognitive aspects, xviii
    synchronous, 170, 242
Web-based materials, 75, 93, 184, 185
Web-based note-taking, 60
Web-based survey, 173
Web-based technologies, xiii, xvii, xviii,
    5–7, 80, 98, 188, 190
Web-based text, 58
Web-based tool, xviii, 80, 98, 192, 193,
    196
weeding, 35–38
    (*see also* cognitive load, cognitive
        overload)
work made for hire, 211–213, 219, 226
working memory, 10, 11, 21, 26, 28, 32,
    34, 39, 40, 43
working memory (*see* memory)
World Wide Web, 20, 85, 156, 206